Contents

Part One
Theories, Issues and Perspectives in British Family Support

Part Two

Developing Practice in Family Support

Part Three

Resources for Working in Family Support

The RHP Companion to

FAMILY
SUPPORT

Edited by

Nick Frost
Andy Lloyd
Liz Jeffery

LEARNING RESOURCES
CENTRE
Havering College
of Further and Higher education

Russell House Publishing

First published in 2003 by:
Russell House Publishing Ltd.
4 St. George's House
Uplyme Road
Lyme Regis
Dorset DT7 3LS

Tel: 01297-443948
Fax: 01297-442722
e-mail: help@russellhouse.co.uk
www.russellhouse.co.uk

British Library Cataloguing-in-publication Data:
A catalogue record for this book is available from the British Library.

ISBN: 1-903855-16-0

Typeset by Sheaf Graphics Ltd, Sheffield

Printed by Antony Rowe, Chippenham

About Russell House Publishing

RHP is a group of social work, probation, education and youth and community work practitioners and academics working in collaboration with a professional publishing team. Our aim is to work closely with the field to produce innovative and valuable materials to help managers, trainers, practitioners and students. We are keen to receive feedback on publications and new ideas for future projects. For details of our other publications please visit our website or ask us for a catalogue. Contact details are on this page.

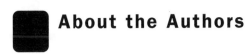

About the Authors

Pam Acaster – is a Volunteer Co-ordinator at West Leeds Family Service Unit

Jenny Brown – is the Senior Co-ordinator of Castleford Home Start

John Clark – is the Restorative Justice Co-ordinator for Leeds Youth Offending Team and Chair of Yorkshire Association of Youth Justice

Christine Clavering – is the Unit Manager of Bradford Family Service Unit

Kevant Coates – is a Principal Caseworker (Child Protection) with Leeds City Council Social Services Department

Mary Delaney – is a Volunteer Co-ordinator at West Leeds Family Service Unit

Nick Frost – is a Senior Lecturer in Continuing Education at the University of Leeds

Dawn Higgins – is the Crèche Supervisor and PaTH Worker at West Leeds Family Service Unit

Charlotte Jackson – worked as a PaTH Worker at West Leeds Family Service Unit, and now works for the Carr-Gomm Society

Rosie Jakob – is Deputy Manager of Browning House in Leeds

Liz Jeffery – is a Development Officer with the Leeds Children's Fund

Asher John–Baptiste – works at Checkpoint, Bradford, a community organisation for African (Caribbean) women

Andy Lloyd – is the Unit Manager of West Leeds Family Service Unit

Tracey Race – is Children's Service Manager at an NSPCC team based in Barnsley

Nicky Ryden – is an independent Social Worker, teacher and researcher

David Saltiel – is the Service Manager of West Leeds Family Service Unit

Mike Sells – works in the Communications Section of Leeds Social Service Department

Warwick Turnbull – is employed at Bradford Family Service Unit

Acknowledgments

We would like to thank the following people:

*Carol Wales, Alison Hodgson, Angela Williams and Carol Coyle
for their help and advice.*

*Fiona, Jonathan, Elizabeth, Sarah
Stevie, Lindsay and Alice
for their support and patience.*

█ Editors' Introduction

This book brings together reflections on theoretical and policy approaches to family support with a range of practice-based chapters that we hope will provide practical guidance for those working in family support and a useful source of reference and stimulation for those studying and researching in this field.

The Scope of This Book: A Practice in Search of a Definition

First, let us address the scope of the book. We argue throughout the book that 'family support' can be a somewhat slippery concept - in many ways it is a practice in search of a definition, an issue explored further in Chapter 1. For this reason readers may at times become a little frustrated with the text: a reader may ask why isn't there a chapter on a particular (missing) topic. The answer to this question may not always be very clear - potentially the book might have been double or even treble the length it is now. We have attempted to cover in our theory and practice chapters what we would regard as the major challenges and issues, but inevitably a reader might disagree and feel that an important topic has been neglected. Sometimes an absence will be for purely logistical reasons - a chapter on working with men, for example, fell through for practical reasons, which we regret - although we hope that gender is squarely addressed as an issue across a range of chapters.

Second, we wish to address the issue of the geographical basis of the book. Writers on contemporary policy in the United Kingdom in the 21st century face the shared challenge of addressing the recent emergence of the four separate and discrete nations - England, Northern Ireland, Scotland and Wales. In relation to family support there are now real variations across the four nations. The Health Boards in Northern Ireland, the Children's Commissioner's role in Wales, the Reporter's system in Scotland all lead to profound differences between the nations in terms of the structure and delivery of family support

and related issues. We have based this book on an English perspective. This is not meant to imply any superiority or narrow nationalism - in fact we look with some envy at developments such as the Children's Commissioner in Wales - rather that we wish to base our analysis on our direct experience of practice. We therefore draw mainly on the practical English examples with which we interact everyday. However, regardless of some organisational and legal differences, we feel that the main thrust of the book does have a trans-national application. Rather than detail each nuance of difference we trust that a trans-national readership will feel able to reflect critically on the English experience and apply any strengths and weaknesses as they think best.

How the Book is Organised

Part One: Theories, Issues and Perspectives in British Family Support

In Part One of the book, as editors, we hope that we have provided a sound framework for the practice chapters. The first seven chapters draw together academic, local authority and voluntary sector perspectives forming a basis for Part Two of the book - nine chapters written by practitioners which describe, analyse and reflect upon their practice experiences.

Nick Frost, in Chapter 1, reflects on the definitional issues, theories and concepts which underpin family support practice. Whilst some of the discussion might appear to be a long way from the day-to-day realities of practice we believe that a consistent, and thought through, theoretical approach helps to support high quality practice. Frost argues that we need to work with an all inclusive definition of families and that practice should be seen as empowering. He goes on in Chapter 2 to reflect on some of the underpinning statistical evidence on family and household change which impact on the reality that practitioners confront everyday. This chapter also reflects on the contemporary policy framework provided by the New Labour Government elected in 1997 (and still in power at the time of writing).

Liz Jeffery, in Chapter 3, reflects in detail on the key child welfare debate of recent years - the 're-focusing' debate. Drawing on her extensive personal experience of developing policy and practice in this field outlines the parameters of this debate and reflects on its limitations and possibilities. In the following chapter she examines the local authority context - can the local authority deliver family support? What are the strengths and weaknesses of the local authority in this field? There has probably been too little analysis of this key question - we hope this book develops the debate.

Following this Andy Lloyd analyses the key role of the voluntary sector. In Chapter 5 he charts the recent rapid pace of change in the voluntary sector – reflecting on how the sector has risen to the challenge of family support. Andy describes his own personal experience as a manager in the voluntary sector and draws on his experience participating in voluntary sector networks and developments. In Chapter 6 he develops his analysis by reflecting on the nature and reality of voluntary sector/local authority partnership - are they indeed partners, rivals or innovators?

Liz Jeffery concludes Part One with a chapter which reflects critically on two of New Labour's major policy initiatives in the field – *Sure Start* and *The Children's Fund*. We have taken an editorial decision not to focus in this book on the third leg of New Labour's joined up strategy for young people – the development of the Connexions service. Whilst clearly relevant to our concerns we feel that any serious discussion of Connexions would take us too far from our central themes – and into discussion of issues such as youth transitions and employment, which are important but distanced from our central concerns in this text.

Part Two: Developing Practice in Family Support

Part Two of the book provides an extensive outline of a range of practice approaches to family support, building on the more theoretical tone of the first seven chapters. The chapters differ in their style and approach – we wanted to give a real flavour of the practice

outlined rather than impose a 'party line' on our practitioner contributors. We trust that the variety and richness of their practice comes across.

If one issue has emerged in recent years to challenge family support practitioners it is that of substance abuse. In Chapter 8, Christine Clavering outlines how to engage most effectively with children whose parents use drugs or alcohol, an issue that presents a growing challenge to staff working across a variety of agencies. The chapter helpfully describes the impact on individual behaviour of different kinds of drugs and how their use is likely to affect and impair the quality of their parenting and the welfare of the children concerned.

Bringing up children single handed can be a lonely and difficult task, irrespective of material circumstances. When single parents are poor, are subject to racism or who are suffering with poor mental or physical health those difficulties are compounded. In Chapter 9 Pam Acaster and Mary Delaney provide an insight, utilising 'real life' case studies, of how an innovative family support scheme can offer real support and encouragement for single parents.

Asher John-Baptiste and Tracy Race reflect on the particular experiences of Asian and African communities in relation to family support. They argue that family support services should be far more culturally empathetic and informed by a clearer perception of the needs and requirements of diverse communities. The importance of listening to women as individuals and hearing what they have to say, rather than generating stereotyped assumptions about their needs and backgrounds is emphasised.

David Saltiel and colleagues outline the importance of play as a focus for working supportively with parents and as a means of encouraging them to engage with local community networks. Chapter 11 also illustrates how individual projects can evolve over time, in response to the changing social context. The Parenting At Home (PaTH) project moved to a wide focus on parenting support for families where child protection was a concern. Their practical approach seems to prove helpful in such situations with an emphasis on developing the parent-child relationship.

In Chapter 12, Nicky Ryden draws on her experience as an evaluator, to reflect on the challenges of delivering family support in a rural area. For those living stressful lives in our large towns and cities it is easy to imagine that life in the countryside is tranquil and relatively prosperous. Ryden's chapter however firmly denies the myth of the 'rural idyll'. She highlights poverty, isolation and distance from resources as the challenges that are frequently encountered in rural communities. She outlines the kind of flexible and responsive family support services which are required in such communities.

Chapter 13, written by Jenny Brown, a Home-Start co-ordinator, reflects on her experience of recruiting and working with volunteers. Brown analyses the valuable contribution of volunteers to the family support process and is keen to emphasise the importance of volunteers being properly recruited, trained and supported. They also need to be respected as individuals in their own right with their own needs.

In recent years close connections have been made between family support and youth crime. In Chapter 14 John Clark provides some critical reflection on these developments. In particular he outlines the nature and role of the Parenting Order and how this has attempted to bridge the parenting support and youth justice systems.

Chapter 15 analyses the central question of assessment, an issue which has recently received much official attention, and Rosie Jakob and Kevant Coates discuss the issues relating to assessment of families. Sometimes family support services are unable to prevent situations developing and then child protection issues come centre stage. This chapter analyses the issues relating to assessment, what it means to ensure that the best interests of children are promoted, how to work in partnership with parents, and, crucially, how to work with the strengths and positives of families.

In Chapter 16 Warwick Turnbull shares his experiences of the difficult and challenging issue of working with children who have lost a parent or a carer. He gives some useful practice advice, informed by theory and research, for those working in these complex and demanding situations.

Part Three: Resources for Working in Family Support

In Part Three we provide a brief guide of resources, which can be used to guide and develop family support policy and practice. This part of the book includes Mike Sells reflections on an issue which receives little attention in written texts – the utilisation of information in family support services. Information is not only power, but a central tool for the family support practitioner and for families themselves who need to know what service and resources exist and how to access them. In his valuable contribution to this book Sells very helpfully outlines how individual practitioners can acquire the information they need to work most effectively with families. Sells also describes how, when information resources do not exist, they can be built and developed.

We complete the book with a selection of some of the resources we have found most useful and provide contact details for a range of family support organisations.

Part One

Theories, Issues and Perspectives in British Family Support

1 Understanding Family Support: Theories, Concepts and Issues

Nick Frost

Introduction

This book is about family support – a form of child welfare practice that aims to assist and empower parents and carers in raising their children. Whilst the second part of this book consists of a range of chapters about how professionals can support families in a range of very practical senses, this first part of the book aims to explore some of the theories, concepts and issues that underpin the everyday practice of family support.

What is Family Support?

The concept of 'family support' may seem a fairly straightforward one to begin with – but is argued here that it is actually a very ambiguous and complex one. First of all we need to examine its two components – 'family' and 'support' – and then explore the implications of coupling them as 'family support'.

The word 'family' is in itself a complex, and in many ways, a political concept. When we speak or write about 'family' and 'families' it tends to trigger associations such as 'family life' or 'family values' and thus immediately becomes a value-laden and politically significant concept. For example, many hold a view that the family might be in some sort of 'decline' or 'crisis', or there can be profound differences about whether single parent families or gay families are in some way inferior to two parent, heterosexual households. As David Morgan argues:

> In at least some political usages of the term 'family' there was a kind of slippage, deliberate or otherwise, from the use of this single term to the construction of some kind of normative standard of family living, compared with which other family practices may be seen as more or less deviant.
>
> (Morgan, 1999: p16).

The practitioners who read this book will come across families in many diverse forms – single parents, married parents, re-constituted, adoptive and so on. To some extent the debate about the family will seem abstract to them – as good practice will quite simply be an attempt to promote the best interests of the children and young people who live in any given household. For this reason in this book we wish to explore families and households in all their diversity and not to assume that policies and practices should draw on some perception that any particular family form is superior to others. Therefore wherever the terms 'family', 'families', or 'households' appear they should be taken to apply to the full range of living arrangements which people make for the up-bringing of children.

Now to move on to the word 'support'. 'Support' implies some sort of help, assistance or preference for the object that is being supported. In social work this support can take a variety of different forms – it can include 'doing to' families, 'doing with' families or enabling families 'to do' something. In this book we prefer to focus on the latter two elements of support. We recognise that sometimes we do have 'to do' something to families but this is often a short-term approach which does not always enable families to take more power and control over their lives in the future.

Having argued for an inclusive view of the 'family', and having examined what 'support' might imply, what then can we understand by the term 'family support' – the practical topic of this book?

The term has a fairly short history in the United Kingdom. It has come to prominence over the last decade following emphasis in Section 17 of the 1989 Children Act on supportive work with families and also in the more recent 're-focusing' debate which attempts to shift the focus of child protection practice towards more supportive interventions.

There are many definitions of family support, a variety which is reflected throughout this book with different examples being explored at different stages in this book. A useful starting point is that provided by the Audit Commission whose report in many ways provided the parameters for the current debate. They argue for a very wide definition in stating that family support as a social care practice can include:

Any activity or facility provided either by statutory agencies or by community groups or individuals, aimed at providing advice and support to parents to help them bringing up their children.

(Audit Commission, 1994: p39).

Whilst this definition uses the wide-ranging phrase of 'any activity or facility', Ruth Gardner attempts to provide a more specified range of definitions, as follows:

*Family support can mean **self-help** or volunteer help for family members with minimal outside involvement until the family itself identifies the need. It can mean a **continuum** of advice, support, and specialist help starting in the community and signposting the family towards early, less traumatic intervention to avoid a crisis. And it can mean a **specific approach** that is a way of dealing with life crises and problems, including abuse within families, which takes account of any strengths and positive relationships within these families which could assist recovery.*

(Gardner, 1998: p1, emphasis in original).

The National Family and Parenting Institute argue that family support has four key features:

Four Principles of Family Support

There is no single policy that can meet the many needs of Britain's families. And help needs to be sensitive to the subtle distinctions in people's feelings and values. A balance between the needs of children and the broader needs of families should be maintained; although in many areas they are indistinguishable, it is important that children's separate needs are not marginalised.

Public policy to support families needs to be universal, non-stigmatising, wide-ranging and accessible.

Support for all families

Government services exist to support parents and families to lead a decent life, and raise their children. A large body of research into the direct needs of families shows that all families need access to support during the course of a child's life and that support services should be as available as other universal services which we take for

granted. Universal support needs to be supplemented by services targeted at those in greatest need.

No stigma attached

Raising children is not the sole responsibility of the individual parents. Parents must rely on others, both from their families and from outside the home. It is a task for the whole community. People who use services should be seen as valued users, rather than passive recipients of services. There is no stigma to asking for services or for help. How, for example, can disabled parents find the support they need without their children being labelled 'in need' by local social services departments.

Support across the board

Services must be wide-ranging and overlapping. Measurement of success is not always possible, and services that are easily measured may not always be the best option. Services supporting families range from supporting couples' relationships, direct services for children and young people, play, youth and leisure services, transport, fiscal policy, housing and education policy, as well as direct services to help families. The Government must work hand in hand with local authorities and the voluntary sector, which are providing many innovative and effective ways of helping parents. Cross-cutting and multi-agency work must become the norm.

Accessible

Accessible services means thinking creatively about providing or enabling affordable help. Informal ways of helping parents can play as important a role as voluntary or statutory provision. Accessibility also means easy access to information about services and information about parenting issues which encourage parents to find their own solutions and help. A willingness to think creatively about sources of support and advice can lead to other solutions than simply calling for more of the same. Supporting existing community and faith-based organisations to provide support opens other doors to parents (National Family and Parenting Institute, 2001: p1).

The NFPI definition is particularly interesting as it refers to services for all families, not necessarily those in contact with social workers or voluntary organisations. It is apparent from this discussion that family support has a broad range of meanings, and indeed some might say that it is an ill-defined concept, and therefore of questionable value. We agree that there is a challenging, underlying tension in the term family support, which arguably is underplayed in some of the family support literature. This tension comes into focus crucially when there is a difference between the best interests of the children and the wishes of the parents, a tension which is played out every day in family proceeding courts across the country. It is such tensions and practical difficulties that make the concept of 'family support' potentially a fragile one. For example, how can we say we are supporting a 'family' if it is in the best interests of the children to be separated from their parents? How can we say we are supporting a 'family' where the father is abusing the mother? Here it becomes helpful to 'disaggregate' the family – that is not to see it as a unit, but as made up of a diverse elements (parents, mothers, fathers, children, sons and daughters) who may indeed have a fluid and diverse range of different, and perhaps, conflicting interests. For this reason both gender and generation are crucial concepts in helping us understand and analyse family support.

This tension in working with families has for a long time been at the heart of social welfare practice. In some Victorian agencies any tensions were resolved quite simply through the practice of 'child rescue' (see Parker, 1990). Child rescuers, such as Thomas Barnardo, focussed on removing children from their parents – who were sometimes seen as being immoral or feckless. The extreme example of 'child rescue', in many ways we could say the 'ideal type' of child rescue, was the practice of sending children to the far flung corners of the British Empire, even if this meant some form of deceit in terms of how family background was reported to the children (see Melville and Bean, 1989).

Since Victorian times social welfare practitioners have wrestled with the problems of how to support families in practice. Perhaps the most helpful historical account of this struggle is Linda Gordon's *Heroes of Their Own Lives* (1985) which provides an analysis of how some of the early child protection practitioners

in the United States struggled with the complex issues of family support, child rescue and child protection. Gordon's work demonstrates how practitioners reach complex decisions in their work with families based on the idea of desegregation, with a central focus on issues around gender, generation and ethnicity.

When critics of social control perceive social work simply as unwanted intervention, and fail to recognize the active role of agency clients, it is in large part because they conceive of the family as a homogeneous unit.

There is an intellectual reification here which expresses itself in sentence structure particularly in academic language: 'the family is in decline', 'threats to the family', 'the family responds to industrialisation'. Shorthand expressions attributing behaviour to an aggregate such as the family would be harmless except that they often impose particular cultural norms about what 'the family' is, and mask intra-family differences and conflicts of interest.

(Gordon, 1985: p296).

Sometimes professional practice would attempt to shift power, for example, from a violent father to a caring mother. Gordon's numerous case studies illustrate how a straightforward adherence to 'family support' would neither have made sense conceptually nor have safeguarded children and young people. Gordon argues that it does not make sense to think of social work as 'social control', when the primary role was to shift power imbalances within families, often to the benefit of those with less power.

We therefore need to recognise these tensions, contradictions and problems inherent in the term family support (see Parton, 1997). Whilst the editors of this book are in many ways active proponents of family support we also recognise that it has a complex relationship to child protection practice and that a crude adherence to 'supporting the family' would, in some ways, be as simplistic as Victorian 'child rescue' seems to us now.

The reader may be thinking following from this discussion that the most theoretically consistent position is to reject the concept of 'family support'. However, in this book, we see family support as a concept which now has a real meaning in the field, and that has something of a 'critical mass' behind it

– we would therefore be making a mistake to abandon the basically humanitarian and progressive notions which are implicit in the deployment of 'family support'. In our view, for all its' difficulties and complexities, we suggest here that the term 'family support' forms the basis for a progressive form of social welfare practice with children and their families. Many of the practice chapters in this book provide evidence for this proposition: the readers will be able to judge for themselves if utilising family support as a concept generates a body of coherent ideas and practice models.

How can we try to pin down the illusive concept of family support? In terms of thinking about what family support looks like the framework developed by Hardiker and colleagues in a number of publications (see Stevenson, 1999) has become perhaps the most influential. The authors have attempted to provide a four level analytical framework which specifies and defines the use of family support in different ways and at different levels.

This framework provides a method for analysing and, indeed, planning family support services.

The first level refers to projects and services which might serve whole estates or communities. For example, if a housing estate had a common problem of a shortage of play facilities, a community group, perhaps supported by a voluntary organisation who faced a shared problem of lack of play space for children and young people, an intervention at this first level could be to analyse and then hopefully provide a range of play facilities. This approach attempts to address a collective problem to the benefit of all local parents and their children. It is important at this level that there is an emphasis on joined-up thinking – a discussion on play, for example, might involve schools, police, leisure services, planning and many others.

The second level refers to a more targeted service which is aimed at addressing expressed needs. At this level, according to Hardiker et al., it involves some sort of social casework. Second level services will usually be aimed at identified individual families rather than whole communities. In contrast to the play example given above the service is likely to be focussed on specific, identified families – perhaps referred by health visitors or social workers to an organisation such as Home-Start or a single parent support scheme (see Chapters by Brown, and Acaster and Delaney in this

volume). Such services offer informal befriending and support to families on a voluntary and negotiated basis.

Third level services are designed to help with more severe problems, maybe including child care and child protection issues, where services at the lower levels are regarded as insufficient. They require a more intense and targeted service than that outlined at level two, being provided by alcohol and drug rehabilitation agencies (see Chapter 8 by Clavering in this volume).

The fourth level of services, which is not particularly considered in this volume, is concerned with the 'rehabilitation' of those who have been looked after by the local authority, for example, returning to their birth families.

This framework then may provide a practical base for the development of policy and practice development. It allows us to understand more clearly what the role and purpose of different forms of family support is. It also enables us to map, in a very practical sense, which services exist and what purpose they serve.

Theories and Approaches to the Family

Underpinning much of the discussion in this book is exactly how we understand 'the family' (see Featherstone and Frost (2002) for further discussion of these issues). There are a whole variety of different theoretical approaches to understanding the family and households – we cannot explore all of these in this context (however, see Bernardes, 1997). We have selected here to analyse what we might call communitarian or 'Third Way' approaches to the family. This perspective is personified by two key theorists: Amitai Etzioni, in the United States, and Anthony Giddens, a leading British social scientist. We have chosen to examine these approaches as they have been influential in the United Kingdom and such ideas are reflected in the policy of the British 'New Labour' Government (elected in 1997 and in power at the time of writing). Following an examination of communitarianism we then look briefly at a school of thought on the family which might be less familiar to practitioners – the family practices school. This, we argue, is particularly relevant as it sees families as active parties that construct their own social reality – thus being consistent with a family support approach to social work practice.

The Third Way approach to the family

The New Labour project, which resulted in the election of a Labour Government in 1997, is sometimes identified as a 'Third Way' approach to politics. Giddens identifies the following as the key values of a 'Third Way' approach to politics:

- equality
- protection of the vulnerable
- freedom as autonomy
- no rights without responsibilities
- no authority without democracy
- cosmopolitan pluralism
- philosophic conservatism

(Giddens, 1998: p66).

Here we see the beginning of a way of thinking about the family – a focus on freedom and diversity, but within a framework of responsibilities. These ideas are developed and elaborated upon by Giddens in his Reith lectures that are published as *The Runaway World* (1999).

Probably the most pre-eminent British social scientist, Giddens has argued that changes in the family should be understood in the context of both globalisation and change. Giddens states that with the current trend towards global social change (globalisation) there is a key tension between tradition and modernity. In other words there is a tension between our feeling comfortable with society as it used to be and the many challenges of rapid and global social change. When applied to the family this tension has an effect on us all in a very intimate way. For those in the child welfare field there is a double significance – we are living with the change in the family **both** in the way it impacts on us in our private lives and in our public role, as professionals working with children and families.

These changes have a real significance for our everyday lives. Even those of us living with a spouse and with dependent children living at home will have a less traditional family living next door or in our close

family. But also as child welfare professionals will be working with diverse family structures, with married and single parents, with reconstituted families, with those separated and divorced. The decline of traditional family structures since the 1950s, which we outline statistically in the next chapter, is a reality.

Crudely there are two positions we can take on these changes – either a nostalgic attempt to re-create the 1950s family, or an attempt to work with the recent changes in the family. Giddens argues that recent changes should be welcomed as they are premised on a new democracy in the family – a shift towards giving a voice for women, and crucially in the context of this publication, for children:

> *The inequality of men and women was intrinsic to the traditional family...In (mediaeval) Europe, women were the property of their husbands or fathers – chattels as defined in law...In the traditional family, it wasn't only women who lacked rights: children did too. The idea of enshrining children's rights in law is in historical terms relatively recent...One could almost say that children weren't recognised as individuals.*

(Giddens, 1999: p55).

For Giddens then the traditional family was a site of silence and inequality for women and children – the post-traditional family, for all its faults, tensions and problems – is at least an attempt to give a voice to women and children. In fact it is this attempt to empower women and children that leads to many of the challenges of the fragmenting and changing family. Giddens argues for a democratic family – drawing on many of the same principles as political democracy:

> *A democracy of the emotions...is as important as public democracy in improving the quality of our lives...Children in traditional families were – and are – supposed to be seen and not heard. Many parents, perhaps despairing of their children's rebelliousness, would dearly like to resurrect the rule. But there isn't any going back to it, nor should there be. In a democracy of the emotions, children can and should be able to answer back.*

(Giddens, 1999: p64).

Giddens, then, emerges as a champion of recent changes in families. But what does Giddens propose in terms of policy? Consistent with much of the social welfare literature he argues that promoting the best interests of children is the most important thread that should inform and guide family policy. Giddens argues that women and children, previously oppressed in the family, are now able to seek freedom from traditional constraints and to take some control of their own lives.

What can we draw from this discussion on Third Way approaches for this book? Arguably there are three main points:

1. First, Giddens acknowledges that he draws on much of the therapeutic literature about relationships and families to help with shaping his broader sociological ideas. Marina Warner (1984) in her book about childhood draws on social work literature in a similar way to Giddens. This suggests that the work being done in the child welfare field is having wider ramifications in terms of how modern Western societies think about and conceptualise children and childhood.

2. It is also helpful to note the call to actively engage with modernity and change. There is a part of all of us that yearns for times past, the long hot summers playing unsupervised, the security of knowing that Mum and Dad would be there – but that is nostalgia in both senses of the word. It is nostalgia in the sense that it is past, and that it is, at least partly, 'imagined'.

3. Consistent with much social work literature Giddens also argues that promoting the best interests of children is the most important thread that should inform and guide family policy. Giddens argues that women and children, previously oppressed in the family, are able to seek freedom from traditional constraints and to take some control of their own lives.

There is a close link between 'Third Way' approaches to the family outlined above in our consideration of the work of Giddens and the communitarian approach, embodied by the American thinker and activist Amitai Etzioni. Etzioni is the most influential theorist of the communitarian school. In this context we draw on his book *The Spirit of Community* (1993b) and the related publication *The Parenting Deficit* (1993a) (this section draws on Featherstone and Frost, 2003).

Etzioni begins his chapter on the 'communitarian family' by arguing that:

> *Making a child is a moral act. Obviously it obligates the parents to the child. But it also obligates the parents to the community.*
>
> (1993b: p54).

The emphasis on morality and responsibility is important here. A primary aspect of what Etzioni argues is that two-parent families are both pre-dominant and preferable. Thus:

> *It is no accident that in a wide variety of human societies...there has never been a society that did not have two-parent families...in the hundreds of known societies throughout recorded history, two parent families have been the norm.*
>
> (1993b: p60).

From Etzioni's perspective this is largely a practical, rather than an ideological issue – child care and education are demanding both physically and emotionally and is, therefore, better carried out by two people. It follows then that for Etzioni the increase in divorce rates is undesirable because of the consequences particularly for children's educational development. As we have seen this is a different emphasis to that provided by Giddens.

Drawing on empirical data on family trends Etzioni argues that as a consequence of the increased time spent in employment there is what he identifies as a 'parenting deficit' in modern Western societies. It is this aspect of Etzioni's work which has become most widely known. Parents, he argues, are working unduly long hours often because they are choosing to do so in order to sustain a particular living standard. The impact of this trend is socially significant as it leads to many social ills – including substance misuse and youth crime:

> *The millions of latchkey children, who are left alone for long stretches of time, are but the most visible result of the parenting deficit.*
>
> (1993b: p56).

Thus for Etzioni lack of effective investment in parenting has a widespread social significance – crucially communitarians believe that individual choices have wider social implications. It is important to note that Etzioni does not see the communitarian family necessarily as the same as the traditional family. His focus is very much on parenting as an activity which should be shared by both genders – and which should not be seen as the sole responsibility of the mother. In practical terms Etzioni wishes to see many reforms which can be seen in the *Supporting Families* Green Paper (Home Office, 1998). Etzioni advocates reforms such as waiting periods before marriage, pre-marriage counselling programmes and the discouragement of divorce. The focus is on parental responsibility and the reinforcement of this in a way that will benefit the wider community.

There is a direct line from the work of Etzioni and Giddens to the New Labour Government's *Supporting Families: A Consultation Document* (1998), which takes a pragmatic approach to families recognising that there is considerable diversity. The paper also explicitly sets itself against preaching or moralising about families. However, it is also clear that it sees children's welfare as being best safeguarded within a structure comprising married parents residing together looking after dependent children.

The family and 'family practices'

Moving on from 'Third Way' approaches we wish to examine one more theoretical approach. In recent years analysts of the family have been critical of approaches to the family that have seen the family as a 'structure' or as a passive instrument which responds to changes elsewhere in the social structure. The 'family strategies' approach has emphasised the ability of families and their individual members to act, to take decisions, and to make their own history. Sociologists, most notably Morgan (1999) and historians such as Davidoff and colleagues (1999) have developed and applied this approach.

Discussion which emphasises family 'strategies' has gradually replaced older portrayals of families as the passive objects of historical change. Morgan, for example, argues that 'family', 'represents a constructed quality of human interaction or an active process rather than a thing-like object of detached social investigation' (1999: p16). This concept was further refined when feminists noted that families have not only joint interests, but also internal conflicts over resources, power, autonomy and choices (Davidoff et al., 1999).

This approach is relevant to this book as it has the advantage of recognising agency and difference in families and that as human actors we do not simply respond, we also calculate and take decisions about how to respond to situations. Thus, for example, Davidoff et al. examine concrete families across the last four centuries and assess how they have responded to the social events and other pressures on them. Coontz, the American historian, explains succinctly the implications of this for our understanding of families actually work:

> *Understanding the specificity of social location and the importance of context...directs our attention to the tension between the institutional or historical constraints under which people operate and the tool kit of personal cultural and social resources they use to make choices.*
>
> (Coontz, 1999: p294).

This is very helpful for family support workers and social welfare agencies. Indeed this approach in social welfare has tended to be represented through the concept of 'partnership' – which suggests, minimally, that families are other than simply passive recipients.

The editors of this book would argue that these theories are relevant and important for family support practice. Theory helps us to think critically and constructively about the work that we do. Theory can provide an underpinning which informs our practice in a dynamic way.

Evaluating Family Support

In many ways underpinning this book are issues relating to research and evaluation. The initiatives we outline in the practice chapters have been subjected to varying degrees of evaluation and may draw on research to influence their development.

In recent years there has been a focus on developing what is variously referred to as 'evidence-based' or 'evidence-led' practice (see Lloyd, 1998). The key argument of this school of thought is that all welfare practice should be able to provide some evidence for the forms of practice which they adopt. In this section we examine how family support practice can be researched and evaluated.

Peter Pecora (1998) is probably the most important and influential American researcher in the family support field. Pecora has emphasised the importance of utilising an analytical framework for the planning and the evaluation of family support. The framework provided by Pecora is consistent with that utilised by Hardiker et al., which is outlined above, although the emphasis of the language and concepts vary slightly. The levels of prevention – which Pecora calls universal preventive interventions, selective preventive interventions and indicated preventive intervention – are effectively similar to those identified by Hardiker et al. (1999). Such frameworks are crucial to evaluation and research as Pecora argues that:

> An important first step in a renewed prevention effort is to arrive at commonly agreed upon definitions of the terms prevention and prevention research. Without this, prevention will continue to be a confused field with disagreement on its scope.
>
> (1998: p6).

Pecora is deploying prevention here in much the same way that we have been using the idea of family support in this book. What is important here is to make the links between family support practice and the wider social policies which help and support all families. As Pecora has cogently argued:

> Family based services will not replace other types of child and family services or broader societal and service system reforms…it is incumbent upon researchers and program staff to point out the place of family based programs within the larger network of services, and to emphasise to policy makers that both the short and long-term success of these programs is dependent upon the family's ability to access a range of community services and other societal supports.
>
> (1998: p16-7).

Whilst in this book we focus on child welfare services – as provided by statutory and voluntary welfare agencies – it is important to note that these services play a relatively minor role compared to the main state services such as education, health and social security.

What is the role of research and evaluation in relation to child welfare? The following quote from Lloyd has summarised the current debate well:

> Within the developing debate around evidence-based social work practice, two trends can be distinguished. One could be described as being towards a more strict or hard-line approach, the other veers toward eclecticism, or pragmatism. As

> far as the more hard-line approach is concerned the case for the use of methodologically sound research, in particular randomised controlled trials…has been strongly made.
>
> (1998: p164).

As Pecora has argued in relation to family support, 'we need to pursue a rigorous long term research agenda' (1998, p34). This rigorous approach, or what Lloyd refers to as 'methodologically sound' usually involving the randomised controlled trial, is rarely used in family support. As McCroskey and Meezon argue:

> Traditional, experimental evaluation designs have seldom been used in this area, because random design to a treatment or control group is difficult in a program whose doors are open to all interested.
>
> (1998: p61).

As a consequence of this problem and also for more positive reasons:

> Some evaluators advocate studying family support with non-traditional approaches that draw the evaluator into direct interactions with the program staff and participants…some also emphasise qualitative understanding over quantitative assessments of program effects.
>
> (McCroskey and Meezan, 1998: p61).

In the chapters in this book the reader will perceive that a range of research and evaluation methods and techniques have been used. What are the issues for research and evaluation which arise from our consideration of family support? Six particular issues are identified here:

1) The growth of evaluation

One emphasis in New Labour policy has been on evaluation and the related issues of evidence-based practice. Most of the social and family initiatives launched by the New Labour Government are subject to extensive evaluation at both national and local levels. Programmes which are being evaluated and for which evaluative evidence is beginning to emerge include Sure Start, the National Youth Justice Boards' parenting programmes, and early years Centres of Excellence. In total these projects will produce a wealth of evaluative evidence relating to the effectiveness of family support services.

2) The Sure Start evaluation

Probably the most influential of all these initiatives is the Sure Start programme which aims to deliver effective, multi-agency family support to those with younger children in disadvantaged localities (Glass, 1999). The national evaluation of Sure Start will produce data on family support initiatives comparable to that of the United States of America Head Start programme which has also been extensively evaluated (see Waldfogel, 1999).

3) A question of method

It will be apparent from this book that there are a wide range of methods that can be used in family support research and evaluation. We would argue that there is a place in family support research for qualitative and quantitative methods, surveys, evaluations and Randomised Controlled Trials (studies where participants are allocated to an intervention group and a control group). No particular method should assume a privileged position.

4) Involving stakeholders

It would be a fundamental contradiction if family support practice placed an emphasis on partnership and user involvement and yet excluded users from the research and evaluation process. Family support research, perhaps more than other forms of research, needs to recognise the importance of user involvement in the research and evaluation process. Many of the projects outlined in this book have value positions such as 'partnership' with parents. Researchers and evaluators are striving to practice together with professionals and services users to devise methods and instruments for use in the research process and in the discussion and dissemination of findings. Family support evaluation has to avoid the assumption that the evaluator is the sole person who can find the true worth of a project or service. As I have argued elsewhere:

> The traditional 'expert' model would hold, probably in an implicit rather than explicit way, that the evaluator has a privileged position in relation to 'knowledge' and has some form of privileged access to this. An alternative model would rather emphasise a process of evaluation which is empowering – which shares knowledge and expertise, and which mobilises, for example, practitioner and service users' perspectives on how the project works.
>
> (Frost in Adams et al., 2002: p52).

Ray Pawson and Nick Tilley in their key text *Realistic Evaluation* (1997) identify clear roles in the evaluation process for the various stakeholders. These are as follows:

> *Subjects, or service users*, 'are likely to be far more sensitized to the mechanisms in operation within a program' (Pawson and Tilley, 1997: p160). These can be uncovered through the use of in-depth face-to-face interviews or through focus groups.
>
> *Practitioners*, 'translate program theories into practice and so are to be considered the great 'utility players' in the information game' (ibid, p161). They can act as partners in the process or as self evaluators.
>
> *Evaluators*, according to Pawson and Tilley, 'carry theories into the encounter with program' (ibid, p161).

It follows if this analysis is correct that each and every stakeholder has a valuable role to play in the process.

5) An investment in research and evaluation

Short-term evaluations, such as those which some of our practice chapters draw on, are valuable, and individual projects can learn important lessons from project specific evaluations which can help them to become 'learning organisations' (Argyris and Schon, 1996). Long-term, comparative and controlled studies too have a crucial role to play in helping to influence both policy and practice development. Investment in evaluation and research is important in contributing to the development of family support.

6) The dissemination process

The evaluation process does not finish with the production of a 'report' or a book. The dissemination process is essential if stakeholders are to receive adequate feedback. Trinder has argued that the dissemination process is in itself 'a political process', rather than a neutral or technical process (1996: p238). Dissemination is about sharing knowledge and therefore power in the family support process. Effective evaluation findings should be part of a process by which family support practice is reflected upon. Family support projects also need different and user-appropriate methods of feedback. The author was involved in a study which was disseminated as part of a 'fun day' which involved jugglers and other entertainment (Frost and Ryden, 2001).

We also need to think about developing more traditional modes of dissemination. One example of this is the Barnardo's *What Works* series, which now consists of almost 20 publications (see Stein, 1997, for example). The Department of Health have adopted a strategy of producing readable summaries of their funded research projects, which have been accompanied by sophisticated publicity and dissemination processes (see Weyts, Morpeth and Bullock, 2000 for an evaluation of Department of Health strategy) and a very effective website.

Conclusion

In this chapter we have attempted to set the scene for the remainder of the book. The chapter has argued for certain approaches to the family and family support. It has also argued that certain theoretical approaches can be mobilised to help establish these approaches. The chapter concluded with a discussion of the role of research and evaluation. We now move on to some of the evidence and data which can be used to underpin some of the arguments made in this chapter.

Families, Change and Policy Reponses
Nick Frost

Introduction

The aim of this chapter is to provide a wider policy context for the remainder of the book. We commence by examining some of the data which provides a backdrop to recent policy developments. This data is concerned with what is happening in families and households – addressing both household structure and issues around poverty and wealth. We then move on to examine some recent policy initiatives which aspire to address some of the issues arising from our statistical investigation.

What is Happening to British Families?

The State collects a mass of data which can give us an insight into patterns and trends within families and households. Statistics do not of course tell a story in any straightforward manner – the statistics are dense and mask complex, and sometimes contradictory, trends and patterns (this discussion draws on Frost, 2001). These statistics are important for family support policy makers and practitioners as they have a real impact on the type of families and households that they work with.

First of all let us examine the structure of households in Great Britain, over the period 1961-1999. This period is significant as it is often identified as a period of crisis within the family (Gordon, 1985). Here, we can note the changes in family structure since 1961. There has been a decline in the number of children in individual families – in 1961 8% of all households had three or more children and by 1998-99 this had halved to 4%. At the beginning of the twentieth century the average household size was about 4.6 people: by 1998-99 this had declined to 2.4 people (Social Trends 30, 2000: p34). Thus, given that there has been an overall increase in the size of the population, more households have developed but of a smaller size over recent decades.

There has also been a discernable trend in postponing the birth of a first child which helps to

explain an increase in the number of couples living in a household without children (from 26% of all households in 1961 to 30% in 1998-99) and therefore also the decline in the proportion with 1 or 2 children (from 30% to 19%). It should be noted that this trend towards later childbirth for women is an uneven one and that there is an association between the postponements of the birth of a first child with the mother possessing a higher educational qualification (ONS, 2000: p11). For family support workers usually working with poorer families, with perhaps fewer educational qualifications, the impact of this may be less visible.

Significantly in terms of family support it can be noted than in 1961 48% of all British households were couples with children (dependent and non-dependent), but that this declined to 29% of all households by 1998-99. One implication of this is that the view of 'the family' as parents and dependent children is, therefore, no longer the majority experience of British households.

Part of the crisis of the family is sometimes identified as the decline in marriage. The number of first marriages in Great Britain peaked in 1970 at about 390,000. By 1995 it had just about halved to 192,000, and by 1997 had declined further to 175,000. This could be read superficially as a decline in the popularity of marriage. However, the picture is more complex, as the rate of re-marriage has increased steadily since 1961, and by 1995 about two fifths of all marriages were actually re-marriages. Thus whilst first marriage is declining in frequency, a significant number of people are electing to re-marry. It follows that the frequency of re-marriage must reflect previous divorces: the number of divorces more than doubled between 1961 and 1995. By 1997 the number of divorces per annum was only slightly less than the number of marriages – about 175,000. However, these tend to be uneven trends due to legal changes. For example, the Divorce Reform Act 1969, (which came into force in 1971) contributed to increases in divorce and subsequent re-marriages in the early 1970s (Social

Trends 30, 2000: p50). Family support workers will often come across the impact of divorce and separation in their work.

Family support workers may also find that they work with large numbers of lone parent families. Lone parent households with dependent children increased from 2% of the total households in 1961 to 7% of the total by 1998-99 in Great Britain. It is important to note that whilst births outside marriage have risen steadily throughout the period and reached about 38% of all live births in 1998 the vast majority of births outside marriage are in fact jointly registered. The percentage of all live births registered by only one person is therefore only about 8% of all live births. As Ford and Millar comment:

> *Statistics on single, never married women are misleading...the number of couples living together without marriage is rising. Women who separate from a cohabiting relationship usually appear in the statistics as single, but they are really separated.*
>
> (1997: p2).

Another important factor for family support staff is to understand that the structure of families and households will vary when examined in terms of ethnicity. This will of course differ considerably on a local basis but we can detect and suggest national patterns and trends.

The statistics suggest that South Asian (Indian, Pakistani and Bangladeshi) people are less likely to live in single person households than the rest of the population. For example, only 7% of Pakistani and Bangladeshi households live in single person households compared to 28% of all households in Great Britain (Social Trends 30, 2000). This partly reflects the more youthful age structure of these groups and also attitudinal factors towards family life.

South Asian households are more likely to be couple households than other groups in the population. For example, in 1999 56% of all Pakistani/Bangladeshi households fall into this category, compared to 21% of the Black population. It follows that Black ethnic groups are more likely to live in lone parent households. In 1999, 24% of all Black households were single parent households. There were more lone parent households than couple households with dependent children in the Black population. These contrasts with the Pakistani/Bangladeshi group where fewer than

10% of households were lone parent households and over 55% were couple households with dependent children (Social Trends 30, 2000).

The only ethnic groups with enough multi-family households to register in the statistics were Indian (7% of all Indian households) and Pakistani/Bangladeshi (10% of all Pakistani/Bangladeshi households). These statistical differences have been given a qualitative dimension in studies such as Beishon et al. (1998) and Exploring Parenthood's study (1997) which help to explain the cultural, social and attitudinal factors underpinning the statistical differences.

Why do all these rather dry facts and figures matter for family support practitioners? Inevitably any one worker confronts only the individual, unique family. However, when trends within families are aggregated the trends we have discussed will emerge and have to be taken into account by practitioners and policy makers alike.

Social Exclusion, Family Support and Poverty

Perhaps the major issue which influences the nature of family support practice is that of social exclusion. Social exclusion has a major impact on the day-to-day work of family support workers and again we would argue that the underpinning trends and statistics do matter.

The context for this discussion is provided by the government commitment to end child poverty:

> *Our historic aim will be for ours to be the first generation to end child poverty, and it will take a generation. It is a 20-year mission but I believe it can be done.*
>
> (Tony Blair, Prime Minister, 18. 3. 1999, quoted by Bradshaw, 2001: p16).

The statistics on poverty are complex and difficult to understand. In this section we draw mainly on the Office of National Statistics (ONS) report, *Social Inequalities* (2000). The *Social Inequalities* report provides evidence for the extent of poverty and inequality in Great Britain. These figures, it should be noted, are subject to rapid change due to policy developments and wider economic changes.

Using a definition of poverty as less than 60% of median income, excluding housing costs, the ONS report makes it clear that around 3.2 million children in Great Britain were living in poverty during 1997-98 (ONS, 2000: p42). This situation was worse for ethnic minority households: 'in 1997-98, individuals in households headed by people from the Black, Indian, Pakistani or Bangladeshi groups were particularly likely to be in the poorest section of income distribution' (ONS, 2000: p42). Nearly two thirds of Pakistani and Bangladeshi people lived in low-income households. Poverty is therefore a reality for many people in Great Britain and this has particular implications for family support policy and practice.

Sometimes it is argued that poverty does not really exist in contemporary Western societies. However, it is a sobering challenge to this view to recall that:

Clear evidence exists to demonstrate a strong association between father's social class and heightened risk of mortality for children at all ages.
(Quilgars, 2001: p38).

When we examine lone parents in particular we can note that lone parents:

...are much more likely than those living in other household types to have low incomes. In 1997-98 just under 2 in 5 individuals in lone parent households were on incomes of less than 60% of median (income). After adjusting for household costs this figure rose to just over 3 in 5.
(ONS, 2000: p36).

There is therefore a clear association between poverty and living in a single parent household. Again this has profound policy implications.

As already stated, these statistics tend to take a 'snapshot' approach to poverty and social inequality, that is, they 'freeze' time and examine the existence of poverty at that time. In contrast to this approach Hill and Jenkins (1999) have used data from the British Household Panel Survey to examine the persistence of poverty over time. They point out that children are more likely than other members of the population to suffer the impact of persistent poverty:

Almost three quarters (71%) of the total poverty experienced by pre-schoolers was chronic, compared to three fifths (60%) for all children and just over one half (56%) for the population as a whole.
(1999: p1).

Hill and Jenkins argue that New Labour policy of movement from benefit to work for families is a useful way of addressing poverty from a 'persistence' perspective.

Piachaud and Sutherland (2000) have also examined the impact of the early stage of the New Labour Government on poverty. It is clear that child poverty grew during the period of Conservative Government – from less than a million children living in poverty in 1979/80 (using less than half of median income as the measure) to more than three million children in 1997/98. In response to this Tony Blair made the pledge we have already referred to – that New Labour would 'end child poverty'. Piachaud and Sutherland argue that the effect of tax and benefit changes under the Labour Government: 'has been to increase incomes of the poorest more than those of the better off and of households with children more than others. Nine out of ten children are living in households where income has gone up...' They estimate that 'By 2002 the proportion of children in poverty will fall by six percentage points' (2000).

The complexity of these figures is demonstrated by the argument made by Walker that whilst an impact has been made since 1997 on child poverty the measurement of any change remains difficult:

Labour's measures up to and including the 2001 budget did significantly boost the incomes of the poorest households. If poverty had stayed put at 1997's levels Labour would have pulled 3m households above the poverty line, cutting the number of poor households from 19.4% to 14%, an amazing achievement. Unfortunately poverty has to be measured relative to incomes at large.
(Walker, *The Guardian*, 2002).

As Walker points out the figures are less rosy when this is taken into account. Poverty and social exclusion are actually related to inequalities in wealth. In 1996, 1% of the population owned 20% of the total wealth. Additionally, the wealthiest 50% of the population owned 93% of total wealth – leaving 7% for the remaining 50%, the poorest element of the population (ONS, 2000: p49).

It is clear then that poverty, and the resulting outcomes, remain a major challenge for family support.

The Child Welfare Response

From the Second World War to the re-focusing debate

Thus far in this chapter we have examined the wider context of family support – the changing nature of families and households, and the impact of poverty and social exclusion. How has child welfare responded to these challenges? In the context of this book we commence by examining developments since the Second World War (for a discussion which as a longer historical perspective see Frost, Mills and Stein, 1999, on which this section draws).

We begin with the 1948 Children Act which introduced a duty to receive children and young people into care on a voluntary basis, emphasised that the religious needs of the child must be met, and placed stronger after-care duties on the authorities. The Child Care Act also placed a duty on the local authorities to restore the child to the family wherever possible. This is important for family support as it can be seen to represent a breaking with the Poor Law and the child rescue thinking of the Victorian era and the early child care philanthropists.

During this post-war period there was an emphasis on the development of preventive work with families, or what might now be conceptualised as family support, using mainly casework skills to prevent the need for children and young people to enter the care system. Caseworkers employed by local Child Care Departments offered a personalised and skilled service to children and their families. The move towards prevention was reinforced by the Ingelby Committee, which reported in 1960 and whose concern with prevention was enshrined in Section 1 of the 1963 Children and Young Persons Act. The Ingelby Committee also furthered the trend of bringing together responses to both delinquent and deprived children and young people.

Meanwhile, the trend towards viewing neglected children as having shared problems with those children and young people who had been involved in offending reached a highpoint with the passage of the 1969 Children and Young Persons Act (see Frost and Stein, 1989: p81). The Act was in many ways the embodiment of a welfare, rather than child rescue, approach to working with families. However, before the Act could

be implemented a withdrawal from this position had begun. The election of a Conservative Government in 1970 witnessed a retreat from welfare to a justice model (see Frost and Stein, 1989: p82-6).

Probably the major landmark for a contemporary discussion of family support was the passage of the Children Act, 1989. Family support is a major theme of this Act, which was enacted in late 1989 and came into force in October 1991. It has been argued that the Children Act is complex and sometimes contradictory (Frost, 1992). However, there can be little doubt that it has raised the profile of family support work in England and Wales, and also influenced developments in Northern Ireland and Scotland. The crucial section for this book is Section 17 of the Children Act which states that:

> *It shall be the general duty of every local authority:*
> *(a) to safeguard and promote the welfare of children within their area who are in need; and*
> *(b) so far as is consistent with that duty, to promote the upbringing of such children by their families, by providing a range and level of services appropriate to those children's needs.*

This section introduced the sometimes controversial idea that local authorities should identify children and young people who are 'children in need'. Where they fall into this category, family support services should be delivered to them.

Following the passage of the Children Act, a policy shift which became known as the 'refocusing debate' was initiated. (This is discussed in detail in Chapter 3 of this book). The debate followed the emergence of an authoritarian style in child protection during the 1980s – largely as a result of political and media concern about child deaths and subsequent inquiry findings (see Parton, 1985) emphasising firm and clear action to protect children seen to be abused or at risk of abuse. The terms of this debate began to be shifted by events in Cleveland (Campbell, 1988) where it had been perceived that child protection practice was in danger of acting against the best interest of both parents and children.

Partly in the aftermath of Cleveland and reflecting a commitment to research-led policy making, the Department of Health commissioned a programme of wide reaching research. This research eventually took the form of 20 publications. These studies were brought together in the ground-breaking publication *Child Protection: Messages from Research* (Department of Health, 1995). This however went further than simply summarising research and engaged centrally in a crucial child welfare policy debate which had been emerging throughout the 1990s. Thus *Messages* became the trigger for the so-called 're-focusing' debate. The focus, it was argued, had been on 'child protection' in the narrow sense of ensuring that children were protected from inter-personal abuse or neglect by their parents or other caretakers. *Messages* questioned this narrow focus, arguing that it led to an investigatory mentality, often leading to no particular intervention or support for the family:

> *The research studies have questioned whether the balance of child protection and the range of supports and interventions available to professionals is correct. This is an issue area child protection committee and professionals associated with this group must consistently raise about services in their region.*
>
> (DoH, 1995: p54).

The focus on Section 17 of the Children Act was strengthened by *Messages*, again suggesting that this is the key Section of the Act:

> *An approach based on the process of Section 47 enquiries and the provision of Section 17 services, might well shift the emphasis in child protection work more towards family support. This, in turn, might encourage local authorities to review the type of Section 17 services provided and to consider how well these are matched to their priority cases.*
>
> (DoH, 1995: p55).

This debate and the research findings encouraged local authorities, often working with voluntary organisations, to develop their family support policies and services. Much of this book has been stimulated by the debate and the events surrounding it, and the chapters in Part Two allow the reader to explore particular practice initiatives in some depth. The debate flowing from *Messages* suggested that the new focus should be more broadly based on the welfare of the child and family – thus the key question shifts from 'how can this child best be protected' to 'what can be done to best promote the welfare of the child and family'? The key theme of this book, family support, is central. Again, as *Messages* argued:

> *In fact a continuum exists between child protection, family support and child welfare. Agreement leads to better outcomes and agreement can be reached without recourse to the child protection process*
>
> (DoH, 1995: p55).

Wendy Rose, a key promoter of re-focusing argued that it follows that services must:

> *...intervene with a lighter, less bureaucratic touch in a number of cases, integrate family support services both practically and conceptually more with child protection, and thereby release more resources from investigation and assessment into family support and treatment services.*
>
> (Wendy Rose, Assistant Chief Inspector, Department of Health, 1994).

The American commentator Frank Farrow has produced an interesting perspective on this debate – reflecting not least that the re-focusing debate has some international currency. The table below is an adaptation of Farrow's work.

Child protection	Current approach	Envisioned approach
1. Case entry and finding	• Referrals mix appropriate and inappropriate cases • Over 50% found 'unsubstantiated' for child maltreatment • Offers no preventive assistance	• Referrals are more appropriate because community alternatives exist • An estimated 80% of referrals are found appropriate • Targeted interventions before referral
2. Assessment or investigation	• 'One size fits all' investigation process • Absence of comprehensive family assessment	• Comprehensive family assessment for all after initial screening • Differential responses
3. Service provision	• Few services available • Little involvement of natural helping networks • Highly centralised agency control of services	• Access to a customised array of services • Strong involvement of community supports and natural helping networks • Neighbourhood-service delivery
4. Substitute parental care	• First choice rather than last • Children linger in substitute care	• Triggered only after intensive family preservation has been tried or considered • Timely and fair decisions about re-unification and adoption
Broader community supports to improve outcomes for children	• No defined mandate to promote well-being • No defined community governance • Few community services • Categorical funding	• Clear community commitment and mandate • A community governance entity • Comprehensive array of early family supports • Finance is flexible
Accountability for child protection	• SSDs are the only accountable agency	• Accountability is shared by network of community agencies

Adapted from: Frank Farrow: Getting From Here to There (unpublished paper, 1995).

This then begins to shift the parameters of child welfare – representing both a move towards family support and a re-focusing of child protection practice to emphasise a family support approach.

The Impact of New Labour

Since the re-focusing debate was initiated in 1994 the major event in terms of child welfare has been the election of the New Labour Government in 1997, and its re-election in 2001. This has arguably both taken forward and re-aligned the re-focusing debate. Policy has developed with a central focus on childhood and child poverty as a key area of state intervention. Whilst child welfare may have been marginalised at various stages of social history at the early stages of the twenty-first century it is clearly centre stage. New Labour family policy has been extensive and has included a mass of initiatives, many of which could be defined as 'child welfare' in its broadest sense. In the context of this chapter we can mention only a few of the most pertinent:

- The 'Supporting Families' Green Paper.
- The National Child Care Strategy.
- Sure-Start.
- The Children's Fund.
- The Working Families Tax Credit.
- Parenting Orders.

In this context we will discuss the first three of these. A useful starting point for our discussion is the *Supporting Families* consultation paper which was an attempt by the newly elected government of 1997 to address some fundamental issues around family policy. New Labour was elected partially in the fallout from the Conservatives association with 'sleaze' and the related failure of the 'back to basics' campaign. The later was perhaps ill-defined but had at its heart a family values agenda. This gives a context for New Labour's attempt to re-think family policy. Would it be possible to devise a family policy which held on to some concept of 'family values', but managed to avoid the pitfalls which the Conservatives had fallen for? The fact is that the *Supporting Families* paper is an attempt to balance the recognition of family diversity and a more authoritarian communitarian approach which bears the imprint of the American social theorist and activist Etzioni (1993 a and b). But this is not simply a theoretical problem – is fundamentally a political one which informs the whole of the New Labour family agenda.

Explicitly recognising many of the issues around diversity discussed in Chapter 1 of this book, the paper states that, 'we must not give the impression that members of the Government are any better than the rest of the population in meeting the challenge of family life' (Home Office, 1998: p4). It argues that there are five areas where government can make a difference:

- Ensuring that all parents have access to the advice and support they need, improving services and strengthening the ways in which the wider family and communities support and nurture family life.
- Improving family prosperity, reducing child poverty, and ensuring the tax and benefit system properly acknowledges the costs of bringing up children.
- Making it easier for parents to spend more time with their children by helping families to balance home and work.
- Strengthening marriage and reducing the risks of family breakdown.

- Tackling the more serious problems of family life, including domestic violence and school-age pregnancy.

Each of these is addressed in detail and the paper attempts to develop a coherent family agenda – engaging with the real problems of change and modernity, of the role of the state and of personal choice. However this remains a discussion paper – we go on to review in brief two important initiatives which have emerged during the New Labour period: the National Child Care Strategy and Sure Start.

The National Child Care Strategy

Arguably the most important initiative in the more practical family policy initiative is the National Child Care Strategy, which has at its heart the Early Years Development and Child Care Partnerships (EYDCPs) established to deliver enhanced and co-ordinated services in each local authority area (DfEE, 1998; Lloyd, 2000). The entire emphasis of the National Child Care Strategy is one of joint working and partnership.

The overall aims of the strategy include:
- *raising the quality of child care*
- *making child care more affordable*
- *making child care more accessible by increasing places and improving information*

(DfEE, 1998: p6).

These aims are to be delivered through the establishment of the EYDCP's. The Government suggests two acid tests for achievement of these aims, both of which are clearly measurable:

- *Better outcomes for children, including readiness to learn by the time they reach school and enjoyable, developmental activities out of school hours.*
- *More parents with the chance to take up work, education or training because they have access to diverse, good quality childcare.*

(DfEE, 1998: p7).

Child care, a crucial element of any family support strategy, is clearly seen as a key driver of family policy and indeed of wider economic policy. It is too early to produce the definitive results in terms of the outcome of the National Child Care Strategy; however, some early analysis has argued that some of the outcomes have been disappointing. According to Helen Wilkinson:

> *Having children remains a significant barrier to the employment opportunities of mothers; and the lack of accessible and affordable childcare is having an adverse impact on mothers returning to the labour market.*

> *(The Guardian, 26.3.2002).*

In many ways effective early years care underpins any family support strategy. Without extensive child care there are a number of knock on effects: stress on families, difficulties of access to work, in particular for single parents, and a lack of social stimulation and care for young children. For these reasons effective child care and family support go hand in hand.

Sure Start

As well as day care, family support requires more targeted and designed early years interventions. The most high profile example of this sort of programme under New Labour is the Sure Start initiative and is described by one of its architects as:

> *A radical cross-departmental strategy to raise the physical, social, emotional and intellectual status of young children through improved services. It is targeted at children under four and their families in areas of need.*

> *(Glass, 1999: p257).*

By 2004 there will be 500 Sure Start schemes and government funding will have risen to almost £500m. This initiative is a central plank in the New Labour project to abolish child poverty within a generation, and is discussed in more detail in Chapter 7 of this book. Sure Start is subject to a Public Service Agreement with the government for 2001-04. This reflects a central theme of New Labour public policy- that there should be clear and measurable outcomes for public policy initiatives. The Objectives in the Agreement are as follows:

Objective 1: Improving social and emotional development

Reduce the proportion of children aged 0-3 in the 500 Sure Start areas who are re-registered within the space of 12 months on the child protection register by 20 per cent by 2004.

Objective 2: Improving health

Achieve by 2004 in the 500 Sure Start areas, a 10 per cent reduction in mothers who smoke in pregnancy.

Objective 3: Improving children's ability to learn

Achieve by 2004 for children aged 0-3 in the 500 Sure Start areas, a reduction of five percentage points in the number of children with speech and language problems requiring specialist intervention by the age of four.

Objective 4: Strengthening families and communities

Reduce the number of 0-3 year old children in Sure Start areas living in households where no one is working by 2004.

These targets reflect a pressure on Sure Start to produce real and measurable outcomes. Whilst these measures may seem narrow on a first reading, some are regarded as proxy targets reflecting in an empirically measurable form more wide reaching aims. In this book we argue however that there are real problems with reducing complex social intervention programmes to measurable outcomes (see Chapter 7). At the time of writing there is little actual research available on the outcomes of Sure Start, although an early survey produced the following positive results:

- Nine in ten parents felt that services for young children have improved significantly over the past year, which they largely attribute to Sure Start.
- 88% were satisfied with services for young children and families with just over half saying they were very satisfied. No one was dissatisfied.
- Over 80% of parents who think services have improved said there was now more for them and their children to do and that there was more support for them as parents.
- One of the main early benefits identified was the provision of high quality play and learning experiences for children. These were perceived as very beneficial for children in acquiring new skills, formally (e.g. learning through play) and particularly informally (e.g. socialising with other children).

- The provision of more and better quality child care facilities is also seen as a key improvement.
- Sure Start has given both parents and their children more confidence. Parents are more confident in playing, teaching and dealing day-to-day with their children and children are more confident in socialising with their peers.
- Support and advice for parents in bringing up their children was felt to be of great value, particularly in introducing them to other parents and giving them more confidence in how to bring up their children.
- There is an increased level of 'community spirit' with parents working together to improve their local community as a result of Sure Start.
- Parents identify greater parental involvement as a key component of the success of the Sure Start programme.
- Most parents felt that their children will be different in five years time having benefited from Sure Start, particularly in their children being more 'ready' for school.

(Source: Sure Start website surestart.gov.uk).

It remains to be seen what the outcomes of the Sure Start programme will be. There are concerns that its concentration in small areas might encourage geographical inequalities of provision and that it might increase the visibility of poor families to interventions around child protection. However there can be little doubt that it is an exciting and innovative programme which will be fundamental to the future of family support in the United Kingdom.

Conclusion

In this chapter we have attempted to explore the context for current New Labour policy and, briefly, some of the content of that policy. The following chapters examine the contribution of the local authority and the voluntary sector to the process of developing family support, before Part One concludes with a more detailed examination of the key elements of New Labour policy, with a particular focus on Sure Start and the Children's Fund.

3 Moving on From Child Protection: 'Messages From Research' and 'Re-focusing'

Liz Jeffery

Introduction

The death, in 1973, of Maria Colwell, a child who had been in the care system but subsequently placed by social workers at home with her mother, marked the beginning of a chain of events and consequences which, over the next 20 years was to change, fundamentally, the role of social workers involved with children and families. Maria's death at the hands of her step-father resulted in a public enquiry, published in 1975, into the circumstances surrounding the tragedy, an event which seriously called into question for the first time the professional accountability of social workers and challenged the assumptions on which they had acted, or in the case of Maria, failed to take action (see Parton, 1985).

Other child abuse enquiries followed in the 1970s when again children were injured or died after being left at risk in their birth families. However, those tragedies that attracted most attention were the ones that took place in the 1980s. Jasmine Beckford, Tyra Henry and Kimberley Carlile were all children who died at the hands of their parents or their partners and who social workers either did not or were unable, because of their existing powers at the time, to protect (see London Borough of Brent, 1985, for example). The issue was portrayed in the media as comparatively simple: social workers were failing in their duty to keep children safe; they were listening only to their parents and not giving sufficient weight to what the children themselves said about their circumstances. Indeed, in some cases they were not seen or spoken to at all.

The events of Cleveland in 1987 (Campbell, 1988), where children were removed from parental care on suspicion of sexual abuse, provoked however, a backlash from the public. Opinion now swung in the opposite direction and social workers were seen as over-zealous in their efforts to protect children and disregarding the rights and privacy of birth families, claiming evidence of abuse where it did not exist. Instead of failing to listen to children and leaving them in danger, they were now accused of over-credulity in their acceptance of what children told them, and to be taking their views too seriously. The mandate for effective social work intervention with children and families had now been completely called into question and the profession was in crisis.

Responding to Enquiries

Maria Colwell's death and those that followed in the 1970s and 1980s prompted a number of government-led responses directed at more effective protection of children who were either in public care or otherwise known to social workers. Starting in 1974, a number of DHSS circulars (DHSS, 1974, 1980) gave rise to the creation in local authorities of Area Child Protection Committees (ACPCs) formerly known as Area Review Committees, which continue to exist and which bring together in an inter-agency meeting management representatives from Health, Social Services, Education, Probation and the Police. The role of these Committees is to formulate and oversee child protection policy and procedures within the local authority, with many of the associated responsibilities being devolved to specialist sub-committees.

In 1987 these procedures were reviewed and gave rise in 1988 to the first *Working Together* document (DHSS, 1988). This national guidance replaced what were known as 'at risk' registers with the Child Protection Registers that continue to exist today, and clarified and standardised the way in which they were to be used. Children's names were to be entered on the register only after a multi-agency case conference which would agree to registration if a child had either been seriously harmed or was assessed as being at risk of harm. The register was to be held either by social services or NSPCC on its behalf and managed by an experienced worker with specialist skills in child protection. It was these new responsibilities and the procedures that accompanied them which led, in the late 1980s and 1990s to the steady growth of what has since become known as the child protection 'industry'.

Alongside and associated with these procedural changes, further developments were taking place. Concerns about social work accountability and responsibilities, highlighted by Maria Colwell's death and the others that followed, raised awareness that more research was needed into how professional decisions were made and what actually happened to children once they were admitted to public care. This feeling was reinforced by the need, in times of economic restraint, to determine whether the steadily increasing social service budgets could be justified. So, for the first time, the DHSS published an overview of research which they had commissioned, with *Social Work Decisions in Child Care* being published in 1985 (DHSS, 1985). This publication achieved considerable significance, not only in terms of the particular findings it produced but also because it inaugurated a new era in social work, one in which practice was to become more grounded in research and evidence which would be commissioned, by government who would thus, indirectly, become more involved in overseeing and influencing the profession.

A further influential development was the report in 1984 of the Short Committee (Social Services Committee, 1984) which recommended a total review of all child care law. This was arguably not before time. Ever since the Children and Young Persons Act, 1933, the volume of child care legislation had increased apace until by the mid-1980s children's welfare was covered by more than 50 legal instruments. The Children Act 1989, implemented in 1991, repealed all previous legislation and in bringing together for the first time both public and private matters, became the first totally comprehensive piece of child care law (Frost, 1992).

The Children Act, 1989

...the most comprehensive and far-reaching reform of child-care law which has come before Parliament in living memory.

(Lord Chancellor, quoted in Department of Health, 2001: p4).

The timing of the Children Act, which was being drafted just as events in Cleveland were unfolding, was highly significant. Conceived at a time when the rights of children to be protected from harm were generally viewed as needing to take precedence over those of their parents, the experience of Cleveland led to the pendulum swinging the other way, and to a clamour for parents themselves to be protected from what was seen by some as the unwarranted intrusion of social workers into their lives. The Act then had, in some way, to steer an acceptable course between the Scylla of children's rights and the Charybdis of the parents' lobby, and try to avoid being shipwrecked along the way.

A further influence on the Act were the research findings of 1985 (DHSS, 1985) which have already been referred to, which highlighted both the way in which professional decisions were made and their impact on the lives of children. This was the first time that child care legislation had been so directly influenced by research and the Children Act was therefore seen as a landmark in this respect. In fact, further research was commissioned immediately after the Act was passed to explore how far certain key aspects were being addressed during implementation and highlighting in particular the experience of black and ethnic minority families.

So what did the Children Act have to say and what impact did it have on professional practice? First of all, the Act introduced a number of guiding principles. In summary these were that:

- The welfare of the child is paramount.
- Wherever possible children should be brought up and cared for in their own families.
- Parents of children in need should be helped to bring up their own children themselves.
- This help should be provided as a service, in partnership with parents and meet each child's identified needs, appropriate to their race, culture, religion and language, and draw on effective partnership between local authority and other agencies, including voluntary organisations.
- Children should be safe and protected if in danger.
- Children should be kept informed about decisions affecting them and participate in decisions about their future.
- Parents retain parental responsibility even when their children no longer live with them and should be kept informed and participate in decisions about their children's future.

The Act consists of twelve parts of which the most significant in terms of social work practice are Parts

III, IV and V. Guidance and regulations were also produced to assist in the implementation of the Act. As we saw in the previous chapter the key element of the Act in terms of family support is Part III, and in particular Section 17.

The Act proceeds to outline firstly the *powers* of a local authority to provide day care for under fives; accommodation; out of school and holiday provision; and importantly social services power to request support from other agencies in achieving these functions (Part III, Sec.18); and secondly, their *duties* to 'take reasonable steps to reduce the need to bring care or supervision proceedings...'; 'to avoid the need for children...to be placed in secure accommodation...'; 'to take reasonable steps through the provision of services to prevent children suffering ill-treatment or neglect;' 'to provide Family Centres as...appropriate;' and 'to publish and make available information about services.'

Parts IV and V clarify social services' statutory powers and introduce some new measures in terms of child protection, substituting, importantly, Emergency Protection Orders for Place of Safety Orders which had allowed parents no legal means of challenging the removal of their children into care for the first 28 days; and introducing Child Assessment Orders. Of particular significance in Part V is Section 47, which states that the local authority is required to make or cause to be made: 'such enquiries as they consider necessary to enable them to decide whether they should take any action to safeguard or promote the child's welfare' and that 'the enquiries shall, in particular, be directed towards establishing whether the authority should make any application to the court, or exercise any of their other powers under this Act, with respect to the child.'

The various influences on the Act, referred to at the beginning of this section, are clearly discernible both in the general principles of the legislation and, more specifically, in the way in which it is framed. So, for example, the primacy of the family in relation to children's upbringing is recognised and upheld, with firstly, local authorities being specifically empowered for the first time to support families and children in need, with the aim of enabling children to grow up safely with their parents, and with examples of how to achieve this being offered, through, for instance, the provision of family centres; and secondly, with

parents retaining responsibility for their children, even when they are looked after away from home. In addition, the rights of children are similarly upheld, most notably through the paramountcy principle, which states that their welfare must be the first consideration; but also in the way the Act requires both that children are consulted about any decision that affects them and that their wishes and feelings are taken into consideration, according to their age and circumstances.

How far in practice the Act has proved successful in balancing the competing demands of family support and child protection is what was specifically addressed in *Child Protection: Messages from Research* (1995) and what we will now move on to consider.

Messages from Research – A Key Moment

Although not published until 1995, four years after the Children Act was implemented, the decision to commission the various pieces of research which together comprise *Messages from Research* was taken in the late 1980s.

This was at a time when the country was reeling not just from the spate of public enquiries following the various child deaths of the 1970s and 1980s, but was also stunned by the events of Cleveland and the professional disarray this revealed. The positive way in which the research previously commissioned by the DHSS had been received was an additional factor influencing the decision to fund new research into child protection issues, looking specifically at 'when to take action, how to intervene, when to remove children and when and how to withdraw services.' (DoH, 1995: p7). Research was to focus not simply on child sexual abuse – inevitably in the limelight, following Cleveland – but also on wider issues of physical harm and neglect.

Although preceding publication of the Children Act, the content of the forthcoming legislation would already have been substantially known to those commissioning the research. An additional objective then was to determine how far the Act had promoted positive and appropriate interventions in the sensitive interface between supporting families and protecting children at risk of serious harm.

The impact of *Messages from Research* was intensified by the prior publication of the Children Act Report 1993 and the Audit Commission Report (1994), both of which drew attention to the fact that Section 17 of the Act was proving slow in implementation, and family support services were not developing as readily as had been hoped. Indeed, it appeared that local authorities had in general failed to appreciate that Section 17 as well as Section 47 could be used as a means of accessing these services. As the Children Act Report very pointedly noted: 'some authorities are still finding it difficult to move from a reactive social policing role to a more proactive partnership role with families.' (Children Act Advisory Committee, 1993: para.2.39)

When *Messages from Research* was finally published it was, as Parton points out (Parton (Ed.), 1997), to a fanfare of publicity. Not only was it personally launched by the then Minister of State, John Bowis, it also achieved maximum coverage in the media, in a way that was totally unprecedented in terms of child care policy, and which was also still able to revive raw memories of Cleveland and the impassioned feelings evoked by those events. Once more, the social work profession was the centre of attention and yet again it had been found wanting.

So what were the main messages and how were they received? In all, twenty pieces of research were brought together in this document and summarised in an accessible format. Taken as a whole, they covered a wide range of issues, ranging from what could be seen as 'normal' expressions of sexuality within a family, to parental perspectives on abuse and including analysis of how child protection procedures were operating in practice. The introduction acknowledges the limitations of the research – that it pays too little attention to the specific needs of children with disabilities, and that there is insufficient emphasis on 'issues of race, gender and rights' (1995: p8). It also explains that '*Messages* does not purport to be a statement of best policies with regard to child protection; but it does explain how society's response to maltreatment has changed over time... and offers ways in which practitioners can see if the results are true for their particular areas of work' (1995: p18)

Looking at the research as a whole, various messages emerge, the majority of which can be thematically grouped together for a more general understanding:

- Firstly, when a child protection investigation takes place, there is far too little account taken of the *context* of the abuse or harm, and far more emphasis placed on the abusive act or incident itself, which is seen in isolation and not against a wider background of family functioning. So, for example, '...non-abusing parents' requests for psychiatric help were overlooked, non-resident parents were rarely engaged, the needs of siblings were ignored...' (1995: p43) and domestic violence often went unrecognised. Such a narrow focus has two possible disadvantages: it may lead to a failure to recognise and make use of sources of help and support for a child or family that lie in the wider kinship group or neighbourhood, for example; and it can reduce the likelihood of co-operation from a family who feel, often justifiably, that the whole story is not being heard and that they are being assessed on incomplete criteria.

- This finding links with the second: that parents are generally left feeling alienated and angered both by the intrusive nature and process of a child protection investigation, and by the formality and bureaucracy usually associated with child protection conferences. This was particularly true where the original concerns were not upheld, when, in the majority of situations the matter was closed, even when there was a clear need for help and support and the family would have welcomed some assistance.

- Thirdly, those situations deemed to be most damaging were those where children were emotionally neglected, characterised in the research as 'low warmth, high criticism' families, where the harm was associated with the parenting style, rather than with specific abusive acts or events. Indeed, it was noted that '...long-term difficulties seldom follow from a single abusive event... but...are more likely to be a consequence of living in an unfavourable environment.'(1995: p53) Ironically, if neglect was the main concern, a child's name was less likely to be placed on the child protection register, resulting in fewer resources and services being offered to families where perhaps they would be most beneficial and best received. Indeed, registration was independently recognised as a passport to resources, and was on occasion used with that aim in mind.

- Fourthly, the amount of human and financial resources committed to investigations was found to be out of all proportion to the eventual outcome. A large number of families were drawn into the child protection 'net' but of these only 15% of the children were registered and a mere 4% were ultimately removed from home. For this small percentage, the process worked well in protecting children from serious harm. For the rest, the consequences were distressing and often counter-productive, in that these families were less likely to turn to social services for help in future. Moreover, social work time that could have more usefully have been spent delivering services to users, had been wasted on unnecessary investigations.

- Fifthly, although *Working Together* (DoH, 1998) and the Children Act had each explicitly advocated working in partnership both with families and with other agencies as the best means of delivering support, this had not, in most instances been achieved. Partnership was helpfully defined by Thoburn et al. (DoH, 1995: p37) as being marked by:
  - respect for one another
  - rights to information
  - accountability
  - competence and value accorded to any individual's contribution

In short, each partner is seen as having something to offer, power is shared, decisions are made jointly and roles are not only respected but backed by legal and moral rights.

It could be argued of course that, in relation to families, particularly those on the receiving end of an investigation, the degree to which power is shared and decisions made jointly is inevitably limited, and indeed, as has already been noted, they are less likely to seek help from social services subsequently. Nevertheless, as an ideal to be worked towards, and particularly when the partnership in question is between agencies, this definition still has something to offer. So far as partnership with other agencies was concerned, it was found they were 'glad to share information and spread pressures created by suspected abuse' (DoH, 1995: p26). However, this was assessed as being due more to the function this served in managing their professional anxiety, since 'once protection plans had been made' this inter-agency work 'tended to decline' and 'social services were frequently left with sole responsibility.' (Farmer in Parton (Ed.) 1997: p159). In relation to teachers, it was noted there was a particular need to raise awareness about the protection process.

- Finally, and far more positively, if parents were successfully engaged, then the child protection process was likely to prove effective with the quality of the relationship between the social worker and parents seen as the key determining factor. There was general agreement between studies as to what personal attributes were most appreciated by families. These included, first and foremost, honesty and reliability, together with clear information about what was happening and the options available to them, in addition to advice about what sources of support existed. In situations where parents felt they had been listened to, treated fairly and had their own needs as parents understood, then even if an outcome went against a parent's own interests, repeated abuse was less likely to occur and accordingly, a child was more likely to be protected in future.

In summary then, how can we encapsulate briefly the main lesson emerging from *Messages from Research*? Regrettably, it was not a positive one. To quote one of the researchers:

The balance between services was unsatisfactory... The research studies suggest that too much of the work undertaken comes under the banner of child protection...Child protection work – frequently thought of as investigation rather than enquiries was seen to dominate...many investigations are undertaken, many families are visited and case conferences called but...in the end, little support is offered to the family.

(Hearn, 1997a: pvii).

Re-focusing the Need for a Lighter Touch

Following the publication of *Messages from Research*, further central guidance was issued (Department of Health, 1996). This called on local authorities to refocus their practice in relation to child care to redress the balance struck between work characterised as child protection, and what was seen as family support. Where concerns about abuse did exist, a 'lighter touch' was called for, seeking to establish the circumstances in a spirit of enquiry, rather than conducting an investigation, with all the accompanying overtones of police activity associated with this term.

In requiring social work practice to change in this way, the government was again demonstrating its desire to shape and take some control over professional practice, rather than allowing it the autonomy it had largely enjoyed in the past. This was true not only of social work, but also of the police, health and the teaching profession, all of which were coming under increasing pressure to demonstrate accountability to the public, in terms of meeting targets and measuring outcomes and effectiveness. This approach was reinforced by the incoming Labour administration, when it assumed power in 1997. The need for social workers to refocus their practice was again vigorously stated, alongside the requirement for them to work in closer partnership with other agencies and most importantly with families themselves.

So how were social service departments expected to approach refocusing and to what extent have they managed to achieve any change?

In the aftermath of the publication of *Messages from Research*, the government encouraged open debate about how practice could be re-focused, and in this context, funded new research into how this could best be achieved. Some of this was carried out by the National Children's Bureau, published under the title *When There's A Will There's A Way* (Burton, 1997). Drawing from *Messages from Research*, several key points were made:

- Firstly, large amounts of additional resources were not essential for practice to change; rather this depended more on existing resources being deployed differently and to better effect.
- Secondly, an approach that built on a family's strengths, rather than focusing on their difficulties was more likely to prove productive, not least because it enabled parents and professionals to move forward more in a spirit of partnership.
- Thirdly, and linked to the previous point, re-focusing was not concerned with developing a totally new way of working. On the contrary, it was reinforcing the core skills and values of the social work profession, of which perhaps the most important was 'building relationships based on trust and respect, without which any positive change was unlikely to take place.' (1997: p2).
- Finally, the authors identified that 'the refocusing of practice requires that work with children at risk of significant harm is placed within the context of family support, and that children in need become the primary group for intervention...Re-focusing... requires that children's needs are placed at the centre of all practice and service considerations. (1997: p2-3).

Exactly what steps have been taken by social service departments since 1995 to re-focus their practice has inevitably varied considerably from one authority to another. So, for example, in certain areas, new teams have been created, some concentrating on child protection, others on the delivery of family support. This approach has been criticised in some quarters for preserving the artificial divide between child protection and children in need, rather than seizing the opportunity radically to rethink service delivery and see child protection as part of the continuum of response to children in need. In other authorities, a more generalised attempt has been made to reduce the number of child protection conferences held and to work more closely alongside families, making use of formal procedures only as a last resort. Given the complexity of demographic factors, and the differences in pre-existing practice, it is by no means surprising that the response to a call for re-focusing has proved so varied across the country. It will perhaps be helpful then to look in more detail at how one large metropolitan authority has been attempting to rise to this challenge.

A Large City Re-focuses

This section outlines one large city authority response to re-focusing. The northern city of Leeds response to the publication of *Messages from Research* and the call for re-focusing, was to stage a major one-day conference in early 1997, to look at the future role of Area Child Protection Committee (ACPC) and how a new balance between child protection work and family support could be achieved. From the outset, and reflected in the ACPC membership, there was a strong emphasis on a multi-agency approach, with the project worker who was subsequently appointed being required to report to an inter-agency steering group, and with training delivered by and to professionals from all relevant statutory and voluntary organisations.

As a result of this conference, a pilot project was launched in one area of Leeds, aimed at directing the less serious child protection referrals away from formal procedures and case conferences and into family support meetings. Other objectives were to develop alternative assessment procedures for children in need and to facilitate an integrated inter-agency response to meeting those needs; to stimulate community activity to provide support to children in need; and to enable families to take on more responsibility for the care of their children. The overall aim was to 'encourage a process which will promote and support the well-being of children within Leeds, creatively using the resources of families and local communities to reduce the need for child protection.' (Frost et al., 2000). The project was evaluated from outset, and its expansion over the rest of the city was seen as dependent on the findings of this research.

The area selected to pilot this initiative was carefully chosen. Not only did it have, in comparison with other parts of Leeds a comparatively low rate of child protection referrals, it also had a long-standing ethos of trying to work closely in partnership both with families and other agencies, helped, in this respect, by the existence locally of a number of key voluntary organisations. The project was therefore offered the best chance of success and was indeed enthusiastically received in the locality.

The evaluation at the end of the first year produced encouraging findings, with both social workers, other professionals and importantly families themselves responding positively to family support meetings. The few teething problems that were identified were not sufficient to cause major concern. Moreover, a statistical analysis over this first year also indicated that, in the

selected area, the incidence of child protection conferences and registration of children had fallen dramatically.

On the basis of this positive evaluation, a decision was taken to extend the pilot to a second area, known to have the highest rate of child protection referrals in the city. If it could flourish there, it was reasoned, this would provide sufficient evidence for the initiative to expand city-wide. This next phase was, in fact, successful and the project is currently in the process of moving across Leeds, where the new procedures will soon be in place in every area.

So what are the particular hallmarks of the Leeds re-focusing project? First of all, families invited to family support meetings will be those who would otherwise have been the subject of child protection conferences. The process is not, therefore, offered to all families where children are 'in need' but only to those where child protection concerns exist that are serious enough to consider convening a conference. Decisions as to which routes to adopt are taken by social services in consultation with the police, as the two lead agencies in child protection. The decision to hold a family support meeting can subsequently be reversed if concerns increase to an unacceptable level, when a family will instead be invited to attend a conference, or, if appropriate, court proceedings will be issued. Similarly, a family that has come to conference, may, if not requiring registration, be followed up via the family support route.

Next, the kinds of referrals likely to lead to a family support meeting rather than a conference, are those where neglect is probably the main issue. Typically, these will be families where there are particular problems and there is insufficient support from family or community, for example, where parents have mental health problems or learning difficulties or are perhaps struggling single-handedly to bring up several children. Meetings are also sometimes used where physical abuse has occurred, most commonly where this has been an isolated occurrence and the parent has expressed regret. They are only rarely used in circumstances of sexual abuse, exceptions being when the perpetrator has been positively identified and has moved out of the house and the caring parent accepts their responsibility for keeping the child safe in future. The 'bottom line' for all referrals is that parents acknowledge the concerns that have led to the meeting and are prepared to work in partnership with the professionals in trying to address them.

Lastly, the style of the meetings differs considerably from child protection conferences. Instead of being chaired by a child protection co-ordinator, this role is assumed by the social service team manager, who will have direct management for the social worker involved with the family and may indeed have met the parents themselves. The parents are invited to bring along other relatives or supportive friends and children old enough to participate in the discussion; and the only professionals to attend are those who already know and are working with the family. A typical family support meeting is therefore much smaller than a child protection conference and everyone there will be known to the family. The style of the meeting is also more informal: instead of it taking place around a conference table, it is usually held in an ordinary family room, often not on social services premises but in a school or nursery where the family feel comfortable. There are no written reports and after the concerns that have led to the meeting have been identified, the format is as flexible as the circumstances require. The central purpose is to draw up a written plan to support the family and this will rely on contributions from the professionals present, the family themselves and any other agencies who it is felt will have something worthwhile to offer and whom the family find acceptable. A key-worker, whose task is to co-ordinate the plan, visit the family and liase with the other workers is appointed. This may or may not be the social worker and is ideally the person enjoying the closest professional relationship with the family. Finally, a review date is set. This will be after no more than three months and is often sooner, depending on the particular situation.

Three years on from the start of the project, re-focusing is well on the way to becoming established practice in Leeds. Those with most experience of family support meetings are unanimously enthusiastic. Professionals recognise their potential for supporting and keeping together families whose children would otherwise have almost certainly ended up 'looked after', but who instead remain safely at home with their parents. They also welcome the endorsement provided by the project of existing good practice and the opportunities for working in closer partnership with other agencies, both statutory and voluntary. Of particular importance, is the fact that family support meetings work equally effectively with families from mainstream and minority ethnic backgrounds; and with families where disability, for either parent or child, is an issue, where the flexibility inherent in the process is seen as particularly helpful. Even when situations deteriorate, as is sometimes unavoidable, the co-ordinated inter-agency plan that has been devised and delivered is not wasted. If, for example, court proceedings become necessary, the time-scale can be considerably reduced since lengthy further assessments are usually unnecessary and parents are less likely to contest the proceedings. Importantly, at a time when there is often pressure for work to be short-term only, and cases closed as soon as possible, family support meetings can demonstrate very persuasively the value of working in a longer-term and focused way with families where problems are enduring. Moreover, in providing a framework for working closely in partnership both with professionals and more importantly with families themselves, family support meetings enable parents to gain or retain a sense of dignity and self-respect. In the words of an experienced social worker, they can demonstrate to professionals and families alike that 'dependency need not necessarily mean failure', or, as a mother expressed it, whose older children had all been previously removed, but who was now successfully managing to care for her 18-month-old daughter, family support meetings represent '...a chance to prove you're a good parent, not an uphill struggle to prove you're not a bad one'.

Seen in the context of *Messages from Research* (DoH, 1995), the Leeds re-focusing project specifically addresses all of the main findings:

● Harm is seen in a wider context with other resources, both from within the family's own network and from different agencies, brought to bear on the situation.

● Parents feel involved, supported and helped by the family support process and are more likely to be offered appropriate services, often at an earlier stage.

● Parents are more likely to turn to social services for help in future.

● Stronger partnerships are established, not only

with families but also with other professionals, who feel more involved in the process and whose attendance at subsequent reviews is far more reliable.

● Because families tend to feel supported and understood, rather than 'named and shamed', positive relationships develop with social workers and other professionals, which in themselves promote self-respect and self-confidence and increase the likelihood of children being protected from future harm.

Conclusion

In this chapter, we have seen how the rise in significance of child protection issues, starting with the death of Maria Colwell in 1973 and reaching a crescendo in 1988 with the crisis in Cleveland, came to dominate the child care agenda and the profession in general. The Children Act itself represented an attempt to redress the balance between child protection and family support by introducing the concept of children in need. By indicating, in Section 17, the kinds of services that could assist in supporting families and by emphasising that it was not social service departments alone who were to deliver these but the corporate responsibility of all local authority agencies, it was hoped that the Children Act would re-establish a climate where help was offered to families as a right, when they were in need, rather than concentrating almost exclusively on 'child rescue'.

The findings brought together in *Messages from Research* however indicated that family support services had been less well developed than originally hoped. The government therefore called for a re-focusing of child care activity to bring child protection and family support into a healthier balance. The Leeds re-focusing project provides an example of how one local authority attempted to translate the principles of re-focusing into practice.

In 2001 the Department of Health published a further review of research *The Children Act Now* (DoH, 2001). These new messages from research effectively take up the story from where those published in 1995 left off. There is encouraging evidence in *The Children Act Now* that the re-focusing initiative, launched in 1996, is now beginning to take effect, to the advantage

of a broader group of children and families and that three out of seven authorities 'had enthusiastically accepted the challenge...that encouraged them to put more of their resources into Part III services.' (2001: p45). Nevertheless, they also felt that 'the balance between safeguarding and promoting welfare for children in need had not yet been achieved.' (2001: p46).

There are a number of important issues that are raised both in *Messages from Research* (1995) and reiterated in 2001.

Firstly, there is 'evidence that well-planned services and casework support, made available after consultation with family members about what *they* would find most helpful, can lead to dramatic improvements in the well-being of the *child and parents*' (our italics) (Thoburn et al., in Parton (Ed.) 1997: p190). Although, as suggested earlier, the re-focusing of services is not ultimately dependent on the provision of **new** services, nevertheless there is certainly an argument that existing services could be made far more flexible and responsive to the expressed needs and wishes of service-users. More imaginative use of carers, for example, to provide planned short breaks to support children to remain with their own families whilst at the same time providing predictable periods of respite, could reap substantial rewards in terms of helping families to manage over the longer term. This is also a service that families themselves would like to see in place and value if and when it is provided, with both children and parents benefiting. Similarly, as the government have acknowledged in their Sure Start and Children's Fund initiatives, families and children need to be consulted about any new services that are developed in their localities. Only then will we be certain that services are truly responsive to their needs.

Secondly, the needs of the child and parent cannot be seen in isolation from each other. One of the regrettable consequences for the social work profession of the child deaths in the 1970s and 1980s, and the subsequent events in Cleveland, was that a polarisation developed between children's rights on the one hand and parental rights on the other, as if the two were in opposition. The more recent focus, encouraged by the Children Act, on the concept of *need*, has offered a helpful way forward, a direction that has been reinforced by the recent Framework for Assessment with its emphasis on looking at the needs of the family as a whole. As Farmer points out: 'for children who remained at home, there were severe limits as to how far it was possible to enhance their welfare if the needs of the parents on whom they depended were not addressed.' (Farmer, in Parton (Ed.), 1997: p156). Possibly the most significant and helpful way in which we can refocus, is to adjust our vision to keep children and their parents simultaneously in our sights.

Finally, we need to remember, particularly those of us whose work includes elements of child protection, that despite what may sometimes feel like evidence to the contrary, most parents do in fact want what is best for their children, and it is a very small minority who are not committed to their child's welfare. We would argue that there is an irrefutable logic to family support. As a policy document from Kent Social Services stated:

> *Our intention is to support children in their families and communities because this is where their roots are: the place to which the majority will return; and the base from which they can most satisfactorily grow into adult life.*

> (quoted in Parton (Ed.) 1997: p225).

4

The Strengths and Weaknesses of the Local Authority: Can They Deliver Family Support?

Liz Jeffery

All happy families resemble each other, each unhappy family is unhappy in its own way.

Anna Karenina (Tolstoy).

Introduction

The Children Act, 1989, central in many ways to the current debate about family support, was also significant in emphasising the concept of corporate responsibility. This theme had already been anticipated in the earlier versions of *Working Together* (1991, 1998) which established operational guidelines for those responsible, in different agencies, for child protection. However, it was not until the Children Act was implemented in 1991 that this co-operative relationship became mandatory. The introduction of the notion of corporate responsibility clarified legally for the first time, that the welfare of children was no longer an issue for social service departments alone, but as the guidance to the Act clearly stated '...agencies are no longer merely exhorted to co-operate but are legally required to do so.' In terms then, of family support, it was no longer simply the social services department that would be held accountable for its delivery: it was the local authority as a whole.

Setting up strategies for change and translating them into practice is, however, a difficult matter. Local authorities found it very challenging to break down long-established patterns of working separately and independently of each other. This inability, or perhaps reluctance, to move forward on a corporate level, led, in the mid-1990s, to the requirement on local authorities to produce Children's Service Plans with different local authority and other agencies called on to work together to plan collectively how to address the needs of children in their area. The need for 'joined up thinking' was reinforced by the incoming Labour administration in 1997, to the extent that the phrase has now entered the public lexicon. Indeed, the whole notion of joint working is central to much of the current Labour administration's agenda and provision for families and children.

The Changing Role of Social Services

It may be helpful to consider the current emphasis on corporate responsibility in the light of the changing context within which social services departments have been operating during the last 30 years. In 1969, the climate in which social service departments were ushered into being was one of positive growth and heady optimism (see Frost and Stein, 1989). These departments brought together under one roof both mental health, adult and children's services, and the new generic social workers they employed were seen as the knights in shining armour who would rescue children from deprivation and lives of squalor or delinquency and successfully deal with the 'multi-problem families' on their individual caseloads. Thirty years on, and after many child-care tragedies and the inevitable enquiries that have followed, the context in which social workers currently practice could not be more different. When tragedies occur, individual practitioners are now not merely seen as professionally culpable following, for example, a child death, but are held personally responsible for the tragedy. These events have, over time, contributed to a decline in confidence in the social work profession, but also to a growing awareness that it is unrealistic to expect that they alone can safeguard children without the assistance of other agencies and professions (Parton, 1985). In fact, this was one of the influences behind the first *Working Together*, and also identifying the need for corporate responsibility. Indeed it can be argued that the very definition of social work is becoming blurred as with the advent of Primary Care Trusts, health and social service departments work more and more closely together. As a result, 'social care' is delivered not just by trained social workers but also by a wide variety of other staff with different qualifications and professional backgrounds.

Secondly, the worsening economic climate in the 1980s and 1990s impacted heavily on social service departments, and, in particular, on the nature of their relationship with the voluntary sector (see Chapters

5 and 6). Thus, in recent years, there has been an increased emphasis on looking to the not-for-profit sector to deliver some of the basic functions previously associated with social services, particularly if they can do so at less cost. Indeed, Section 17 of the Children Act specifically states that every local authority '...shall facilitate the provision by others (including in particular voluntary organisations) of services which the authorities have the power to provide by virtue of this section...' This message was further reinforced by the accompanying 'Guidance and Regulations' which stated that '...in putting together packages of services, local authorities should take account of the services provided sector and other agencies;' and was further reiterated by the current Labour administration in its requirement on local authorities to deliver services at 'Best Value', or, in other words, as economically and efficiently as possible, if necessary looking to other agencies as service providers.

This expectation has contributed to the role played by voluntary organisation and community groups changing considerably. As Andy Lloyd argues in Chapter 5, until as recently as twenty years ago, their contribution was to identify existing gaps in statutory provision and to move in to fill them, until such time as the local authority might be convinced of the need for the particular service and choose to take over this responsibility themselves. However, with these recent changes in service provision, it is now often the local authority who are becoming aware of the need for new resources and who are specifically looking to the voluntary sector to meet these needs by means of service level agreements. Moreover, local authorities are also beginning to devolve responsibility for some of their existing services to voluntary organisations, with, for example, supervised contact of children with their parents, in the context of care proceedings, sometimes being devolved in this way. Thus, the essence of the long-standing relationship between the local authority and the voluntary sector is being radically altered and arguably turned on its head.

Family Support: The Search for a Definition

In any consideration of family support in relation to the local authority role, a useful starting-point might be to consider whose task it is or should be to determine what exactly this phrase means and how it should be translated into practice. How far, for example, should any definition be left to professionals, and to what extent should the views not only of service users themselves but also of their communities be canvassed and allowed to influence the shaping and delivery of services and resources?

The Children Act 1989 provides an interesting basis to start from, not least because although Section 17, in Part III of the Act, is devoted to family support, nowhere within this section, or indeed elsewhere in the Act, is this phrase specifically defined. Instead, Section 17 refers to 'children in need' and the duty of the local authority to provide ...'a range and level of services appropriate to their needs'. The Guidance comments that the definition of 'children in need' is left deliberately vague to emphasise the possibility of developing a wide range of supportive services and resources to meet the extent and type of need identified by each individual local authority. The inference at this stage is that it will be professionals, operating within different local authority departments who will develop, hopefully corporately, a working local definition of 'children in need', which will, in turn, inform and shape the services they deliver, and indeed this has subsequently become a requirement on local authorities, through the Children's Services Planning process.

This notion, of a 'top down' definition of family support and what it should or should not include, persisted for some time. So we read in the Audit Commission's Report *Seen But Not Heard* (1994) that family support is: 'an activity or facility aimed at providing advice and support to parents to help them in bringing up their children'. The assumption is again made that it is the task of professionals, and not of those with whom they seek to engage, to define what support or help is required.

Barbara Hearn, in *Child and Family Support- a practical approach* (1995) takes issue with this interpretation. She suggests her own, broader definition, as follows:

> *Family support is about the creation and enhancement, **with** and for families in need, of locally based (or accessible) activities, facilities and networks, the use of which will have outcomes such*

as alleviated stress, increased self esteem, promoted parental/carer/family competence and behaviour and increased parental/carer capacity to nurture and protect the children.

(emphasis added, 1995: p19).

This definition is, it can be argued, preferable. Not only does it put forward some idea of the desired outcomes to be achieved as a result of supporting families, it also goes some way towards suggesting the process that ideally needs to be adopted. Importantly, as the emphasis implies, it introduces the notion that the families concerned should be consulted about the type and form in which this support should be delivered through an essentially inclusive process. Parents and children in Hearn's definition, are not merely seen as the passive recipients of services, they are themselves contributing to the debate, attending meetings, and stating from their own experience and in their own terms, what services and resources they would find helpful and would like to see developed and perhaps be in a position to contribute to their delivery themselves.

This is a theme now enthusiastically embraced by the Labour administration and absolutely central to the philosophy of the Sure Start and Children's Fund initiatives, which are discussed in Chapter 7.

Can Social Services Departments Deliver Family Support?

Hardiker and colleagues (1991) devised a very influential model of preventive work which has subsequently proved particularly helpful in conceptualising family support services (for further discussion, see Chapter 1). The authors identified four tiers of services, each with its own targets and aims of intervention, and emphasising, in particular, the part to be played by social service departments in the provision of these services, with the role of the voluntary organisations being implicit rather than fully spelled out. As Nick Frost pointed out in Chapter 1 the model was as follows:

● first-level prevention or 'diversion'
● second-level or 'early' prevention
● third-level or 'heavy-end' prevention
● fourth-level intervention or 'early restoration'

In practice, the degree to which child and family workers based in social service departments have proved able to deliver support at all four levels or tiers is open to debate. Firstly, social workers have tended to focus their efforts, more or less exclusively, on child protection work, and on children seen to be at risk of serious harm or neglect. Put another way, they have been engaged in what Hardiker would refer to as Level Three and Four activities, rather than in delivering the kind of family support envisaged in Part III of the Children Act and associated, perhaps, with Levels One and Two. Indeed, it was the need to shift this balance of priorities which was highlighted in *Messages from Research* and which was further emphasised in the call for refocusing (see Chapter 3).

Parton (1997) argues that trying to move the emphasis from child protection services towards family support is not necessarily achievable, as the lack of human and other resources within social service departments mean there would be too few staff to cope with the volume of work this would produce, a factor often highlighted by social workers themselves. Indeed, given the intention to shift social work priorities away from such an exclusive focus on child protection, and more into the delivery of family support, it is ironic that the implementation of the Children Act has in itself made this harder to achieve. The rights of parents and children to proper representation of their interests in the court arena, the proliferation of experts at a hearing and the rigorous testing of evidence have all contributed to a situation where involvement in care proceedings is now extremely costly in terms of social work time and energy. So, in areas for example where there is a high rate of child protection referrals and subsequent court proceedings, families requiring 'only' support are often closed to make space for these other more pressing demands.

Secondly, the difficulties encountered by social services in delivering family support are compounded by the fact that the very nature of supportive intervention suggests that it should be both reliable and, if necessary, long-term. Indeed, Gordon Jack in considering how assessment can be translated into purposeful action, highlights 'the value for those children who live in adverse family circumstances of an *enduring* relationship with a special person outside the household' (Jack, 2001: p46) and the consistency

of this finding in the existing research. Other recent research suggests also that for families, 'practical services were understood best, but there were a surprising number of parents who valued what might be best described as a casework service, where social workers both co-ordinated other services and offered social work support within the context of a focused and purposeful professional relationship' (2001: p74).

Looking, for example, at those families where parental mental illness is a problem, the continuing nature of any support offered is usually crucial in most if not all of these situations. Clearly, difficulties such as these are often enduring rather than short-term, and it is particularly where these issues are significant that families are arguably most in need of support to enable them to care for their children effectively. Continuing research has in fact highlighted the correlation between poor parental mental health and families where child protection is a concern, with over three-quarters of parents, in a recent study on significant harm, rated to be depressed on a standardised test (DoH, 2001: p29). The argument for on-going assistance is probably equally strong where physical health problems or learning disabilities impact on parental ability to care for their children. Although, in all these situations, there may be periods when the parents can cope well with relatively little outside help, there will also perhaps be times when there is a need for intensive support, ideally provided by agencies and professionals who are already known to them, and who are able to work closely together. Therefore, although many, if not most, area-based social workers would prefer to be engaged more directly in family support, the demands made on their time by activity associated with child protection, and the often long-term nature of support needed by families, means that, in reality, this assumes relatively little priority.

What Support Do Families Want?

In recent years, and especially since the implementation of the Children Act, there has been considerable research undertaken into the kind of help particularly valued by service-users and the nature of the resources they most welcome or would like to see developed (DoH, 2001).

One finding to emerge strongly has been the importance service-users attach to being treated as individuals. Each family and each child has its own individual perception of the world and of their own difficulties, and an offer of assistance that might prove invaluable to one family, may for another, whose circumstances appear outwardly similar, feel intrusive, insulting or simply inappropriate. This could be the case, for example, in the case of an Asian family, who are offered over-night respite care, when, in fact, day-care would be far more acceptable and less stigmatising within their community. Or again, whilst one single parent might welcome help from a Home-Start volunteer another, similarly struggling to bring up several children single-handedly, might find someone visiting her house unacceptable, but appreciate the offer of monthly weekend breaks, provided by a carer whom she knows has been approved by the local authority (Frost et al., 2000). Services need therefore, to be flexible and developed wherever possible according to the expressed needs of those receiving them, rather than simply expecting families to accept whatever services are on offer. In addition, the capacity of children to live in and tolerate adverse circumstances varies considerably. As Brandon et al. argue in *The Children Act Now*, 'individual children will respond differently to similar events and lifestyles. What is significantly harmful to one child may not damage another' (2001: p45). This is an area where social workers, drawing on their core skills in assessing service-users and individualising their needs can have a great deal to offer.

Secondly, research stresses the importance families attach to offers of practical help and assistance, and to straightforward and accessible information and advice. So, for example, the provision of a washing machine for a family with two children still in nappies, or transport to enable a sick child to keep hospital appointments, are likely to be perceived as especially helpful and will also demonstrate that the family's particular circumstances are being sensitively addressed. Equally important is the opportunity for parents to access support directly themselves. Family centres that offer a range of services may mean, for example, that a mother can call in for advice on housing or legal matters, whilst knowing that her child is being well cared for next door, and importantly that she can meet other parents in similar circumstances to her own. This type of provision is particularly important when families are socially isolated, or are living at a distance from relatives or have none they can call on for support. Indeed, 'in two...family support studies, lack of emotional support was the factor that tipped the balance, turning a previously manageable situation into one that was untenable' (2001: p27). Accessible resources are important too, in terms of parents' dignity and self-respect, in that they themselves are able to identify their own problems and needs, and seek appropriate assistance and this, in itself, can help promote self-confidence. It is important then, for those working with families to have as comprehensive a knowledge as possible of what resources exist in their area and what practical help can be made available to them, so that this can, in turn, be passed on to families.

Thirdly, despite what might appear to be consistently negative publicity about social workers, social services were often approached directly by families needing help. In fact, they were 'the agency of first choice in over half the cases' in one particular study (2001: p97). This was evidently particularly true for families of dual heritage and where families needed help with specific issues, who were often the most socially isolated.

Finally, the findings repeatedly highlight the value placed by service-users on their relationship with a social worker who was deemed to be helpful and positive. Particularly appreciated by parents were openness, honesty, reliability and an ability to empathise. 'She listened to my problems. I thought she'd think I was hopeless but she didn't. She said she'd helped lots of parents like me' (2001: p68). Clearly, it was also important to this parent to learn that she was not alone but that other families experienced similar difficulties. This realisation, by itself, can be particularly helpful and reassuring. Families also welcomed acknowledgement of their strengths as well as their difficulties, but importantly, just 'being listened to equated with helpfulness even if no other service was offered' (2001: p81). and 'simply talking over problems in a brief casework relationship with a social worker was sometimes enough to enable families to gather their often considerable strengths and find their own solutions to the problems they had presented to Social Services' (2001: p122).

A Continuum of Services

So what do these views have to tell us about the way in which family support should be delivered? The crucial message to emerge from this new body of research is that social work is by no means dead or even seriously ill. On the contrary, what families appreciate and find most helpful in the delivery of services mirrors very accurately the traditional skills and values of the social work profession: an empathetic understanding of another's situation; honesty and integrity; openness in defining concerns; an appreciation of a family's unique circumstances; an acknowledgement of their strengths as well as their difficulties; encouragement of self-determination; understanding when practical services are particularly helpful; and a knowledge of available local resources. All of these qualities are particularly valued in social workers by parents and children alike.

There are occasions then, when social workers are both the first choice in terms of service delivery and also, because of their particular skills and values, are those best-placed to deliver support, as for example, if a parent wants short-term accommodation for a child, whilst they themselves are in hospital. There will be other situations, however, where, as already suggested, because of pressures of work and time constraints, social workers cannot offer the help required. Yet again, there will be families for whom social services are not the preferred option. These will include those whose previous experiences have left them with ambivalent or angry feelings towards social workers, for example, if they have a history of an unhappy childhood in care; or if the services need to be particularly local, accessible and flexible, and available, perhaps, out of working hours. Nevertheless, in these situations too, social workers still have a role to play. They will not perhaps be the primary means of support. As Parton suggests, this is not always either appropriate or possible, but as professionals who can accurately assess the needs of a family and as brokers of resources, using the local knowledge and information they have acquired from working closely alongside families to access more informal services, and drawing on community facilities they are still crucial players in ensuring that families receive the support they need (Parton, 1997). The recent national guidance (DoH, 2000) on assessing the needs of parents and children demonstrates helpfully the form in which assessments can take place, identifying the different domains in which families operate and highlighting areas where support is most needed.

Let us now look at an imagined scenario to illustrate some of these points:

Jimmy Brown, aged six, has been referred anonymously to social services by a neighbour, who is concerned that he is poorly clothed, looks thin and under-nourished, and has been seen wandering the streets alone after dark. The neighbour is worried about his safety and has tried to talk with Karen, Jimmy's mother, with a view to perhaps offering some support but Karen has been difficult to approach. Karen is known in the neighbourhood as having 'a short fuse' and as being something of a loner, and appears to have no family or friends. Jimmy is a child of dual heritage but lives in a predominantly white area where he has been subjected to some racial abuse by older local youths.

An initial assessment undertaken by the social worker, Jenny, ascertains that Karen is a single mother and is indeed quite isolated, after growing up in local authority care in a neighbouring authority. She had moved to this city in search of a new beginning after her abusive relationship with Jimmy's father broke down. She and Jimmy now have no contact with him. Her own background has resulted in her having had little if any positive experience of parenting to draw from, and as her concerned neighbour suspected, she has no close friends or relations. Perhaps not surprisingly, she appears to Jenny to be suffering from depression and to have little self-esteem. She understands the concerns about Jimmy but seems to lack the ability or energy to do anything to change the situation. Jenny knows of a local voluntary organisation which runs a project supporting single parents in the community and Karen reluctantly agrees to a visit by the co-ordinator. This meeting, which Jenny also attends, goes well and Karen agrees to the suggestion of being linked up with one of the project volunteers. It turns out that the scheme is able to link Karen with a black worker, something she particularly appreciates as she hopes this will help Jimmy to develop a sense of cultural identity. Social services convene a meeting which Karen attends and Jimmy's schoolteacher is also there,

in addition to the project organiser at the local voluntary organisation. Karen is apprehensive about attending this meeting, remembering different ones that she attended as a child in care, where she felt unable to speak and resentful that other people were trying to run her life, some of whom she had not even met before.

In fact, Karen feels comfortable and able to participate in the meeting. She feels that her views are heard and her wishes respected. Drawing on the local knowledge and skills of the professionals and on Karen's own views of what she needs a plan to help her and support her in parenting Jimmy, is put in place. In addition to the continuing help from the volunteer, it emerges that the school, which have also been very concerned about Jimmy, have been considering starting a breakfast club, but have so far lacked the funding to set this up. Jenny is aware of sources of funding and since the plans are otherwise in place, it is arranged with Karen's agreement, that once this has started, Jenny and the volunteer will help Karen take Jimmy to school in time for him to attend this. The neighbour, with whom Jenny has been back in touch to let her know the outcome of the referral, has also told Jenny of local community outings that have been arranged over the summer. As a grandmother whose own grandchildren live at the other end of the country, she would be interested in going on these herself but feels uncomfortable at the thought of going alone. She would however be very happy to go with Karen and Jimmy if they want to come along themselves. This suggestion is put to Karen in the meeting and she indicates she would like to take the neighbour up on this offer.

Clearly many situations that social workers are presented with are not so straightforward as this. However, this example hopefully demonstrates both the importance of social work skills in engaging quickly with service-users and assessing their needs as well as the benefits for families of close working between statutory and voluntary organisations. By working closely together, an individualised, sensitive response to a particular family's needs becomes more achievable, and it is also easier to tailor the support plan to meet the needs of, for example, a disabled child or a family threatened with homelessness. Such an approach enables the family to be seen in a wider overall context, where the community is a resource to be called upon, as appropriate, to assist in meeting their needs. Importantly, as the research indicates, such a response is also more acceptable to families (Jack, 2001) and in accordance with what they would choose for themselves, at its best providing them not only with assistance with immediate difficulties, but also encouraging them to engage more with the wider community generally.

If, however, this situation were to deteriorate, Jenny, as her social worker, might become a more central source of support to Karen, both by becoming more directly involved herself and more available to listen and respond to her needs and also by accessing other more targeted and specific services for her. For example, if Karen were to become re-involved with her ex-partner who again became violent towards her, Jenny would, with Karen's agreement, be in a position to approach specialised counselling and support services and perhaps accompany her to at least the first appointment. Alternatively, if this situation were to improve, Karen might feel not only more able to manage her own problems, but also in a position to offer support to other parents who were encountering similar difficulties to those she herself has worked through. As Hearn pointed out 'the potential for some families to move from apparent state dependency to independence and then to contribution is not sufficiently tapped.' (1997: p235).

By viewing family support in this way as a continuum, the possibility of families being able to move easily through different levels of support and to contribute themselves to the delivery of services becomes more of a reality. The increased flexibility that could be achieved would also increase the likelihood of services being responsive to the particular individual circumstances of a family.

Conclusion

In any consideration of family support, it is important firstly to emphasise that the need for it is essentially unremarkable. All children can, at some point or other, be seen as 'in need', whether as a result of bullying at school, on account of a difference in skin-colour or sporting ability, or arising from a parent's illness or death. Most families are fortunate enough to have relatives or friends to call on when their own resources are stretched or insufficient, but there are many who, for whatever reason, lack these informal support networks and have to look elsewhere for help. It is important that these families are not pathologised and that any services they need are as accessible and delivered in as informal a way as possible.

In trying to assess how services to support families might be shaped and delivered, I have identified that service-users often view social workers in a very positive light and as the first port of call if they encounter difficulties. However, the time constraints placed on the profession as a result of their central role in child protection, together with the long-term nature of much supportive work, means they are perhaps not often able to be the primary source of help. Nevertheless, their professional skills and knowledge are of fundamental importance in assessing a family's needs and co-ordinating a supportive plan, and in this context their own role in terms of offering support to a family, may have greater or less significance.

I have suggested that a helpful way of conceptualising family support is to think in terms of a continuum of provision with services made available through a mixed economy of care, drawing on both the statutory and voluntary sector and also including resources based in the community. Between them, agencies can in this way provide a range of services and resources in different forms and levels of intensity according to the particular needs of a family. It is also possible, in this way, for any plan of support to be not only tailored to an individual family's particular needs, but also to be responsive to those needs changing over time, at different stages of the family's life-cycle.

For such a continuum of support to operate smoothly and be of most benefit to families, it has become even more important that some of the traditional rivalries and divisions between agencies and departments are broken down. Not only do inter-agency partnerships need to exist at both operational and management levels, there should also be clear communication channels from service-users right through to director level, so that the ideas put forward by children and families can produce a readier response from those who have the power to initiate services. The need for this open, on-going dialogue is something that has been highlighted by the current Labour administration in its Sure Start and Children's Fund initiatives, and the kind of innovative thinking by inter-agency groups coming together with local residents to plan how best to make use of these new sources of funding, provide an excellent model of the way forward.

We are moving hopefully into an era where the skills and knowledge of individual workers are more important than the boundaries between the agencies which employ them. Local authorities, through their different departments, already help families in a multitude of ways, but if 'working together' can become even more of a reality in the future, then the impact on the lives of families will be all the greater. In delivering this support, we need also to hear not just the voices of children, so often silenced before the Children Act, but to hear what their parents are saying too. For '...professional practice which reduces a family's sense of powerlessness, and helps them feel and function more competently, is likely to improve the well-being of both parents and children' (DoH, 2001: p46).

5

What is Happening in the Voluntary Child Care Sector?

Andy Lloyd

Introduction

In the previous two chapters we have examined the central role of the local authority sector. We now move on to explore how the voluntary child care sector has grown and become increasingly influential in recent years. The central focus of this chapter is to discuss and analyse the impact of this sector, with an emphasis on family support in particular. The sector can be classified using the following general typology:

- The 'big' five child care organisations who have budgets of many tens of millions of pounds each year – a group which includes the National Society for the Prevention of Cruelty to Children (NSPCC), NCH Action for Children, the Children's Society , Barnardo's and the Save the Children Fund.
- The smaller, but often national organisations, with an annual turnover of perhaps £10-20 million each year such as Family Service Units.
- The local voluntary sector groups, with comparatively small budgets (perhaps less than £100,000 per year) and those very specific local – often community-based – groups with very small levels of funding.

Clearly the issues confronting these organisations vary significantly. However, many of the issues and challenges that will be discussed in this chapter are shared, whatever the size, nature and funding of the organisation.

Why has the voluntary child care sector grown in both size and influence? One relevant recent factor here is the introduction of the National Lottery Charities Board (now the Community Fund) which has had a remarkable impact. Small groups can now apply for small grants (up to £5,000) – a significant amount of money for a local parent and child group meeting in a local hall and being run by volunteers. At the other end of the scale, grants of hundreds of thousands of pounds over three years for the largest organisations mean that this source of funding cannot be ignored. The inevitable knock-on is that, for many

organisations within the sector, the NLCB changed the nature of their working practice quite substantially.

For this and for other reasons these are exciting times for the voluntary child care sector. There are opportunities for growth, with many new government initiatives (such as those explored in Chapter 7) insisting on partnerships between the voluntary and statutory sector providers. There are, too, very real threats. Those organisations that fail to keep up with current thinking, suddenly find their access to money severely restricted, and thus they may well face a funding crisis. This chapter will consider the changes the sector has seen in recent years and some possible motors of change for the future.

A Brief History of the Voluntary Sector

The voluntary sector, for the very most part, has its' roots in the late Victorian era when many philanthropic individuals felt that they had identified a need and chose to address this need in some practical way. Thomas John Barnardo (the eponymous founder of one of the key organisations) and Reverend Thomas Bowman Stephenson of National Children's Home (now NCH Action for Children) both saw the extreme poverty of street children in British cities and resolved to do something to alleviate their plight. As Owen argues, philanthropy can be seen as a response to the 'growing pains of an urban society' (1964, p.163).

Very often, these individuals were willing to invest both substantial personal finance and also their time and commitment to the cause they had espoused. To give the example of Barnardo:

One evening a boy at the mission, Jim Jarvis, took Thomas Barnardo around the East End showing him children sleeping on roofs and in gutters. The encounter so affected him he decided to devote himself to helping destitute children.

(www.barnardos.org.uk/aboutBarnardos/history).

Barnardo was horrified by the poverty, degradation and hunger in which he saw children living in 1870s

London. Following the death from malnutrition and exposure of an 11-year-old boy who had been previously turned away from the boys home, Barnardo vowed that 'no destitute child ever refused admission' – a legend which the boys home bore from that day on. Smaller homes for girls, felt better able to meet their needs, followed some years later (Parker, 1990).

In the same decade, the Reverend Thomas Bowman Stephenson, along with his colleagues Francis Horner and Alfred Mager, saw the same levels of need amongst the children of London and so set out to 'provide education, training, and…a good home for orphans and destitute children'. They established the Children's Home in London, an organisation which grew, and in 1907 became known as the National Children's Home. The founders of the National Children's Homes were all Methodists – Stephenson himself being an ordained minister. Within a year of the Children's Homes being founded, the organisation was adopted by the Methodist church, a link that remains strong today:

> *Ever since a Methodist Minister founded NCH in 1869, the link between the charity and the Methodist Church has been strong. Both our Methodist roots and over 130 years of work inform our values as a charity…We are proud to be the child care charity of the Methodist Church and our continuing relationship with it enriches our work in many different ways.*
>
> (www.NCH.org.uk/aboutNCH).

The proliferation of voluntary organisations is significant as David Owen argues:

> *The distinctive modern technique…was the charitable society. Throughout the nineteenth century, especially, such organisations multiplied at a fantastic rate…*
>
> (Owen, 1964: p5).

Probably the most significant philanthropic child care organisation founded during this period was the National Society for the Prevention of Cruelty to Children. Following a visit to the United States where he came across the New York Society for the Prevention of Cruelty to Children, Thomas Agnew, a Liverpool banker was instrumental in starting the Liverpool Society for the Prevention of Cruelty to Children. We should not get the impression that philanthropy was a male preserve. Many of the philanthropic organisations were organised and led by women. One

such woman was Hesba Stretton, who in a letter to *The Times* printed on 8th January, 1884 pointed out that:

> *In Liverpool, a 'Society for the Prevention of Cruelty to Children' has been started, and the report of one months work gives 86 cases in which children have been taken under the protection of the Society. In none of the cases, however, did the committee find it necessary to resort to legal proceedings, firm and kindly remonstrance's with the parents and guardians have prevailed…Prevention is better than punishment.*

The points made in this letter, by a woman who was to become a founder of the NSPCC, are crucial to a full understanding of child protection work carried out with the Society and how this can be contrasted with the child rescue work carried out by organisations such as Barnardo's (Holman, 1988). The NSPCC had a conception of prevention, a major concern of this book, and this helps us to understand why they have no legacy of large institutions.

Throughout the late 1800s, then, there is a clear pattern emerging that saw highly motivated individuals, driven by a philanthropic sense of responsibility, directly intervening in the lives of children in order to create for them what philanthropy perceived to be a better and safer existence. These individuals either had a private income which they used to fund ragged schools, homes for boys or campaign for better treatment for children, or else they were able to persuade others by the strength of their arguments to fund these ventures.

Lord Shaftesbury, the great social reformer, orator and philanthropist – and founder of the Shaftesbury Society – played a more directly political role. On one occasion, when speaking in the House of Commons, proposing reforms for those – particularly young children – working within the coal industry:

> *The House heard Ashley (Lord Shaftesbury) in deepening silence as he disclosed what was happening to children and women down the mines. Some members wept.*
>
> (Pollock, 1985: p63).

Shaftsbury's ability to speak persuasively about issues of welfare reform ensured that, while he had little private income himself, he was able to speak so persuasively that the resources required for his ragged schools and other practical welfare provision became available from those who were in a position to endow such ventures.

The motivation for many of these individuals to develop their ideas into reality appears to be a strong commitment to the Christian faith:

> Throughout the history of English philanthropy religious motives appear strikingly – in secular as well as in directly religious philanthropy.
>
> (Owen, 1964: p3).

If not motivated by their personal faith, the founders of voluntary organisations were motivated by political commitment. While Family Service Units (FSU) was formed half a century after those already discussed, its genesis is very similar. Originally the Pacifist Service Units, it was begun by 'small groups of conscientious objectors' (Welshman, 1999: p462).

In describing the workers involved in the Liverpool Branch of the Pacifist Service Units, Welshman goes on to say that 'Many of the members of the Unit were Quakers, and the approach was essentially pacifist and religious...' (Welshman, 1999: p462).

So, the early years of the voluntary child care sector were typified by individuals motivated by strong religious or political commitments, who invested their own time – and often money – into a lifetime of service to those children and families who were living in extremes of poverty and need. The lack of formalised state provision meant that all the income for these organisations was from what is now known as 'voluntary income'- that is donations made by individuals or groups of individuals. As Welshman notes it was only from 1954 that 'the Ministry of Health allowed Local Authorities to provide grants under section 28 of the National Health Service Act' (Welshman, 1999: p463).

Whilst the motivation of these people seems to be beyond reproach the tension between philanthropy and social control is a difficult and complex one – which is still with us today in many forms (see Frost, Mills and Stein, 1999). Philanthropy, however seemingly well-motivated, always contains within it the exercise of power. Mauss sums this tension up well:

> To give is to show one's superiority...To accept without returning or repaying more, is to face subordination, to become a client and subservient.
>
> (Mauss, 1969: p15).

Assessing the balance sheet of Victorian philanthropy is therefore a complex exercise, balancing progressive social reform against methods and systems which tended to impose values and methods which were not necessarily in the interests of children and their families.

Into the Twentieth Century

We have seen that the early years of the voluntary child care sector was typified by individuals driving through personally and religiously motivated agendas for social change. Either with their own money or with resources begged or levered from rich benefactors, they pursued a path which they saw to be 'right' – often gauging that sense of being right from their understanding of Christian faith or other moral or religious basis.

This was not going to last for ever. The increasing acceptance, through the first half of the 20th century, that the State had a role to play in meeting the welfare needs of the children of this country began to change the way the voluntary sector child care provision was organised.

It was no longer acceptable or possible for one person to drive through such agendas of social change. Politics became more complicated and less open to individual influence – particularly from those with money or status to use as a lever. Parliamentary seats were no longer 'handed down' the family line. With this came increasingly strong arguments commending official recognition of the need for there to be organised welfare provision for children living in difficult circumstances. The development of the organised Welfare State symbolised the growing acceptance of a role for the State: a development which had profound implications for the development of the voluntary sector.

The growth of the Welfare State changed the circumstances of the voluntary child care sector very significantly. Within the political rhetoric and fanfare of new universal services was an explicit and clear acceptance that the welfare of those members of society who are living in need was a responsibility of the State. Until relatively recently, when Mrs Thatcher famously declared that there is 'no such thing as society' and the merits of individualism were professed to be the new way forward, this way of thinking has gone reasonably unchallenged.

As a result, there became a need for voluntary child care organisations to re-think their raison d'être. The niche which they had filled – that of making basic, but important, provision for all destitute and needy children – had been, to some extent, usurped. Universal provision did not immediately eradicate child poverty. It did, however, begin to provide, in an ordered and universal manner, the sorts of provision that Stephenson, Shaftsbury, Barnardo and others were so motivated to establish.

At this point, it is clearly vital to stop and acknowledge the plethora of small, locally based voluntary organisations working in their own locality to improve the lives of children and families in their area. These organisations represent the heart and spirit of the great social reformers of the 19th century. They are motivated, on the whole, by altruism and the recognition of the need for social change, and who work long and often anti-social hours to further the aims of their organisation. Residents Associations who bid to trust funds for relatively small amounts of money to develop a safe play area for children on their estate are not doing so for personal gain or profit. There is a need for locally focussed and managed groups struggling with increasingly complex bureaucracy to provide a huge range of different services that children need.

There can be a tension between the role of the large voluntary organisations, which can be perceived as dominating voluntary provision for children, and the smaller, more locally-based organisations. Very often, small local organisations can be both more cost effective and efficient than the bigger organisations. Ten volunteers working one evening a week each is the equivalent of a full time worker and is clearly more cost efficient. In addition, in terms of local acceptability, the volunteers may well play a role which is difficult for paid professionals to play. Whatever the size of the organisation there are increasing pressures for clear policies and procedures to be in place. For example, it is no longer acceptable for any volunteer to be given responsibility for children without clear checks and procedures being in place.

The transition of the large voluntary child care organisations cannot be fully understood without reflecting on the legacy of residential provision of organisations such as Barnardo's, NCH Action for Children. The larger provision often characteristic of the early part of the twentieth century was run down as we entered the second half of the century and often replaced by Community Homes with Education (CHEs). CHEs were campuses with a number of house units each housing 8-12 children built together with a school and recreational facilities also on the site. They housed a number of children on the one campus and were very often in rural or semi-rural environments. CHEs were used extensively, mainly by Social Service Departments, and were often full to capacity. The influence of the Care Order made on the grounds of criminal activity as provided for by the Children and Young Person's Act 1969 s7(7) saw a large number of children – mostly but not exclusively boys- needing a residential placement and CHEs were an obvious and apparently ideal choice.

Events in the 1980s and 1990s – most notably the Waterhouse report into homes in North Wales – have aptly demonstrated the real risk of allowing people to work with children (particularly vulnerable children) without there being in place a robust and watertight method of checking the police records of those individuals. Many CHEs have been involved in serious scandals where it has become clear that there had been abuse – sexual, physical and emotional – of the children who were being looked after. Sometimes this abuse was organised and sometimes it was individuals acting alone (Frost, Mills and Stein, 1999).

Such scandals became widespread and it is evident in retrospect that abuse was extensive in the care system in the latter half of the twentieth century. These scandals and a much increased understanding of the behaviour and tactics of adults who perpetrate abuse on children, demanded huge changes for the voluntary sector. No longer was it possible or advisable for these organisations to accept any volunteer who walked through their door. Today, rigorous checks are an essential and inherent part of the personnel function of the voluntary child care sector.

Health and safety at work legislation, the Disability Discrimination Act, employment law and other law and policy have increased the need for the voluntary sector to be highly skilled and vigilant of the changing face of employment practice.

The funding of the voluntary child care sector has also changed substantially over the same period of time. The technique of well connected social reformers visiting wealthy benefactors and obtaining funding for a project over a drink in the drawing room, or by encouraging individuals to take out a 'subscription' to the organisation seeking funds, has now largely passed. Clearly there is still an amount of large one-off or regular donations made by individuals to their favoured charity. However, many such wealthy families, along with companies and other organisations, have preferred to move towards a more organised way of giving by developing a trust fund. Cash or company shares are lodged in a trust fund and the interest from the money or dividends from the shares is distributed to applicants according to the criteria drawn up by the trustees of the fund.

These trust funds, of which there are many hundred in the UK, have clear application criteria and a list of priorities for their funds. There has been, in response to the increasing need of the voluntary sector to raise funds from these sources, the development of the professional fundraiser. There are databases to research, books to buy and courses to go on in order to learn how to be a successful fundraiser. Most of the larger voluntary organisations have dedicated fundraising teams who have targets and strategies which they adopt to meet these targets. The strategic development of fundraising is a highly skilled and complex operation involving statistics, demographics and researching the donor databases.

So, professional fundraising and increased demand for procedures and policy documents around the employment of staff and the use of volunteers has changed the working practice of the voluntary child care sector. This increased professionalism is not, in entirety, a bad thing. It is essential that anyone who is working with children have clear and transparent policies regarding their well-being and protection. We know, often from harrowing experience, that adults seeking access to children for sexual purposes are cunning and manipulative in their endeavours. They will seek work with child care organisations, and the voluntary sector, like all others, must ensure that whatever safeguard there can be in order to minimise the risk must be done.

Similarly, it is not possible for someone with a good idea for working with children to simply have tea with the Chief Executive of a large corporate firm and come out with a handsome cheque. (In fact, on rare occasions this is possible but so rare as to not be a viable fundraising strategy!) A clear and organised fundraising plan is essential. Without it, the employment of many people is placed in jeopardy. Planning must be strategic and logical, and must not be an ad hoc and last minute scribbling. To fail to do so means risking effective work being targeted at the most needy children. Anecdotal working – working with the children who we know or already have links with – means a serious risk of excluding the most disadvantaged (and therefore the most invisible) members of our society. It also risks excluding minority groups – minority in terms of ethnicity, sexuality, disability etc. – as without specific planning and commitment, the harder to reach groups remain harder to reach.

This increased professionalisation of the voluntary sector has led to a move away from the title of 'voluntary'. The suggestion that the work is done without pay is no longer accurate. The size of some of the larger organisations now outstrips the budget of some local authority departments. The use of the phrase 'third sector' (as opposed to the statutory and private sectors or the not-for-profit sector) is becoming increasingly popular. These descriptions assist in the conceptualisation of the sector. The sector contributes an enormous amount both in terms of work and in terms of research, publicity and employment to the provision of services for children. It is no longer appropriate or reasonable to consider the 'voluntary' sector as a small player in the social welfare field; nor is it sensible for the sector to give the impression that all its workers provide services free of charge. It can be argued that it is time we move away from the term 'voluntary' to what is a descriptive and accurate name – the not-for-profit sector. Having argued this, this chapter will refer to the sector as such from this point on.

The Impact of the National Lottery

In 1993 the Government awarded, after a competitive tendering arrangement, the contract to run the National Lottery in the UK to Camelot, a consortium of business and other interests. The terms of the contract was that 25% of all funds raised by the lottery games – initially the draws and latterly scratch cards – should go to 'good causes'. This was to revolutionise the funding of the not-for-profit sector. Suddenly there was a single body with what at the time seemed to be inestimable wealth able to give large grants to charitable organisations who met their criteria. The Child Care sector applied in great numbers and many of them were successful in obtaining what became known colloquially as 'lottery money'. Not only were some of the grants large – tens of thousands of pounds a year for a project, but it also gave grants for three years – a move away from the one year funding roundabout which many organisations had become used to.

Not-for-profit organisations employ the same thinking to their planning and strategy to those in the other two sectors. This includes a long-term vision as well as short-term and medium-term objectives. When such an organisation receives one year – often non-recurring – funding, there is a mixed feeling. Clearly any such donation is welcome and essential for the ongoing work of the organisation. Without such grants, many projects simply would not be financially viable and so would close. On the other hand, it is difficult to recruit into any post within eight weeks and so, with an induction period, perhaps 20% of the time allocated to the grant is gone before it is actually operational. It will then have about 6 months – half the funding time to run the proposed scheme – before needing to spend the substantial time and effort needed in completing new funding bids to seek continuation funding.

Clearly, some projects are funded for one year as they simply want to deliver a specific piece of work which can be done within that timescale. Others will already be in place and there will be no need for a recruitment and induction time. However, there is a real risk that one year funding can lose some of its effectiveness by being so short term. Furthermore, it is increasingly difficult to recruit to social welfare posts, as there is a shortage of qualified and unqualified workers wishing to come into the sector and a one year funded post is not the most attractive proposition for many people with financial commitments.

The introduction, therefore, of three year funded projects from the National Lottery Charity Board (now the Community Fund), was a welcome and hugely helpful innovation.

There were some less welcome repercussions from this introduction. Individuals have become, over the last decade, less willing to give individually to charities, through regular giving or even through putting coins in a collecting tin. By buying a lottery ticket, it can be seen that one has done one's 'bit' for charity and that there is no need for further giving. This is understandable. The message from the National Lottery is that by buying a ticket for a draw, you are not only giving yourself an opportunity to win a life changing amount of money, but you are also making a direct contribution to the good causes the board support.

If a not-for-profit organisation makes a successful bid, and receives a substantial three year funded bid, then this is absolutely unarguable. However, if an organisation's bid is not successful, then a major source of income is reduced with no compensation available in terms of a grant from this major trust.

A further difficulty has been that continuation funding becomes problematic. In the three years of the lottery grant, an efficient and hopefully effective project has been developed and is having a positive and productive effect on the local community. At the end of the funding, it is important that this project does not simply close due to lack of funds. However, continuation funding is rarely available from the Community Fund and many other trusts who could match their level of funding insist on funding 'new and innovative' projects.

It is easy to see why the Trust funds seek to go down that path. New and innovative is often a code for risky and potentially unpopular and so these projects struggle to obtain mainstream support. Some of the projects will not succeed, but others will be a huge success bringing credit to the organisation delivering the service and also the funding body. This is good...but it causes a headache for those projects which were new and innovative three years ago but has now become established and successful. To seek mainstream statutory funding is terrifically difficult in the age of cut backs and tight spending reviews. Again, this is no individual agency or organisations fault. There is a limited amount of money and, in truth, there can only be a limited number of projects. There is, however, a real pain involved when a project closes due to lack of funding. This pain is not simply felt by the staff whose jobs disappear. It is felt, too, by the service users who have benefited, and would have continued to benefit, from that service were the funds available. A pure free market approach to the not-for-profit sector is not a wholly helpful model.

The Community Fund has seen many significant and valuable benefits for the not-for-profit sector. Many projects, big and small, around the country would not have come into being and made a huge impact on local areas – and the children and families living there. It has not, however, been without pain.

The Business Model

The National Lottery Charity Board introduced a requirement for bids over £200,000 that the application comes with a business plan attached. The move towards a business model of development for the not-for-profit sector is a major change that has become part of mainstream thinking in the past decade. For social welfare reformers and campaigners, thinking and planning traditionally had been in terms of how to facilitate change in people whose lives are in some form of difficulty – either by their own fault – or more probably in this line of thinking, the fault of structural inequalities and prejudice. It was more likely to rage against business (that is, capitalism) than to embrace its practices as appropriate and even necessary strategies in achieving the same long-term goal, that of ameliorating the hardship that some families and children live in. This change is a real and significant one. Gone are the days of us and them – with reformers very much siding with the poor against the rich, the weak against the powerful.

The political, economic and social reality of the 21st century is that the not-for-profit sector, who have always gone to business for money, need also to recognise that some models of business planning not only have validity in today's economy, but may help achieve the goals of the organisation. It is folly to argue otherwise – although it is to be hoped that there can be a quid pro quo as business adopts some of the equality of opportunity and family friendly policies of the not-for-profit sector. This, of course, is a little overly simplistic at the edges. Of course, some businesses have adopted a robust welfare approach

to its employment and production policies. Equally, some not-for-profit organisations remain committed to a street level campaign against the powerful and wealthy on behalf of the oppressed. For most, I would argue, the 'mixed economy' has shown a useful way through this particular debate.

This is no better typified than by the introduction of MBAs (Masters Degrees in Business Administration) for the welfare or not-for-profit sector. So great is the conversion to this way of thinking that instead of a small number of managers from the sector enrolling in generalist MBAs, academic institutions now have complete courses – courses which are eagerly subscribed to – for the not-for-profit sector. This is a significant and in many ways important move.

Funding by Local Authority Social Services Departments for the not-for-profit sector usually comes via provisions of the 1989 Children Act, Section 17. Increasingly, however, this funding, which used to come in the form of a grant, now comes as a Service Level Agreement. Targets and conditions are attached to the money and monitoring – including Best Value assessments – is becoming the norm rather than the exception.

This move towards a clearer business like agenda is not in itself a bad thing. Clarity of financial accounting and planning for the future direction and development of the organisation is a wholly valid matter to be addressed – particularly by funding bodies. The not-for-profit sector must accept the inevitable move towards this approach and adopt it and then adapt it to best suit the needs of the people we are working with rather than hang on to a political dogma which is looking and sounding increasingly outdated. The reality is that those organisations which choose not to do this will find themselves, rapidly, running out of funds.

The Future?

So what of the future? It has been argued in this chapter that the 'voluntary' sector should rename itself the not-for-profit sector. This is descriptive, accurate and places the sector alongside the statutory and private sectors as equal partners in the provision of services to needy and often vulnerable families and in particular for the purposes of this publication, children. This is neither revolutionary nor particularly going to further the aims of organisations in the sector. It does, however, reframe the nature of the service delivery that is being sought to provide.

What is more revolutionary is the essential move to embrace business language and to a great extent, business thinking and methods. This will be anathema to some within the sector and it is easy to understand why.

The very nature of the sector is that it's history, as we have seen from earlier in this chapter, is infused with social campaigning; motivated by philanthropic convictions of social justice, the early campaigners eschewed any suggestion of moving away from being a 'friend of the poor and needy'.

It is, of course, important to maintain a balance in this matter. Over the past three years, the NSPCC have launched a campaign – the Full Stop campaign – which was to raise a huge amount of money (several hundred million pounds) to stop the abuse of children. The campaign cost tens of millions of pounds to run with poster campaigns and a mail drop through every letter box in the country asking for individuals to sign up in support of the scheme. In many ways the Full Stop campaign was admirable and ambitious. It was also very costly and failed to reach the huge fundraising target that it had set itself. The business model had been adopted and to some degree was found wanting. The resultant publicity has not been wholly complimentary about the organisation and there has been something of a public relations battle to re-establish itself as a credible campaigning organisation.

It is absolutely essential that, while the not-for-profit sector adopt new techniques, whether these be borrowed from business or not, it must remember its roots and its primary focus. The not-for-profit sector is exactly that. It does not exist for the benefit of shareholders, nor does it want to make a profit. Organisations in the sector should look carefully at their financial reserves. Given that all money within the organisation in this sector is essentially charitable – that is, it has been given or earned to pursue the organisation's charitable aims, large reserves should not exist. Clearly financial prudence is essential and reserves are an essential buffer zone against unforeseen problems or cash crises. There is absolute legitimacy in ensuring that there are sufficient cash reserves to

see an organisation through a difficult patch. However, rather than just as a toy gathering dust on a shelf in an office – being saved just in case someone needs it – it should instead be given to a child who will enjoy it and play with it now, so £100 in a bank account against a never-to-come rainy day is £100 that could and perhaps should be spent on providing a group for parents and their children on a needy estate.

If the not-for-profit sector lose sight of its original aims and objectives, and the charitable aims it is charged to pursue, then it has lost sight of its reason for existence. No amount of business planning can truly take the place of the motivation to work for social justice that motivated Stephenson to quit his plans to go to the Far East to be a missionary and instead, horrified by the squalor and degradation in which London's children were living, committed himself to a lifetime of service to these children.

Conclusion

The not-for-profit sector has changed hugely since the mid 1800s. It has needed to change to reflect the political and economic reality of the current day. It will need to continue to change as the world changes. The effect on share prices as a result of the atrocity on New York on September 11th 2001, is having an impact on the amount of funds that grant giving trusts have available to give away to organisations in the sector. This will directly affect the provision of services. There will always be world or local events that directly and clearly impact on the service delivery of such organisations.

However, in all of this, let us remain committed to the children and families that the organisations in the sector exist to work alongside.

6 Partners, Rivals and Innovators: The Voluntary Sector Role in Relationship to the Local Authority

Andy Lloyd

Introduction

The previous chapter discussed the development of the not-for-profit sector and considered the very major issues which have been faced by the sector over the past two decades. This chapter will develop that discussion with particular reference to the relationship with the local authority, and specifically the local authority social services department. The chapter begins by briefly examining the role of each sector before moving on to consider in what ways there is a need for partnership between the statutory and not-for-profit sectors in order to maximise both the level and quality of services provided in the field of family support. The discussion will then move on to examine in what ways the two sectors are rivals – for resources (often hard cash!) and for the market position within the provision of family services.

Immediately, it is important to explain the reference to market provision. For a worker in the welfare sector, whether within the not-for-profit or the statutory part of that provision, the notion of market position is a novel and perhaps for some, offensive, one. This provision is not selling services and our service users are not in the market to buy them. Clearly this is different for those organisations operating in the private sector. However, for the purpose of this chapter, the focus will be on the relationship between the not-for-profit and the statutory sector.

So, what is the market position that is being discussed here? It is simply the need for all organisations, big or small, statutory or not-for-profit, local or national, to attract funds in order that their operations can continue and develop. This means that each organisation needs to develop strategies in order to 'position itself' in the 'market' in a similar way to those methods adopted by rival supermarkets or car manufactures. The parallel is not exact but there is an increasing similarity in which the welfare sector is choosing to market itself. This is a matter for further discussion later in this chapter.

Whatever the language used, it is indisputable that there is, and always will be, a limited amount of resources, and there is increasingly strong competition for those resources. For the good of the family welfare provision in this country, it is essential that this rivalry is managed properly and with justice. Having considered partnerships and rivalries, the discussion will then move on to consider the way in which, if managed and developed appropriately, innovative projects and service delivery can continue growing throughout the country.

The Role of the Local Authority

Within the remit of the children and family support agenda, the local authority role is fixed largely by the Children Act 1989, in particular Section 17. This Section provides, by any definition, a wide and far-reaching brief. Endless debates can take place about the meaning of some of the words within this section. What does 'in need' mean? What does 'as far as is consistent' mean? What is a 'range and level of services' and who defines what is deemed to be appropriate.

All of these questions are important and require discussion. Further government guidance and case law has helped to clarify some of these matters. There is not the space in this chapter to discuss them in any detail. Suffice to say, however, that the overarching responsibility for children who are in need lies squarely with the local authority – which invariably in reality means the Social Service Department (or increasingly the conglomerate department which includes Social Services).

The fact that Section 17 of the Act is clear that it is a duty of the local authority means that there is no choice in providing some sort of service – and in fact it is unlikely that many would argue that this state of affairs is wrong. So, the local authority has the legal **duty** to safeguard the welfare of the child and to promote them living with their family where at all possible.

Historically, the local authorities have both provided directly themselves for children and families and also commissioned the not-for-profit sector to undertake services on their behalf – usually through a Service Level Agreement. Typically, the local authority will provide a budget (or less frequently posts) and the not-for-profit organisation will agree to deliver an agreed amount of work. Monitoring ensures that the local authority is getting what they have paid for and allows for some scrutiny of the quality of the work.

This arrangement has pertained for a number of years – certainly preceding the advent of the Children Act. It has clearly been a valuable relationship for both sides of the sector and the relationship between the two has been, and remains clear. The 'commissioning' local authority is in a very strong position to insist on the nature of the work which the 'commissioned' not-for-profit sector undertakes. It is less likely, although in no way impossible, that the local authority will insist on the **manner** in which these services are delivered. There is, however, an element of he who pays the piper, calls the tune. This is not unreasonable and needs to be accepted by both parties.

The local authority agenda has, of late, itself been informed by many policy decisions at a national and local level, which has affected the level and range of family support services it is able to provide.

The need for increased services delivered by the local authority has meant that they have been under financial pressure for some time, despite increasing budgets. Each year as the amount of money that central government allow local authorities to spend is announced, there are real concerns expressed by the Local Authority that the amount does not match the need within the area. When the local budgets are then produced, the Social Services Departments will again express anxiety that the figure they have been allocated will not meet the needs within the Department. This is an unfortunate, but seemingly annual, event which can lead to cuts in services. It also not infrequently means that the grants and service level agreement funding paid by the local authority to the not-for-profit sector is cut. Rarely is the entire amount cut – often a percentage is cut or a cost of living increase is not awarded (which amounts to a percentage cut in any event).

The Best Value review regime, which has been introduced by central government recently, has again challenged the budgets and planning of the local authority. An insistence, which in many senses is a reasonable one that services delivered must demonstrate good value for money, has meant that streamlining of service provision has been required across family support services.

The Quality Protects agenda, which has had additional central government money attached to it, has allowed social services departments to increase spending, particularly on child protection services along with services for children who are looked after by the local authority.

This relates to the main policy debate of recent years, which has ranged from one side to the other over the past two decades and is that of long-term family support versus short-term focussed intervention.

Long-term family support argues that for some – possibly most – families, the task of raising children in a manner which will not see those children perpetuating the difficulties which brought the family to the notice of the Social Services Department in the first place will take some time. Some parents/carers will not come to a point of change quickly and it is unreasonable to expect them to do so. Supporters of long term intervention would argue that given some of these people have suffered from inappropriate abusive parenting themselves, it is not reasonable to expect them to bring about change in a short period of time. Indeed for some families, low level, long-term support is going to be required for many years.

On the other hand, many would argue that long-term support is creating an unhealthy dependency which victimises and de-skills the families. They would argue that speedy and educative intervention will often provide the skills that the family need and, once that has been achieved, the work should be withdrawn and the family should be allowed to continue the parenting process without interference. In the case where the family encounters a further difficulty, a similar short-term programme should be introduced which again addresses the matter which is causing the immediate difficulty.

Each side of this debate has its merits. The paternalistic attitude of some of the early founders of the major child care organisations appears to have very much played in to the dependency model. To insist that a family cannot move on and will need a lifetime of support risks being a self-fulfilling prophecy.

The short-term intervention model certainly seems attractive.

However, some families have multiple problems and do not solve them by going on, say, a twelve-week parenting skills course. To expect that they should be able to move that quickly is difficult to argue.

In reality, a mixture of both models is required to offer effective family support. Some families can and do respond to short and intensive interventions. Other families remain as open cases for many years as a series of interventions are offered but still more is required.

While this argument is fascinating on a philosophical and theoretical level, it also has a very real implication as to what services the local authority may seek to commission from the not-for-profit organisations. If the short-term model is the preferred solution, then 'spot purchasing' – buying in a short term and specific service as and when it is required – is the most cost effective and useful commissioning style. If long-term family support is being advocated, service level agreements with clear targets and reporting requirements make much more sense.

As this debate has been held over the past 20 years, the manner in which the local authority has used the not-for-profit sector to undertake family support work has also changed. This has inevitably led to some insecurity of funding and some organisations have found themselves unable to continue offering services as the whole of their funding base has been changed and they no longer qualify for the grants they once did.

The local authority has faced a huge change – much of which is led by central government policies – which has had significant effects on the financing of family support services. This state of change looks set to continue.

A further debate surrounds the priority of the local authority's work. They are charged, within the Children Act 1989 with the responsibility of promoting the welfare of the child and the whole raft of child protection measures introduced in that Act. As funding becomes more and more pressured, there is an inevitability that the focus of their work will move toward their statutory responsibilities. This leaves the local authority departments with decreasing amounts of time to spend on the therapeutic or developmental work. There is a risk that, without additional funding, the local Social Services Department will be simply involved in statutory child protection work and any other more therapeutically or support minded work will become the domain of the not-for-profit sector. This would not be a helpful development – for two reasons. First, there are very skilled and experienced workers within the statutory sector who have knowledge and understanding of family support. To remove them from the available resources to families – even if only because of financial imperatives – means that families would lose out on that expertise. Secondly, there is already a recruitment and retention problem in many statutory Social Services Departments. A move of this nature would risk experienced and skilled workers moving out of the statutory services, leaving what is arguably the most important part of the family support agenda – child protection – to newly qualified workers who themselves would move on in due course.

The Not-For-Profit Sector

The not-for-profit sector is somewhat more diverse than the local authority. There are large national organisations and there are small locally based and locally managed projects. Each of them will have a mission statement or a statement of purpose and those of them which are registered as a charity will have a set of aims and objectives (often in the terms of a Memorandum and Articles of the organisation) agreed by the Charity Commission. Those involved in family support will write their mission statement differently, but the theme will be, in one form or another, commitment to improve the quality of life and provision for children and families.

The Barnardo's mission statement argues that the:

Barnardo's vision is that the lives of all children and young people should be free from poverty, abuse and discrimination. Our purpose is to help the most vulnerable children and young people transform their lives and fulfil their potential.

(www.barnardos.co.uk).

Along similar lines the Children's Society argue that:

If you believe every child deserves a decent chance in life, you believe in everything we stand for.

(www.the-childrens-society.co.uk).

For the NSPCC their mission is:

...to end cruelty to children. Our vision is a society in which all children are loved, valued and able to fulfil their potential. In other words, a society that will not tolerate child abuse – whether sexual, physical, emotional, or neglect.

(www.nspcc.org.uk).

Whilst these are very different statements, the same theme runs through all three examples. In terms of legal powers, not-for-profit organisations do not have powers under the Children Act to directly act to protect children, with the exception of the National Society for the Prevention of Cruelty to Children. For all other not-for-profit child care organisations, apart from the general responsibility on organisations to ensure the safety of children, there are no specific legal rights in this matter.

This is an important matter. Not-for-profit organisations are not the local authority. They do not, apart from in some circumstances the NSPCC, have rights to apply for legal orders. The implication of this is that it is often very much easier to engage with families who will not engage with the statutory agencies. Families who are convinced, often without good reason, that the local authority social worker will immediately remove their children when there is a difficulty, are reluctant to allow that worker into the home. This image of local authority social services Departments is an unfortunate one and is often not helped by media coverage that place such workers and their departments in a no-win situation. The phrase 'damned if you do and damned if you don't' is not an uncommon one within a local social work office. The development around refocusing projects (described by Liz Jeffery in Chapter 3) will hopefully move families away from this particular way of thinking, but there is still a long way to go.

The not-for-profit sector has a very important role in campaigning and acting as an independent voice within the family support debate. It is important that they keep their distance from the local authority – but only in as much as it retains its independent voice. This campaigning role, however, must not replace service delivery with vulnerable families. It is an absolutely essential part of family support services that issues are addressed and campaigns are undertaken. Great strides have been made in changing,

for instance, the way that who are selling sex are treat police forces will now treat the child abuse rather than charge the is testament to the value of campa However, without practical support se girls, there is only limited merit in the c

One of the major advantages of being not-for-profit sectors is that it is easier to and develop innovative – or possibly risky – pie work. The local authority is ultimately accountabl the local voter, via elected members. This accountabili and the inevitable formalised decision-making machinery mean that risk taking is not always possible. Not-for-profit sector agencies are accountable to their management board or, if a registered charity, the trustees of the organisation. It is often easier for trustees to approve an innovative and possibly unpopular cause than it is for a local authority department. Again, there is a risk of over simplification here. In reality many local authority departments develop highly innovative programmes of work and some not-for-profit organisations make very safe decisions, which may not actually address the needs of the most vulnerable children and families in the area.

Partners?

The government, in recent years, have made it clear that it expects the not-for-profit and statutory sectors to work in partnership in the area of family support. Two major funding streams – Sure Start and the Children's Fund are not available unless it is clear that there is a robust, sustainable and real partnership between agencies (see Chapter 7). The government plan to have 500 Sure Start programmes in the country by March 2004, all based in local areas of disadvantage and working with families who have children aged 4 or under. There is an unequivocal expectation that there is a partnership approach – which crucially includes parents as active and equal members in the development of the programme in local areas.

A Sure Start programme must:

...bring a partnership together involving parents, community organisations, voluntary groups and statutory agencies.

Support

been a vital
dependent
pieces of
only be
gency

lly
even
ut-for-profit
development and
.,ammes. Designed to carry
start programmes, the Children's
at offering a range of services for 5-13
..-olds. In their introduction to the Children's Fund
Part 1 guidance, David Blunket MP and Paul Boateng
MP wrote:

*We want to see local agencies working alongside
voluntary and community groups, faith groups,
children and young people and parents.*

(Children's Fund Part 1 guidance, p1).

Local area Children's Fund development groups
have a mix of not-for-profit and statutory sector
organisations who are charged with developing the
programme in their locality.

This policy appears to be a deliberate choice on
the Government's part to ensure that the two sectors
work as partners, sharing expertise and resources, for
the benefit of the local community and the vulnerable
families in the area.

Partnership has a great deal to offer. The sharing
of ideas and resources is self evidently good for family
support services. What is equally important, but
perhaps less obvious, is that there is a move towards
offering a portfolio of support to a family in need of
that support.

If it is the duty of the local authority to ensure
that, wherever possible, children remain living with
their families, then the wider the package of family
support offered, and the more options available to
the families, then the better the chance of effective
engagement with that family is going to be.

Good quality partnerships will improve the quality
and range of family support to needy families.
Recognising the skills and expertise of each part of
the sector by others is essential if the best chances
are going to be offered to families who are struggling
and, crucially, the children living in those families.

Rivals?

Partnership is, then, a positive development for
providers of family support. However, as was noted
earlier, the two sectors do exist in the same market
place and are often competing for the same money
and resources. As has also been noted, the local
authority has been vested with the primary
responsibility for ensuring and protecting the welfare
of children.

Within the family welfare, and more specifically
the child protection arena, there is a real danger that
the voluntary sector allow themselves to be quoted
in the media being overtly and sometimes angrily
critical of the work of the local authority Social Services
Departments. This is a disappointing and unpleasant
part of the rivalry between the two parts of the sector.

Frontline child protection investigations – going
out into someone's home to investigate an allegation
of abuse – is a frightening and unpleasant job. Whilst
there are many jobs which are frightening and many
more which are unpleasant, the first ten minutes of
an initial child protection investigation, where it is
known that the family are violent and unpredictable,
or that there are weapons in the home, must rank up
in the top half dozen.

When things go wrong, as they most certainly do
from time to time, lessons should be learnt. If
individuals have not acted in the best interest of the
child or unprofessionally, then action may well be
needed against that individual.

What seems unreasonable is when the not-for-
profit sector, who do not engage in front line initial
child protection investigations – and indeed can and
do refer on any child protection concerns to the local
social services departments – campaign against the
social services departments in a way which creates
real division. Family support is a tough and challenging
occupation. Child protection investigations lead the
way in tough jobs. Mistakes should not be ignored
but the not-for-profit sector does not help itself, or
families who need support, by driving a wedge of
criticism between themselves and the local authority
Social Services departments.

The rivalry can become equally fierce where it
comes to funding streams. If the business model is
accepted, then each organisation has to spend time
creating a market share and a reputation and then,

once that is achieved, more time and money needs to be spent maintaining that market position. This is different from campaigning. A campaign on a specific issue can have public relations benefits, but its primary aim remains the issue. The promotional materials and advertising which seems to have no specific and well-defined focus, but is simply marketing a brand name can appear troublesome. There has been consternation in the media in the past year at the amount of money spent on marketing and public relations by the not-for-profit sector – particularly when the percentage of spend on non-family support work is high.

This rivalry can become troublesome when two or more agencies are seeking to attract money from the same source. In these cases, there is a real risk of individual bids being submitted, there being a lack of cohesion between the bids and so either they all fail or, as can easily happen, very similar services are replicated in the same area. This can lead to a situation where there is not sufficient work for all the projects to undertake. This can lead to the farcical situation where agencies are competing to offer work with the same families. This is made even more troublesome on those occasions where the funding is tied geographically and so some areas are over served and others are in need of more services which they cannot access. This represents a very strong argument for partnership!

Innovators?

The Children's Fund, Sure Start and other national and local funding initiatives introduce the possibility of developing innovative and effective family support programmes. As has been argued above, no single agency from any part of the sector, holds all the answers to a complex and difficult issue. The sooner not-for-profit and statutory agencies can work in true partnership, the sooner high quality programmes of work can be developed. Where this requires a 'giving up' of ground, then it should be done with an understanding that this will benefit the families in the area.

The not-for-profit sector still has a role in introducing innovative and new methods of addressing family support issues. The fact that there are no statutory responsibilities on this sector does allow

such organisations the luxury of developing new work. The development of the 'What Works' approach to much of the family support agenda is a welcome one. However, the 'What Works' research necessarily means that some approaches have worked and others have been less successful. This in turn requires there to be the opportunity for trying out different methods of family support, carefully evaluating each method and then drawing conclusions from the research. This is a luxury – and perhaps that is the correct word – that is not available to the statutory sector whose budget is increasingly tight and workload increasingly heavy.

While it is not the case that the statutory sector never engages in innovative work, it is the case that they are less well placed to do so than the not-for-profit sector. In recent decades the not-for-profit sector has developed innovative work with some of the most vulnerable children and young people in our society – young runaways, street children, young people selling sex and unaccompanied refugee children. It is sometimes difficult for the local authority to respond with the speed, flexibility and lack of bureaucracy which this difficult work requires. This has shifted the not-for-profit organisations to the cutting edge, to innovation and towards campaigning on what might at first seem to be unpopular issues.

The Future?

It is clear that the government is not going to move quickly from the agenda of partnership between the not-for-profit sector and the statutory sector. It is also clear that this partnership, if it is worked at by both 'sides' of the family support provision, can have enormous benefits for the families we are all seeking to support. It is absolutely essential that the funding to the statutory and the not-for-profit sector is maintained – it almost certainly requires an increase over the next decade to ensure improving the quality of family support services.

Sadly, too often, workers and managers from both sectors ask the wrong question. Instead of asking 'What can we get out of this for our organisation?' we need to ask: 'How can a joint working arrangement work for the benefit of our service users.'

This is a simple question to ask in theory. However, when the financial pressures are so heavy – in both the not-for-profit and the statutory sector, it is difficult to get these questions in the right order. The truth of the matter appears to be, however, that if either sector is seeking to maximise income and develop projects then partnership is the only practical way forward. To take a 'stand-offish' approach simply risks seeing funds flowing into other organisations and leaving one isolated. I would argue that this is a good thing. No single organisation has the monopoly of wisdom when it comes to family support, and shared planning and service delivery will very often actively improve the service. It is simply a matter of changing attitudes and accepting the new political and economic reality of family support work. As Badham and Eadie say:

The (not-for-profit) sector's interdependence with the state is not new, but does take different forms. The voluntary (sic) sector is like a chameleon, changing its colour to suit the backdrop of the times. This offers opportunities and threats.
(Badham and Eadie, 2002: p34).

Partnership in innovation is the future for family support. We must all embrace it and work towards that goal – not for our individual organisations, but for the well-being of the children and families we seek to support.

7

New Labour, New Initiatives: Sure Start and the Children's Fund

Liz Jeffery

Introduction

When the Labour Party gained power in May 1997, with its historic landslide victory, expectations of what the new administration might deliver were high, both on the part of the government itself and amongst the electorate. These aspirations related particularly to social and domestic policy. The Conservative administration's performance in relation to the Health Service, to education and the maintenance of law and order, had contributed substantially to its downfall. After the infamous denial by Margaret Thatcher of the existence of society, there had been various attempts, none of them very successful, to find a conceptual framework from which to form a coherent policy relating, in particular, to issues concerning the family. What, for example, were the respective roles and responsibilities of the government and of parents in the upbringing and care of children, and how far should the state intervene in private family life? But 'family rhetoric is attractive, family policy politically dangerous' (Kamerman and Kahn, quoted in Fox-Harding, 1996: p214) and their failure to grapple successfully with these issues and present a coherent and politically acceptable position contributed to the Conservative Party's departure.

The Labour Party meanwhile, during its long period in opposition, had had plenty of opportunity to review its own approach to these issues. During the run up to the 1997 election the Labour Party, under the leadership of Tony Blair, developed a philosophy characterised as 'the third way'. This approach differs in many respects from the traditional 'old Labour' socialist principles that had shaped the agenda and policies of the previous Labour administrations of the 1960s and 1970s and draws heavily on the work of Etzioni in the United States and Giddens from the London School of Economics. As Nick Frost highlights in Chapter 1 it is from this new philosophical starting point that many of New Labour's initiatives, since assuming power, have sprung.

A New Approach to Children and Families

Although, as I shall later go on to discuss, Sure Start was originally announced in July 1998 and subsequently introduced in various trail-blazing authorities in 1999, it was not until the Comprehensive Spending Review of 2000 that the Children's Fund was first heralded by the Chancellor Gordon Brown. This announcement took place alongside the creation by the Prime Minister of the Children and Young People's Unit, a new inter-departmental government body bringing together representatives from the Department of Education and Employment, the Home Office and chaired by the Chancellor of the Exchequer. The role of the CYPU was envisaged as being to produce a coherent approach to provision for children and families that cut across the traditional boundaries and divisions between existing departments and provided instead a means of delivering joined-up policies and initiatives. In this sense the CYPU perceived it as providing a model of good practice and positive partnership that would, it hoped, be mirrored in a new way of delivering services for children and families by local authorities up and down the country.

In March 2001 the CYPU document, *Building a Strategy for Children and Young People*, outlined a range of policies aimed at improving the lives of this age-group. These included a new integrated child credit system and a cross cutting review of children at risk led by the CYPU and the Treasury, to ensure that all government departments took account of the priorities for children and young people. This review was translated in turn, into new initiatives for different agencies and departments, including a 'National Service Framework for Children' for the NHS, the expansion of Sure Start, the introduction of the Children's Fund for 5-13 year-olds and the launch of Connexions which, in conjunction with a generally enhanced Youth Service, was to focus on 13-19 year-olds.

The aims of this new strategy were outlined clearly in *Building a Strategy*. They include importantly a recognition that '...families are the foundation of our society...'; that the voluntary and community sector in addition to statutory agencies, have a significant role to play; that 'children and young people themselves should be given opportunities to play a role in the design and delivery of services'; and a determination 'to ensure that all services for children and young people work for the most disadvantaged in our country and that every service can be interrogated to ensure it does so'. It also acknowledges the need of mainstream services 'to better meet the needs of those children and young people who are vulnerable to social exclusion and often fail to get the level of support they deserve' (CYPU, 2001).

This strategy effectively forms the blueprint for New Labour's approach to children and families. Its key elements are those outlined above with the focus on the prevention of social exclusion, an enhanced role for voluntary and community organisations, and with participation of children and young people seen as central to the effective shaping and delivery of services. Finally there is a new emphasis on outcome-based services showing evidence of change.

In terms of both Sure Start and the Children's Fund there is now an expectation that they can produce real and measurable outcomes in terms of the impact that particular services will have on individual children and their families. This emphasis on outcome based provision again derives from the USA, where the practice and language of the market place and private business sector are transferred into public service planning and delivery. Logically, this is a natural progression of the 'contract culture' whereby statutory agencies purchase services from alternative agency providers with a view to providing wider choice, better value for money and better results for consumers (Williams and Webb, 1992). Outcome funding builds on these principles requiring, as in the business sector, that positive and quantifiable returns flow from any financial investment. In terms of both Sure Start and the Children's Fund then, the requirement to make 'a real and measurable difference' is a central prerequisite of government funding and can have, as I will discuss later, both positive results and less desirable consequences. In addition, there is an associated emphasis on evaluation both on a national and at a local level, with an emphasis on 'what works'.

Although the Labour administration have introduced numerous other initiatives, for the purposes of this chapter I shall be focusing entirely on Sure Start and the Children's Fund, and considering to what extent they can and will contribute to the level of support available to families.

Sure Start and the Children' Fund: Descriptions and Comparisons

Sure Start has been described by Norman Glass, a senior civil servant closely associated with Sure Start, as '...a radical cross-departmental strategy to raise the physical, social, emotional and intellectual status of young children through improved services. It is targeted at children under four and their families in areas of need.' (Glass, 1999, in White, 1999: p52)

As a central element of New Labour policy on children and families it was strongly influenced by evidence that had emerged from the United States as to the effectiveness of initiatives like Head-Start and the Perry Pre-School Programme which demonstrated that comprehensive early years programmes could have a beneficial effect. In describing the policy-making process that resulted in the creation of Sure Start, Glass, a leading civil servant, suggests that it was based on 'a review of what the research evidence said about what worked' (Glass, 1999)

Jane Waldfogel (1999) has produced a useful summary of the outcomes of early childhood interventions, which help to illustrate the evidence underpinning the Sure Start initiative. She concludes that 'well designed early intervention programmes can make a positive difference in the lives of children.' She identifies the following measurable results of such programmes:

- higher IQ scores for children
- higher school achievement
- less time in special education
- higher employment
- higher earnings
- lower crime rates
- lower delinquency
- reduced abuse and neglect
- improved mother-child interaction

- higher maternal employment
- increased parental involvement in schools

A particularly striking research statistic from the Perry study suggests that every $1 invested in such early years work would result in savings of $7 in later state expenditure. This statistic has however, and perhaps not surprisingly, been called into question in terms of the impact that particular services can have on an individual child and their family.

The Children's Fund, announced in the Comprehensive Spending Review of July 2000, allocated £450 million to this initiative, launching its initial three-year trail-blazer programmes in April 2001.These were followed, as with Sure Start, by subsequent programmes, starting in 2002, with a final round, to cover all local authorities, planned for 2003/4. In addition and perhaps not surprisingly in view of the government aspirations for the Children's Fund, the most recent Comprehensive Spending Review (July 2002) announced the continuation of the Children's Fund until 2006 – unsurprising since it takes considerable time and effort for such a complex programme to become operational in each local authority, and it would make little sense for funding to cease where this had scarcely happened and where, even in longer-running programmes, the effect of any expenditure would take considerably longer to demonstrate. Targeted at 5-13 year-olds at risk of social exclusion, the Children's Fund aims to bridge the gap between Sure Start and Connexions. It aims to deliver preventive services:

> *...over and above those provided through mainstream statutory services', but going further it 'is not simply about resources' but about 'a change in culture and a change in the way services are co-ordinated and delivered... We want to see local agencies working alongside voluntary and community groups, faith groups, children, young people and parents. Our aim is to provide services that identify those in difficulty early on, and that address the causes of risk. They should be imaginative and innovative, and open and accessible to all parts of the community that need them. Most importantly, we want to secure long-term improvement by building preventing capacity within individual families and broader communities...the aim is to make a difference, reduce child poverty and social exclusion, and improve the life chances of children and young people.*

(CYPU, 2001).

As with Sure Start the Children's Fund is required to work towards specific outcomes. These are:

- Reductions in truancy and exclusion from school.
- Improved educational performance.
- Reduced youth crime and reconvictions.
- Improvements in social care and health-related measures e.g. fewer children and young people needing to enter care.
- More use of existing services by commonly excluded groups e.g. black and minority ethnic families, children and young people and parents with disabilities.
- More involvement of users, children, young people and local adults in service delivery.

(CYPU, 2001).

Again there are specific and detailed requirements in relation to the collection and monitoring of data, the targeting of children and the evaluation of outcomes both at a national and local level.

There are however a number of important differences between the Children's Fund and Sure Start. Firstly, the successive rounds of Sure Start have required all targeted local authorities to decide for themselves which particular neighbourhoods should receive funding. Within the initial Sure Start guidance it states that identified neighbourhoods should typically contain around 700 children in the 0-4 age-ranges, and the services provided should be within 'pram-pushing' distance of families accessing them. Local authorities have handled this requirement to identify the neediest neighbourhoods very differently. In some they have been selected centrally, according to local indices of need and deprivation. In others, there has been open competition between different localities, to demonstrate that their particular neighbourhood is the neediest and most worthy of support, amounting effectively to an undignified and unedifying 'beauty contest', particularly unfortunate in authorities where the case for having a Sure Start programme can be readily made out for any number of council estates and areas of deprivation.

In the case of the Children's Fund, however, the situation is different. Funding is available to a local authority as a whole, once the delivery plan has been approved, and it is the responsibility specifically of the local Children's Fund partnership to determine how funding should be allocated. This means in principle at least, that children and young people living in deprived circumstances have a more equal chance of being on the receiving end of targeted services and resources.

Secondly, whilst it is certainly the case that Sure Start is intended to build on and enhance the role of voluntary and community organisations in terms of service delivery, this requirement is made more explicit and is more fundamental to the thinking behind and delivery of the Children's Fund. As already indicated, the Children's Fund 'is not simply about resources' but a 'change in culture', and in the most recent (July 2002) Comprehensive Spending Review, the Children's Fund was again described as being 'a catalyst for change'. The expectations on the Children's Fund then, and the role it is anticipated as having in terms of changing the face of service delivery for children and young people, is seen as altogether greater and potentially more influential than is the case with Sure Start.

Thirdly and not surprisingly given the target age-range of the two initiatives, the Children's Fund is required to involve children and young people and their parents even more in the shaping and delivery of services. It is a central precept of the Children's Fund that any new project should be developed in response to the express needs and wishes of children and young people and that their views are fed into any ongoing agenda. In this way young people are encouraged not only to participate but to share responsibility in lifting themselves out of social exclusion and building their own capacity for playing a full part in the community.

Finally, and interestingly, the Children's Fund has built into it, an area of potential confusion. Alongside the central Children's Fund that we have so far been describing, there is another strand, known as the Children's Fund Local Network. This Local Network is allocated regionally and not to individual local authorities. An approved voluntary organisation applies for and is granted responsibility for the dissemination of small grants of between £250 and £7,000 to community organisations to help them build their capacity and deliver more effective services. Compared with the main Children's Fund, the Local Network therefore handles far smaller amounts of money and

in addition to the different channels and levels of administration, its remit relates to work with the full age-range of children and young people aged 0-19 years and not just 5-13 year-olds.

Although notionally in place since April 2001, the timescales involved in establishing local Children's Fund partnerships, in recruiting and training staff to local programmes, and in implementing services based on often newly forged alliances between statutory, voluntary and community organisations, mean that it is too early to comment, with any authority, on how services are being delivered and received. It is certainly therefore too soon to predict outcomes of this new way of working. What is already becoming clear, however, is that different local authorities are interpreting the Children's Fund guidance in very contrasting ways. Whereas in one authority small local partnerships between voluntary and statutory agencies are encouraged to submit proposals for new projects and to expand existing areas of work into new areas, with control and oversight being maintained centrally, in other authorities funding is being allocated to different organisations, usually from the voluntary sector, and responsibility delegated to them for the delivery of services in relation to, for example, family support. There are very probably cogent reasons for these contrasting interpretations of the guidance, relating to local demographic factors and the existence or otherwise of voluntary and community organisations with the capacity not only to deliver services, but also to fulfil the various recording and monitoring requirements. It will be interesting and instructive ultimately to discover how these different types of programme fare in any local and national evaluation.

Sure Start and the Children's Fund: A Critique

Sure Start and the Children's Fund represent two major examples of what is arguably a very different way of approaching services for children and young people. Inevitably, as in any radical departure from the norm, gains and drawbacks exist hand in hand, progress is uneven, and lessons need to be learned from the new ways of working. In this section I intend to identify some of both the problems and the advantages of

Sure Start and the Children's Fund as each of these initiatives is translated into practice.

An initial difficulty for any local authority, identified as having serious levels of deprivation, is that these initiatives will inevitably these days co-exist alongside many others. Moreover, since the advent of Sure Start and the Children's Fund, many more initiatives have also been announced such as Connexions, the Street Crime Initiative and Behaviour Improvement Programmes. As and when this New Labour administration finally comes to an end, a post-mortem could well attribute its demise to death by a thousand initiatives! There must be, inevitably, a limit to how many new programmes any individual agency or local authority can reasonably be expected to take on board, understand, and translate into action at any one time, and New Labour, in its enthusiasm for change and action, certainly seems to be pushing at these boundaries. Associated with the sheer plethora of new initiatives is the speed at which the response to them is required. This is a difficulty at an authority-wide level in bringing together inter-agency partnerships, whose representatives have possibly never met or worked together before, and expecting them to deliver coherent plans and strategies in a matter of weeks. It is also problematic at a more local community level. As noted by Freeman et al. 'members of community groups need time to absorb information relating to the future of their community, groups have to meet and discuss'; and importantly, in terms of the participation of this group '...the opportunity...to involve children and young people in discussions about bids has been minimal' (Freeman et al., 1999: p72).

The time taken up in lengthy meetings and discussions to provide this 'rapid response' also takes its toll, particularly on smaller voluntary organisations with fewer staff, and inevitably detracts from their core function of delivering services to needy children and their families. This has been described recently as '...the Sisyphean task of pushing institutional performance up the league tables...' which is '...made harder by constantly redefining and adding targets and introducing initiatives, and of course with no account taken of the costs of competing for initiative funding' (O'Neill, 2002). Additionally, the fact that each new funding-stream appears to have different monitoring requirements, compounds the problems.

A second difficulty, linked with the first, and again presenting particular problems for smaller community organisations, are the demands of evidence-based work, such as monitoring progress and recording outcomes. These are onerous for any organisation, but for those smaller ones, lacking any substantial infrastructure, there are in-built obstacles, which may mean that they preclude themselves, or are precluded from applying for particular funding-streams, such as the Children's Fund. It is to be hoped that these are difficulties which can be overcome with time, as these groups grow in capacity, but in the meantime this is surely an unintended consequence from the government's point of view, since they have highlighted the important role they envisaged for the community sector in terms of delivering the Children's Fund. Larger voluntary organisations are, by contrast, benefiting from the advent of both Sure Start and the Children's fund and are growing in significance and capacity in terms of local service delivery.

The typically short-term nature of many initiatives, including Sure Start and the Children's Fund, is also problematic. Not only does this impact on individual job security, more importantly it may possibly affect the significance and outcomes of any particular project. From the point at which funding is secured, it typically takes several months to advertise for, recruit and induct new staff. Add to this the time already taken by an organisation or partnership to put together a proposal and have it approved, and at least six months are likely to have gone by. In the context of an initiative whose funding is only assured for perhaps two years at a time, it is clear that the impact of any project is likely to be compromised.

There is also a difficulty, in the case of Sure Start and the Children's Fund of the inevitable perceived geographical inequity of provision, when, as already described in the case of Sure Start, some neighbourhoods in a large city will attract funding whilst others, arguably equally disadvantaged, receive none. It may even be that inequalities are reinforced, since typically it appears that it is those neighbourhoods already well-supported by large voluntary organisations and also able to attract, for example, regeneration funding, who qualify for support, whereas those with only small or no organisations operating in their area are penalised. This is a widely voiced concern, and can hopefully be addressed, to some extent at least, by the 'mainstreaming' of Sure Start. Inequality of provision is less of a problem for the Children's Fund, although there are still issues in any authority about where funding can best be targeted.

The strong emphasis, in both Sure Start and the Children's Fund, on producing hard evidence of 'what works', based on statistical data and measurable outcomes, brings with it a further raft of difficulties. Firstly, there is an inevitable emphasis on indices that are susceptible to measurement, such as school attendance and exclusion figures, levels of registration with a GP or dentist, and crime statistics in the over-tens. O'Neill suggests, in this context, that '...the real focus is on performance indicators chosen for ease of measurement and control rather than because they measure accurately what the **quality** of performance is.' (O'Neill, 2002: my emphasis) Whilst these clearly have considerable significance, they do not represent by any means the total picture. Those factors that do not lend themselves to such analysis, such as the general level of well-being of an individual or community, being 'softer' and harder to measure, are given little weight. This focus on quantitative, as opposed to qualitative evaluation, is arguably over-simplistic and fails to register the significance of, for example, a single parent having more friends and feeling happier and more confident as a result of their involvement with a Sure Start programme. This would not necessarily translate into hard evidence, particularly within the brief time-scales within which Sure Start is currently operating, but may, in the long term, have enormous significance for their own future and that of their children. There is, in addition, a particular irony here. In the guidance produced for both Sure Start and the Children's Fund, the government offers numerous descriptions of projects they view as good models of practice, and, in this context, they quote the positive views of those who feel they have benefited from these services. These 'snapshots' and quotations are indeed very instructive in offering a flavour of how different projects operate and what is perceived as helpful by service users. Interestingly, the guidance does not draw on statistics and the type of quantitative data they are now seeking, as a means of demonstrating the effectiveness of a particular project.

Clearly, a balance needs to be struck here, and there is arguably a place for both types of research and analysis.

A second difficulty, arising from a too exclusive emphasis on the 'what works' approach, is the risk that facts and realities can be distorted. For example, one of the targets set for Sure Start is that the figures for re-registration of children on the child protection register within twelve months should reduce by 20 per cent by 2004. This requirement is problematic on two counts: firstly, re-registration is not, in itself, necessarily a bad thing. If, for example, a mother has separated from her child's father, who has convictions for child abuse, her child will be de-registered. If, a few months later, she moves in with a different abuser, it is clearly in her child's interests for re-registration to take place. From the child's point of view, this is an example of positive rather than negative practice. However, in a perhaps less clear-cut situation, where re-registration is also arguably required from a professional point of view, the pressure to reduce statistics could result in a different decision taking place, leaving the child open to further risk of harm.

A third and final problem in this context is the assumption that neighbourhoods and their populations remain, by and large, stable entities, so that data made available at the beginning of a programme can be usefully compared with statistics produced at the end. This supposition fails to acknowledge that for many of the neighbourhoods and estates where Sure Start operates, the population turnover is unusually high. Such areas are often characterised by, for example, high levels of domestic violence, poor mental health, and a large proportion of refugees and asylum-seekers, and possibly of students, all of which contribute to the relative instability of a community. Factors such as this present particular problems for evaluation, particularly in Sure Start areas, but do not seem to have been recognised as a concern.

Lastly and perhaps most significantly, is the way that both Sure Start and the Children's Fund have moved from being, in the first instance, aspirational programmes to now being, in effect, government tools to meet New Labour's own political objectives. So, for example, whereas Sure Start was introduced specifically to improve the lot of children under four, with the stated aim of giving them a better start in life, it has shifted by degrees, to a position where it now operates from a cross-departmental unit, which includes the Departments for Education and Skills and of Work and Pensions. Correspondingly, the main emphasis of Sure Start now appears to be one characterised less by lifting children out of poverty and more by encouraging parents back into work, with services for children being effectively predicated on their parents' employment.

As with Sure Start, so it is now with the Children's Fund. The Comprehensive Spending Review, announced in July 2002, and the briefings that have succeeded it, have made it clear that one of the Children's Fund's original aims – of making provision more generally available to the target age-range of 5-13 year-olds, through increasing, for example, the level of accessibility and the number of self-referrals – is being heavily eroded by new requirements. These are that children and young people, now in the total age-range of 0-19 years, who are perceived as 'at risk', are subjected to identification, referral and tracking (IRT) and that 25% of Children's Fund money, from September 2003 onwards, will need to be devoted to services agreed with local Youth Offending Teams (YOTS). 'At risk' has recently been defined by the Children and Young People's Unit as those young people who are at risk of adverse outcomes such as getting involved in crime or drugs, or teenage pregnancy, school exclusion or being 'looked after'. These recent pronouncements effectively shift the focus of the Children's Fund away from its initial emphasis on supporting children and young people in the context of their families, and heavily into prevention of crime and other outcomes high on the agenda, particularly of the Home Office. Moreover, this change of emphasis could, depending on interpretation, cause problems in implementation, and could lead to legal difficulties with, for example, the Data Protection Act and Human Rights legislation.

The amount of space devoted to the previous section may suggest a belief that nothing positive is considered likely to emerge from either Sure Start or the Children's Fund. This, however, would be very far from the truth, and I shall now move on to explore the positive aspects of both initiatives.

First of all, the commitment on the part of the current Labour administration to try to improve the lives of socially excluded children and young people is undeniably impressive. As recognised by Freeman et al., 'Some of its measures and proposals may arouse controversy, but its determination to make an impact on the issues cannot be questioned' (Freeman et al., 1999: p138). Having inherited a position in 1997 where 3.2 million children were living below the poverty line, such a level of verbal and financial commitment can only be very much welcomed. It also says much for this administration that it is prepared to invest in programmes whose long-term results will not be demonstrated for ten years or more.

Secondly, both Sure Start and the Children's Fund provide a means by which radically new and potentially very positive models of practice can be translated into action relatively quickly. Instead of having to struggle through the bureaucratic processes of various local authority departments, and running the risk of being still-born, innovative ideas and practices are now being actively encouraged and promoted, with examples of positive new ways of working being publicised through Sure Start and Children's Fund networks. This is, perhaps, the 'pay-off' for all the hours of work spent in new partnership meetings, and is no mean achievement.

Thirdly, both initiatives provide a means, albeit an imperfect one as indicated above, of at least attempting to target those groups particularly at risk of social exclusion. In the case of children whose families face homelessness, for example, they have traditionally tended to fall between the remits of different local authority departments, who arguably have some responsibility towards them. As a result, these children are more likely than most not to attend school, or if they do to under-achieve or be the target of bullying; and, because of their unstable circumstances, to elude the help offered by Social Services. It is almost certain that their opportunities for play will also be severely limited. The Children's Fund offers an opportunity for statutory and voluntary organisations with a responsibility for and commitment to working with homeless children, to join forces and try to ensure that their educational, social and play needs is met. Similarly, the low attainment, particularly in secondary school, of boys from African-Caribbean backgrounds, can be tackled through those who share a concern about this situation coming together and devising ways of promoting higher levels of achievement, through, for example, staging a conference for African-Caribbean young people and their parents, celebrating their achievements in wider arenas and identifying the processes that can help or hinder such achievement. This kind of event and the organisation it requires is in fact greatly facilitated by the Children's Fund, with the opportunities it offers of simpler and more effective networking across traditional divides, and of bringing together those with a commonality of interest, whatever their backgrounds.

Indeed, this promotion of positive working relationships is a further very real advantage of both Sure Start and the Children's Fund. Coming together with a shared agenda of tackling mutually identified concerns provides a huge opportunity, not only of effectively addressing the problems, but also of skill-sharing and forging new inter-agency relationships and understanding, and of breaking down traditional barriers and suspicions. Especially to be welcomed in this context, is the enhanced role offered, and already being taken up by particularly the larger voluntary organisations, as already indicated, but also, hopefully, over time, of some of the smaller community organisations, if these initiatives remain in place long enough for them to build their capacity and make use of them. This increased profile for non-statutory organisations is particularly important and significant, since it is they who are more in touch with local neighbourhoods and more likely to be able to address their needs in ways that are seen as acceptable to children and families.

In this context, perhaps the most fundamental and far-reaching aspect to recognise is that both these initiatives are required to develop services that take account of and incorporate the views and wishes of both parents and the children and young people themselves. This represents a radical departure from the previous situation, where participation was very far from being at the centre of the decision-making process. What is important to remember with regard to participation, however, is that '...it is not a process that stands alone with reference to an identified group of children but derives from, and in turn impacts on, the wider society. Participation demands a commitment to listen and react to what comes out of children's participation, especially when such participation challenges the status quo.' (Freeman et al., 1999: p54).

In other words, participation is a process and not an event and as such its consequences cannot be predicted. However, quoting again from these authors '...community development only works when it mobilises the positive interests and energies of people – children as well as adults' (Freeman et al.,1999: p73).

Conclusion

In terms of these two initiatives therefore, despite the problems that have been identified, there is still a great deal to be welcomed. Indeed, it could be argued that the combination of Sure Start, the Children's Fund and Connexions represent the most radical, exciting and innovative approach to provision for children and young people since the 1960s. For the future, however, there are some areas which need to be addressed.

Firstly, there is the practical challenge of deciding how to take account of the more qualitative outcomes of service provision. Richard Gutch, writing recently in *The Guardian*, asked 'How do you define and measure soft outcomes, such as increased self-esteem or reduced risk of being disadvantaged? Projects involving preventative activities can be particularly difficult to pin down...' (Gutch, 2002). We need to think *whose* outcomes we are measuring, and whether they represent real positive change for service users, or merely statistics that can be interpreted favourably by the government, to serve their own interests. As suggested by Cheetam et al. (1992), quoted in Canavan et al. 'A useful distinction ...is between *client based outcomes*, which measure the effects of services on service users, and *service based outcomes* which are concerned with the process of delivery' (Canavan et al., 2000: p218). There is a need to engage with this whole area to ensure that both the qualitative and quantitative outcomes are fully heard and appreciated.

Secondly, as suggested recently by Malcolm Dean, in *The Guardian*, (Dean, 2002) there is a need for a more unified system of recording and monitoring requirements that can address the requirements at least of all the government funded initiatives. This would substantially reduce the pressure particularly on community and smaller voluntary organisations, and would free up considerable time for them to devote to their core activities of supporting families and children.

Finally, using the terminology of Moss and Sharpe (1979), quoted in Fox-Harding (1996: p208) it would perhaps be helpful in any issues concerned with family policy, to think more holistically in terms of a 'family perspective' model. Using this approach, the positive impact of Sure Start and the Children's Fund could be enhanced by consideration of the *family impact* of all aspects of social policy that have a bearing on families and family life. This would result in a more coherent; 'joined-up' approach to all related areas, and hopefully, ultimately to a more family-friendly, and structured approach to social problems. For, as Freeman et al. (1999) observe, there is certainly a need for 'a rigorous analysis of structural problems' since these can 'easily swamp the best-intentioned intervention programmes in neighbourhoods.'

Ultimately then, both Sure Start and the Children's Fund represent a very positive advance in terms of family policy, but there are still problematic areas which will need to be addressed, for them to achieve their full potential.

Part Two

Developing Practice
in Family Support

8

Working With the Children of Parents With Alcohol and Drug Problems

Christine Clavering

Drug use can raise anxiety levels in each of us. Drug using parents can be particularly anxiety provoking. It is important to both recognise these anxieties but also to undertake a full and measured assessment of the child's needs. This chapter discusses the dilemma many professionals feel when faced with parents who are using illegal drugs or alcohol

Introduction

Drug use is a frightening and emotive issue and our responses to it are rarely rational or well informed. Rather, they are influenced by the media and the changeable moral and political attitudes to both legal and illegal drugs. Social workers are as likely as any others to have their judgements coloured by these influences, which makes it difficult for them to carry out an accurate assessment of the needs of children whose parents have problems with alcohol or other drugs. What this chapter argues is that social workers should step outside the fear and emotion and look at the child's safety and developmental needs and the capacity of the carers to provide a safe, warm and stimulating environment for them, as they would with any other child in need. However, in order to make an accurate assessment it is necessary to know what to look for and what questions to ask. This requires knowledge of different drugs, their effects and the accompanying life styles. In addition, I would advise social workers to work closely with drug and alcohol treatment agencies who will have the necessary knowledge and also greater insight into the lives these children may be leading.

Background

As a manager of alcohol and drug services for a total of 12 years in the late 1980s and through the 1990s, I saw considerable change in patterns of drug use and in the response of government to both alcohol and illegal drugs. This was reflected in the response of health and social care agencies and a considerable change in treatment regimes for people with alcohol and drug problems. In the 1980s there was still a belief in the 'addictive personality' and the disease model of alcoholism. Both these theories maintained that total abstinence for life was the only hope for people with these conditions and the only drug treatment regimes were based on American military training and aimed to break down the drug dependant personality and instil an abstinent and disciplined one. At this time, the response of social services to children with a mother with a severe alcohol or drug problem, was almost always to remove the children. The father's substance use was rarely considered, unless it was linked to abuse of the children.

Drugs workers, however, were not convinced that drug use equated with inadequate parenting, and myself and my colleagues put a great deal of effort into convincing social services that illegal drug use was not de facto a reason for child protection investigations and certainly not a valid reason for removing children from their drug using parents. At that time, drugs workers protected the confidentiality of their clients above almost anything else, convinced that a referral to social services would break the trust between ourselves and our clients and equally convinced that social services would act quickly to remove the children.

The change of attitude towards drug users came about with the spread of HIV through sharing injecting equipment. This led to the emphasis switching from trying to help users become abstinent, to protecting the public by providing drug users with clean needles and alternative drugs which could not easily be injected. This in turn led health professionals to a treatment regime which they were comfortable with, that is primarily drug treatment. The irony of giving people addicted to drugs more drugs or different drugs, was lost in the desire to make contact with them and to try and stop them spreading HIV:

There is growing evidence that treatment works. In particular, harm reduction work over the last 15

years has had a major impact on the rate of HIV and other drug related infections.

(Tackling Drugs Together to Build a Better Britain
(1998) DoH, Aim iii).

The 'medicalisation' of the issue of alcohol and drug problems and the funding of services primarily by Health Authorities, separated the dependency from the associated lifestyle and made it more plausible that someone maintained on methadone, or who continued to use illegal drugs in a responsible fashion, could be a good enough parent.

By the 1990s, the introduction of needle exchanges and the expansion of methadone prescribing had brought more and more drug users into services. As a result, drugs workers had much more in depth knowledge of the lives of these service users and much more reason to be concerned about the welfare of their children, who are frequently neglected and abused and almost always emotionally damaged by the fact that their parents cared about their drugs more than they did about their children, for as Dore et al. noted, in observations of children of parents with substance abuse problems:

...there are greater rates of clinical anxiety, depression, low self esteem and lowered perceptions of control over the environment.

(1995: p531).

From 1993 to 1999, still as a manager of alcohol and drug treatment services, I was frequently contacting social services to refer children whose parents we knew to be putting their children at risk through their chaotic drug use and accompanying chaotic lifestyle, only to be informed by the social workers that illegal drug use was not a reason for child protection investigation. They had adopted the 'medicalisation of substance use' approach in which problems are divorced from the accompanying lifestyle. This is not to say that these children are never subject to statutory intervention, as *The Children Act Now* states:

...one third of the families in the emotional abuse and neglect study and two fifths of the parents in the study on making care orders work had problems with the misuse of drugs or alcohol. As might be expected, the incapacity caused by parents' drug use placed considerable burden on the children.

(DoH, 2001: p29).

However, I contend that many of these children could have been identified and supported earlier, and certainly before so much damage had been done, and I would argue that more than issues of parents' 'incapacity' need to be addressed. Again *The Children Act Now* summary concludes that:

Domestic violence and drugs and alcohol misuse are present in families with more severe problems.

(2001: p32).

Unfortunately this failure to confront the issue of cause and effect and how much the alcohol and drug use and the accompanying lifestyle contributes to the problems, rather than being one of a multitude of problems experienced by some families.

The Scottish Executive, in the publication *Getting our Priorities Right* is much clearer about the damage caused by parental drug use:

Children may be at high risk of maltreatment, emotional or physical neglect or abuse, family conflict, and inappropriate parental behaviour (Famularo, Kindscherff and Fenton, 1992; Wasserman and Levanthal, 1993; Barlow, 1996). Children may be exposed to and involved in, drug-related activities and associated crimes (Hogan, 1998). They are more likely to display behavioural problems (Wilens et al., 1995), experience social isolation and stigma (Kumpfer and De Marsh, 1986), misuse substances themselves when older (Hoffman and Su, 1998; McKeganey, 1998) and develop problem drug use themselves (Graham and Hughes, 1995).

Parents with chronic drug addiction spend considerable time and attention on accessing and using drugs, reducing their emotional and actual availability to their children. Conflicting pressures may be especially acute in economically deprived, lone-parent households and where there is little support from relatives or neighbours. (Rosenbaum, 1979). Households headed by problem drug users may be poor, unstable and characterised by criminal activity. Violence may also be a feature of such environments. (Hogan, 1998).

Relationships between drug-dependent parents and their children have been found to be difficult and conflictual. Parents may often provide inconsistent and lukewarm care, ineffective supervision and overly punitive discipline (Kandel, 1990; Boyd, 1993). Deficiencies in parenting skills might, however, also be an outcome of poor role models provided by the parents of drug users themselves. In the long term children of problem drug using parents may have severe social difficulties including strong reactions to change, isolation, difficulty in learning to have fun and estrangement from family and peers. (Barlow, 1996).

(Scottish Executive, 2001: p7-8).

In this chapter I shall look at the effects of problematic drug and alcohol use on parents and subsequently on their children. I shall also look at the consequences of the lifestyle of illegal drug users. I shall then offer some tools for assessing the risks to these children and also suggest helpful interventions for the children.

For the purpose of this chapter I shall be dealing with alcohol, heroin and other opiates, cocaine and crack and amphetamines. There are arguments for including other drugs, but I remain convinced that it is the ones I have listed that give us the most cause for concern. It can be argued that someone can use cannabis on a daily basis without it affecting their ability to look after their children. This is not the case for the other illegal drugs mentioned above. Alcohol can of course be used recreationally and does not have the same implications as illegal drugs, but dependent alcohol use by parents can have very damaging effects on their children and frequently leads to violence in the home.

Physical Effects of Substance Use

Alcohol

We are all familiar with the laws dealing with driving over the prescribed limit, but it is far less often that we hear about someone being charged for being drunk in charge of a child. However, if we consider the effects of getting drunk, it makes us uninhibited and unco-ordinated. The former is dangerous in terms of controlling anger or sexual behaviour towards children and the latter is dangerous in handling and carrying a baby.

Many people become aggressive when drunk and a high percentage of domestic violence is committed by men under the influence of alcohol. A study reported:

...more than three times the risk of domestic violence when husbands or male partners abuse alcohol and drugs.

(Besharov, 1999: p5).

It is now accepted that violence in the home has a damaging effect on children who witness it. It is also evident that violence towards children is much more likely when adults in the home have been drinking. The further effect of intoxication with alcohol is unconsciousness. This is dangerous if a parent is in charge of an infant, but also very damaging for the child who returns home from school to find their mother has passed out on the settee. The child can become very anxious, not knowing what they will find when they get home, some will not want to leave their mother, will stay at home from school and take on the carer role, other children won't be able to wait to get out and will spend as much time as possible away from home. These children would be very unlikely to invite other children home.

Consideration also needs to be given to the effects of withdrawing from alcohol. A parent with a hangover is far more likely to lose patience with a child and hit them and is unlikely to be able to prepare breakfast. Someone who is physically dependant on alcohol will be irritable if they have not had a drink, their hands will shake and in extreme cases will become psychotic and have auditory and visual hallucinations, known as delirium tremens or DTs. Again, this should give rise for concern if there is no responsible adult in a position to care for the children.

Heroin

Heroin is a drug which in simplistic terms takes away pain. This includes physical pain, emotional pain and stress and worries. Users have described it as being like wrapped in cotton wool, where nothing can touch you. This also means that the needs and distress of another person do not impact on you, even if it's your own child. Intoxication with heroin has this effect, further intoxication leads to 'gouching' where the person appears to be nodding off and finally, like alcohol to unconsciousness. A heroin user will not get violent through intoxication, but will not 'be there' for the child.

Someone withdrawing from a drug which blocks out pain, experiences intense pain and anxiety, as all the feelings the heroin has blocked out come flooding back. They are desperate for the next fix and procuring the drug takes precedence over everything else.

It may at this stage be useful to look at the process of drug use that leads to dependence. Most people who start using drugs think they can 'handle it'. However, the effect is so powerful, that they want to feel it again and again. This is especially true for people whose self-esteem is so low, or whose emotional pain is so great that they find it difficult to tolerate the way they feel without the drug. The body, on the other hand, builds up resistance to the drug and more and more is needed to get the same effect. To make matters worse, the user feels worse and worse when they withdraw. This leads eventually to the user needing large amounts of heroin to feel normal and then to needing large amounts of heroin, but never being able to feel as good as 'normal'. Users then start trying other drugs to get a high, for example mixing crack cocaine with heroin.

This desperate quest to block out unpleasant and often unbearable feelings is not compatible to caring for children:

> *Addicted parents have a primary relationship with alcohol or their drug of choice, not with their children.*
>
> (Kaplan-Sanoff and Rice, 1992: p17).

There are very obvious dangers to children of living with someone who is dependent on heroin or any other drug, particularly if they are injecting. The most obvious is children swallowing the drug. This is more likely when the parent is taking methadone, the prescribed heroin substitute, which is often prescribed in weekly amounts and stored in the home. Parents need to be absolutely certain that the children cannot get access to the methadone, as a small amount is likely to prove fatal.

Needle stick injuries are another hazard, as the parent must ensure that anyone else who injects in their home disposes of the needles safely and that children are not taken to places where needles are likely to be left lying around. Used needles and syringes carry the risk of HIV and hepatitis B and C. The last is the most likely to be contracted by family members as it is highly contagious and there is no immunisation:

> *The most significant health risks for this group beyond drug dependency are HIV, hepatitis B and*

> *C, and a wide range of psychiatric and psychological problems.*
>
> (Tackling Drugs Together to Build a
> Better Britain, DoH, 1998: Aim iii).

Stimulants (amphetamine (speed)/cocaine/crack)

I have put these drugs together, as they are similar in their effects. The main difference is that cocaine is smoother and more powerful than amphetamine and crack has an 'orgasmic' high which is greater than either of the others. Amphetamine and cocaine can be used recreationally, but I would argue that crack, like heroin, rarely remains a recreational drug, the effects are too powerful.

The effect of stimulants is to make the user 'high' – self confident, powerful and full of energy. Someone who is high on speed behaves like a hyperactive child, talking non stop and unable to sit still. Crack has the effect of making people feel all powerful and unstoppable. Crack users have been known to walk into a bank with a shot gun, in broad daylight, with no disguise and be amazed when they have been overpowered and arrested. They felt that no one could stop them.

Stimulants also prevent sleep and suppress appetite, so in terms of the overall health of the parents, this is not good.

Withdrawal from a stimulant causes depression and exhaustion. The most severe withdrawal is from crack, with an overwhelming desire to reach the high again. This is what led to the propaganda in the 1980s of 'one rock and you're hooked'. In medical terms, stimulants are not addictive. This means that there are no obvious physical signs of withdrawal, unlike alcohol, tranquillisers and opiates, and therefore no recognised medical intervention for withdrawal. However, this becomes irrelevant when one considers the difficulty of coming off and staying off any of the drugs mentioned. Depending on the amount of stimulant used and the length of time since the body has been drug free, the user can feel irritable or deeply depressed and suffering the effects of severe sleep deprivation.

Children living with a stimulant user will be confused and apprehensive about the parent's mood swings and unpredictable behaviour. There is also concern that a parent whose own appetite is suppressed by the drugs, may not be aware of how hungry their young children have become. Injecting the drugs also carries the same risk of needle stick injuries and subsequent infections.

The use of these drugs should therefore bring up enough issues to start alarm bells ringing about the safety of the children. Some are pessimistic about the parenting skills of drug users:

> *...among mothers who did not abstain from drugs, even high quality, intensive early intervention services were not able to raise parenting skills to a level where the care provided was both stimulating and nurturing. Fully 100% of the children of heavy drug users exhibited weak attachments to their mothers, as compared with one-third of the children whose mothers did not use drugs.*
>
> (Besharov, 1999: p139).

Issues of the Lifestyle of Substance Users

What is less obvious and harder to monitor is the effect the drug using lifestyle can have on the rest of the family. The violence and degradation of the drug using culture is often beyond the imagination of many social workers and is usually well hidden from scrutiny. Social workers will often say they do not have the skills to work with drug users, which usually comes down to lack of knowledge of what to look for and the questions to ask. The scenarios I describe below are extreme and not the experience of all parents who have the misfortune to become dependent on alcohol and drugs, however, their possibility must be born in mind when carrying out an assessment on someone's parenting abilities. The case histories of the heroin user who gets onto a methadone prescription and is maintained whilst holding down a job and being a model citizen are accurate but very rare. A consultant psychiatrist had a slide of the daughter of one of his methadone maintained mothers. The daughter was dressed up for her first communion and sitting on her mother's knee. This was meant to illustrate how people on methadone could be perfect parents. There are also wealthy people, or people who have access to pharmaceutical heroin, who are able to avoid the murkier side of the drug scene. Be this as it may, a very common story is that people prescribed methadone use other illegal drugs on top, that children of drug users are dragged around needle exchanges, drug agencies and drug dealers, are sworn to secrecy and witness drug use and violence on a regular basis.

Alcohol

Most of us would say we know what the lifestyle of a drinker is. Alcohol is legal; therefore there is no need for secrecy and deceit. However it is still not socially acceptable to be an 'alcoholic' nor is it acceptable for a woman to be drunk in public during the day, especially when responsible for young children. A 'good' wife and mother is always ready to mop up tears, bathe grazed knees and have tea ready on time, she does not have to be picked up off the floor covered in her own vomit and urine. The social stigma is such that a woman with a serious drink problem either hides away in the house and leaves the onus on the rest of the family to cover up for her behaviour, or befriends people with the same problem, who will not judge her. Mothers who drink heavily in pubs or clubs tend to be exploited sexually by men and will often take men home for the night. Having drunk strangers in the house can be frightening for children and it brings with it the danger of physical and sexual abuse. Parents with a hangover can be very irritable with young children first thing in the morning, but a stranger will be even more intolerant at being woken up at 6am.

Illegal drugs

The illegal drug scene can be violent and exploitative for parents who are struggling to find the money to fund their habit. It is fairly common for women who are heavily dependent on heroin or cocaine to sell sex for drugs, or to have a pimp who is a drug dealer. In the latter situation, violence and threats of violence are commonly used to prevent the woman escaping from the situation. In extreme situations, women may exploit their children, either by having them witness the sex or by prostituting their children to paedophiles. Parents can often unknowingly put their children at risk of abuse, by bringing them into the company of other adults and becoming so inebriated themselves that they are unaware of what is happening to their children.

Although heroin has become much cheaper over the last five years, a serious heroin habit will certainly take up more than an income of benefits, leaving nothing for food, clothes, bills etc. Ways of funding a drug habit include shoplifting and other theft, credit card fraud, prostitution or drug dealing. This dealing usually involves selling enough of the drugs on to fund one's own habit. Unfortunately, most drug users become greedy, either keeping more of the drug than they can afford, or spending some of the money earned by dealing. This gets them into debt to the dealer, with usually violent results. Flats and houses occupied by drug users characteristically have the doors and often the windows boarded up, after they have been broken down by angry dealers demanding their money, or other users trying to get the drugs, or get drugs or money owed to them.

Parents can protect their children by keeping their address secret, and not socialising with other users. Some succeed in doing this, but most are unable to do so. The nature of addiction is that nothing comes before the drug and when intoxicated, the need to protect one's children is soon forgotten.

As this lifestyle involves a variety of criminal activity, children are trained from a very early age in the need for secrecy and lies. They are worried that to tell tales to a health visitor, teacher, social worker or police could involve the parents going to prison and the child being taken into care. Children learn early, not to open the door. It could be someone wanting to hurt Mummy or Daddy, or someone wanting to take away the children. They learn not to tell their peers, for fear of taunts of 'your dad's a smack head'. They will often be pleased to get to school and have learnt how to disappear into the wallpaper, so nobody notices them. This is why often, when social services make inquiries for possible child protection investigations, often no one has any concerns, because no one must know. Drug agencies know, because they know the parents and the drug scene they are involved in. Unfortunately, the mistrust which often exists between agencies working with adults and agencies working with children comes into play and the views of drug workers are often

not listened to. This of course works the other way round. When social services do become concerned about the welfare of a child, particularly an unborn or new baby, the drugs workers are so accustomed to the behaviour of drug users, that they view unpaid bills and missed appointments as trivial and occasional lapses into heroin use on top of a methadone prescription as normal. However, it is clear that a significant proportion of young people who grow up in drug-using families develop their own drug use problems or problem behaviours such as delinquency, aggression, loss of concentration, hyperactivity, poor school performance and truancy (see Velleman, 1992).

The Scottish Executive is again more confident in detailing the effect of parental drug use on children at different stages of development:

Infancy and pre school years
Babies in general are particularly vulnerable to the effects of physical and emotional neglect and this can have damaging effects on their long-term development. Neglect in these forms can occur while the parent carer is in a drugged state, unaware of what is going on around him/her. Unhappiness, tension and irritability in parents coupled with a lack of commitment to parenting when preoccupied with drug use may lead to inappropriate responses to the child. Poor or inconsistent parenting may damage the attachment process. Poor child care, little stimulation or inconsistent and unpredictable parental behaviour may hinder the child's cognitive or emotional development. Lack of contact with other children when attendance at nursery is irregular or erratic may compound early deficits in social and emotional development. The financial demands of illegal drug use may mean that the child's material environment is poor.

Physical or emotional rejection may prevent children from developing a positive sense of identity and self-esteem. Children may have their physical needs neglected, for example they may be unfed or unwashed. They may be subjected to direct physical violence by parents, and learn inappropriate behaviour through witnessing domestic violence. When parents' behaviour is unpredictable and frightening children may display emotional symptoms similar to those of post traumatic stress disorder.

Primary school years

As children grow older, early problems may be compounded. They may be at increased risk of injury, and show symptoms of extreme anxiety and fear of hostility. The identity, gender and age of the child may affect outcomes: boys more quickly exhibit behavioural problems, but girls may equally be affected if parental problems endure. Children may develop poor self-esteem, and blame themselves for their parents' problems. Parental neglect or disinterest negatively affects academic attainment and irregular routines may make children's attendance erratic or irregular. Unplanned separation can cause distress and disrupt education and friendship patterns. Parents' behaviour can make their children feel embarrassment and shame, and as a consequence they curtail friendships. Children may take on too much responsibility for themselves, their parents and younger siblings.

Secondary school years

Children coping with puberty without adequate parental support may be at increased risk of psychological problems. Children may become increasingly beyond parental control and run a greater risk of injury by parents. There is an increased risk of emotional disturbance and conduct disorders, including bullying, and adolescent boys may become sexually aggressive. They may be increasingly embarrassed and anxious about how to compensate for physical neglect.

If children's family problems affect concentration, attainment in school may not match ability. They may truant. Children looking after their parents or siblings are particularly disadvantaged and experience significant disruption to their education. They may fear family break-up, or reject their family altogether. They are often wary of exposing family life to outside scrutiny, so friendships are restricted, and they become isolated with no one to turn to.

Young people in families where other family members misuse drugs may be socialised into drug misuse and may have an increased risk of developing early problems with drugs and other substances.

(2001, p34-5).

Some readers may be disappointed that this chapter is not providing an answer to the question 'should we remove the children of drug dependent parents?'

Unfortunately life is not so simple. However, it is clear that these children should be regarded as children in need and more resources allocated to them. So, how do we improve this situation? One way is to look at assessments of the protection needs of children of parents with drug and alcohol problems; the other is to look at the need for therapeutic work with the children themselves.

The guidelines produced by the Standing Conference on Drug Abuse for assessments, cover most of the key features. They start from the belief that drug users can be good enough parents, but they need to have safeguards in place, often the support of a network of non-drug users who are partners, relatives, friends or trusted professionals. The following is a useful check list which will make social workers more confident in their ability to work in this field:

The pattern of parental drug use

- Is there a drug free parent or supportive partner?
- Type, quantity and method of administration of drugs.
- Whether drug use is relatively stable or chaotic, i.e. swings between states of severe intoxication and periods of withdrawal or polydrug use, including alcohol.
- Are the levels of care different from when the parent is a non-user?

Accommodation and home environment

- Is accommodation adequate for children?
- Are parents ensuring that rent and bills are paid?
- Does the family remain in one locality or move frequently, and why?
- Are other drug users sharing the accommodation?
- Is the family living in a drug using community?

Provision of basic necessities

- Is there adequate food, warmth and clothing for the children?
- Are the children attending school regularly?
- Are the children engaged in age appropriate activities?
- Are the children's emotional needs being adequately met?
- Are the children assuming parental responsibility?

How are drugs procured?

- Are the children being left alone while the parents are procuring drugs?
- Are the children being taken to places where they can be deemed to be at risk?
- How much are the drugs costing, and how is the money obtained?
- Are the premises being used for selling drugs or for prostitution?
- Are the parents allowing their premises to be used by other drug users?

Health risks

- Where are the drugs normally kept?
- Are the parents injecting drugs? Are the syringes shared? How are they disposed of?
- Are the parents aware of the health risks attached to injecting or otherwise using drugs?

Family's social network and support system

- Do parents and children associate primarily with other drug users, non-users, or both?
- Are relatives aware of the drug use?
- Will parents accept help from the relatives and other professional/voluntary agencies involved?

When is intervention necessary?

- Automatic registration deters contact.
- Are there grounds under one's own local authority's care procedures? Are these appropriate for assessment?
- What is the parents' perception of the situation?
- Do the parents see their drug use as harmful to themselves or their children?
- Do the parents place their own needs before those of the children?

(Local Government Drugs Forum and Standing Conference on Drug Abuse, 1997).

This style of assessment side-steps the argument as to whether drug use is a reason for child protection investigation and looks directly at the parenting and safety of the children. The majority of such assessments will conclude that the parenting is good enough, but that the children have still been adversely affected by their parents' lifestyle. Other children will be looked after by grandparents or other relatives or by the local authority. All these children will benefit from therapeutic intervention, to ensure their emotional and psychological well-being. Some voluntary agencies and local authority family centres already have the skills to work with children traumatised by abuse, bullying and witnessing domestic violence. The needs of children damaged by the lifestyle of their drug using parents are similar:

Early childhood professionals can help children of substance-abusing parents with nurturing relationships, consistency in care, and therapeutic play.
(Howland Thompson, 1998: p34).

Older children need to learn:

- Protective behaviours, with strategies to contact people who can make them safe if necessary.
- They need support from other children who have had similar experiences, both through group work and peer mentoring.
- They need to understand drug use and drug users and be confident that none of the trouble caused was their fault.
- They need to learn alternative coping strategies to provide them with tactics other than drug use as they get older.
- They need to feel that someone cares about them more than about their own need to get off their heads.

Ideally services should be provided in partnership with alcohol and drug agencies, who are working with the parents. Such a project is 'Families First' set up in Rhondda to support and protect the children of substance misusing parents and is a partnership between social services children's division, the community drug and alcohol team and the drug support team. Included among its objectives are: to enhance co-ordination and communication between child focussed and adult focussed services and to improve understanding and awareness of child concerns amongst drug team workers.

This brings us back neatly to the points made at the beginning of this chapter, that drug workers and children's workers need to establish a live dialogue, not work on messages received a decade earlier. It is also worth remembering that children of 'good enough' parents will still benefit from time away from the unpredictability and deceit of an alcohol and drug using environment.

I end by echoing Besharov's final plea:

...it is time to end our wishful thinking about parental drug addiction and recognize its threat to the welfare of children. If the children of drug addicts are to have a fair chance in life, we will have to be realistic about the problem and its likely solution...the continuing tragedy of drug addicted parents and their suffering children imposes a moral duty to respond. To ignore their needs diminishes us all.

(1999: p213).

Supporting Single Parents

Pam Acaster and Mary Delaney

Parenting is hard enough when there are two adults who share the responsibility. Single parents have particular challenges and often need additional support when struggling. This chapter describes a scheme, which aims to support single parents.

Introduction

Since 1992 West Leeds Family Service Unit has run the 'Single Parent Support Scheme' (SPSS). The scheme exists to provide a varied, responsive and flexible way of supporting families. Single parents are linked with a trained volunteer who visits weekly to offer both emotional support and practical help. The help given varies depending on the families' needs and the volunteers' skills and experience. Support may range from shopping, form filling, or taking time to talk to a stressed, exhausted and anxious parent. Such support can also involve assisting in a crisis or dealing with child protection issues. The scheme is managed by two Volunteer Co-ordinators who support both family and volunteer through the link, which can be short or long term. Volunteers are asked to commit themselves to the scheme for a year so that trust and understanding can be built up within a link and so that the volunteer is not someone who appears briefly in a family's life. These are sustained and important links that should make some difference, however small, to a family's life. Families are generally referred to the project by Social Services, Health Visitors, Refuges or Mother and Baby Hostels.

Assessment

The first important point of contact with a family after referral is through assessment. SPSS carries out two assessments so that each co-ordinator has a chance to meet the family. It is important to gather as much information as possible from the referrer as assessments will often have to be done under difficult circumstances and it may be easy to miss vital pieces of information. Assessment takes on extra importance

as it forms the basis for a volunteer to undertake a piece of work that can feel nebulous and unfocussed, certainly in the beginning, and may be the only concrete information that a volunteer will have at their disposal.

Assessments are always carried out within the family home so that the co-ordinators can gain an impression of the living environment, how the children react to strangers and what the family's routine is like. For the latter reason we try to carry out assessments at different times of the day as the atmosphere can change from a busy, hectic morning to a slower, calmer afternoon and may be affected by different family members. This knowledge is helpful when deciding the most appropriate time for a volunteer to visit.

Apart from the opportunity to understand what life is like in a particular family's home there are several very specific aims of our assessment that may be crucial to the eventual success of a link. These are:

- To gain understanding of a family's history and why they are a single parent family.
- To help the family explore why they need a volunteer.
- To find out what other help and support the family has.
- To have an idea of external factors impacting on family life e.g. housing, benefits, ex-partners, neighbours, health issues, school or nursery problems.

Once the first assessment has been completed it is vital that the two co-ordinators meet prior to the second assessment taking place. With the diverse amount of information that has to be obtained from the assessments, inevitably there are gaps in our understanding and factual knowledge of a family. The co-ordinator carrying out the second assessment can then have a specific brief to actively follow up anything unclear or clarify any confusion as well as confirming the facts given in the first assessment. The different personalities of different co-ordinators will also access different information from families.

Although two separate assessments work best for this scheme there are occasions when it is appropriate and useful to do a joint assessment. These are:

- For reasons of safety, for example, a violent ex-partner is still present.

- If the area of housing is unsafe.

- If the woman is in a refuge. Refuge life for single parents affords little privacy and it may need one co-ordinator to occupy the children or just be there to listen as well so that, amid the inevitable distractions and interruptions, information is not missed.

- If the co-ordinators are not satisfied with the information or understanding of a single parent family's needs after two separate assessments have been carried out.

- If you are short of time – not an ideal way to assess but may be the only option given other pressures on a family and the limitations of part-time work.

After both assessments have been completed the combined information is then used to decide if this scheme is the right form of help and if it is, who is the best volunteer for the family. If it is felt that this scheme is not appropriate a discussion needs to take place regarding referring the family to another scheme within the Unit, referring out to another agency or passing the family back to the original referrer with clear reasons why the scheme is unable to help.

Points to keep in mind to ensure that successful assessments of single parent families take place include:

- Asking the referrer to give as much information as is ethically possible.

- Trying to make the assessment happen at convenient times for the family.

- Allowing yourself plenty of time for an assessment.

- Trying to visit at different times of the day.

- Being clear with the family why you are doing the assessment.

- Going back if you do not get the information you need.

- Not giving false hopes about help available.

Linking

If a family is accepted onto the scheme we then have to think very carefully about which volunteer we are to link them with. The information obtained through assessment is utilised to determine the families' needs as accurately as possible. By training the volunteers we are able to build a picture of their skills, abilities and personalities and the type of family they feel able to support. We use all of this information to decide which volunteer should be linked with each family.

The following factors should be taken into account when linking families and volunteers:

- personality
- availability
- geographical area
- shared interests and hobbies
- age
- life experience

Some Illustrative Case Studies

The following case studies have been chosen to show the enormous diversity of needs that single parent families have and to show the reality of life for some families today. The case studies are all very different and despite the challenges and difficulties they face it is clear that with low-key support, single parent families can take control of their lives and make sustainable changes. One example shows that the measure of success for some single parent families may not be about moving on and taking on new challenges but being able to hold their lives in one place rather than slipping backwards. We have chosen one example in particular to show that single parent families may have the same ambition, drive and determination to succeed but that having to meet goals on your own can be far riskier and have greater potential for failure than families with two parents. All the case studies show that what is important in providing support for single parents is really listening to what families say, reliability, commitment and a non-judgmental approach. None of these links could have worked without the volunteers' consistency of visiting every week or the schemes commitment to a family once they are taken on.

Case study 1

The local Social Services team referred a 36-year-old widower with five children to us – he had come to live in England to be near his in-laws. This person was very hostile towards the Social Services, disillusioned with life in England, had a poor relationship with his late wife's family and was feeling increasingly less able to cope with his children and wanted them to go into local authority care. As a male single parent, he found it impossible to join in pre-school activity groups where many single parent mothers are able to access help and support, as such groups are generally geared towards women, not men. He did not know any other men in his situation and felt isolated and frustrated. This was reflected in his home which he kept quite literally boarded up to stop people from seeing in and the children were not allowed to play outside after school. This led to tension and boredom in the home and made parenting the children very difficult. This was one occasion when it was appropriate to do a joint assessment.

This family was linked very quickly with a volunteer. Pete asked for a Black volunteer as his wife had been Black and he wanted the children to stay in touch with their cultural roots. After listening carefully to what he said, we linked him with Liz, a Black volunteer, who was able to give the family a considerable amount of time.

The initial aims were for Liz to establish some routines for bedtime, thus creating space to talk to Pete when the children were in bed. She did this by encouraging a bath time, reading and bedtime routine which Pete, together with the two older children, could maintain on nights when Liz did not visit. This quickly extended as the children made other needs known to her. She then took the children to the library to encourage wider reading, helped with homework and sought out free wallpaper and paint with which to decorate. She encouraged Pete to take down the boards, which he did after some weeks. Pete was unable to braid the children's hair and as a result they were getting teased at school because their hair looked untidy. Liz took them to a hairdresser who braided their hair and the teasing stopped. One morning's voluntary work made their school life more bearable. She also found leaflets about puberty for Pete's oldest daughter, who was twelve, as Pete felt too embarrassed to deal with these issues. Liz also organised a rota for the children to help in the house and each week appointed one child as rota monitor. Liz would take small rewards with her for the ones who had done their work. In addition Liz helped with their school work and baby sat for them to allow Pete time to attend parent's evenings and to go out with friends.

Analysis

This example shows that with some families there are many areas where a volunteer can focus their time. Individually, the pieces of work that Liz did are not unusual on our scheme but the fact that she did them all in six months is. This is because many single parents tell us that they and their children have no constant adults in their lives and in this case Liz, as a volunteer, became that trusted and reliable person. Because she showed that she was committed to them and would help them without judging, the family allowed her to help organise their lifestyle into something more manageable very quickly. The fact that this is a long term scheme helped as this family would not have been able to sustain these changes without the long term reassurance and commitment from another adult.

It is also clear from this example that single parents, who feel they are not coping, often know what changes need to be made. However, the stress and physical hard work of parenting alone makes it difficult to effect those changes and all it may take is the presence of a committed and understanding person like a volunteer to help a parent feel more positive about managing their lifestyle and more motivated to make changes. Pete knew these changes needed to be made which is why he allowed Liz to help him make them so quickly. All the changes made were small yet they drastically changed the home atmosphere reducing the tension in the house and helping Pete to feel stronger about parenting the children and more able to look to a future with the children as part of it.

Case study 2

Shanaz, an Asian woman with a twelve-year-old son, Raju, was referred by the local Social Services team. She felt isolated and that her lack of language skills prevented her from going out. Shanaz was a widow who arrived here with no money but determined to secure a good education for her son.

After assessing Shanaz we felt that her English was not as poor as she thought and were able to link her with a volunteer. Initially after talking to Shanaz, it was agreed that the volunteer's aim was to spend time talking to Shanaz to help build her confidence and to encourage her to go out, to reduce her sense of isolation. The volunteer was able to do this and encouraged Shanaz to attend some groups specifically for Asian women and single parents. With the volunteer's help she also joined a local college to improve her Maths and English. This was a positive and reliable link. However, after a year Shanaz's health began to deteriorate due to heart problems and her needs from the scheme changed. She now needed someone to help her to do the shopping as her son was now taking almost full responsibility for the running of the household on top of attending school. What she needed from the scheme changed from being her needs to those of her and her son. Another volunteer Sally was linked who could take her son shopping every Friday evening to buy the week's groceries saving him doing it every day after school, in addition to cooking, cleaning, translating and interpreting for his mother. An unexpected bonus to this link which might have remained purely practical is that the volunteer, who is the bursar of a local high school is very much in touch with Raju's world and age group and despite their age difference, enjoys a positive and supportive relationship with him. She has also been able to help Shanaz understand the school system in England, exams and university entrance – things that are very different to Shanaz's own school experiences. Sally has taken Raju to buy items for school and supported the family when Shanaz stayed in hospital. She also, very importantly, encourages Shanaz to think of Raju's needs as a child, not a carer.

Analysis

This example shows how the needs of a family can change in a short space of time. For single parent families, changes in circumstances can have a greater effect on the children without another adult to absorb some of the impact. In this case Raju had to assume full responsibility for the household which would normally have been carried out by a partner. In this relationship with the volunteer it is clear that he, as

much as Shanaz, has valued the regularity and commitment from Sally which in turn has allowed him the time and opportunity to talk to a trusted adult. Without any family locally, Sally is his only adult reference apart from teachers. This case shows that in this type of situation it is not only parents who need emotional support but children too, particularly when they are asked to take on more of an adult role than they are ready for or really want. One evening's voluntary work fulfils a practical need which releases Raju from the daily responsibility of shopping plus gives him and Shanaz someone to share their week's news with.

Case study 3

Jane, 29, was referred by a hospital social worker at the end of her first pregnancy. Jane was living in a Family Hostel and there were concerns over her ability to care for a child due to a childlike and excitable approach to life. She also had difficulty with reading and writing and had struggled at school.

As anticipated, when Jonny was born Jane had problems with feeding him, establishing routines and keeping herself and the flat clean. She was also prescribed anti-depressants for post-natal depression – any parent would find this an exhausting and frightening period. For single parents like Jane, this is magnified by having no one to share the role with. Jane's life was further complicated by the stress and lack of privacy of hostel life despite support from hostel workers and she felt confused and overwhelmed by different advice. Jane was linked with Gail to provide someone constant and reliable who Jane could build a relationship with. Gail visited twice a week to help Jane with budgeting, shopping, cooking, sterilising bottles, preparing feeds and keeping the flat clean and clothes washed. She also took Jane to a local drop-in to meet new people and Jane began to manage her life more positively. Gail's visits dropped to once a week. Remarkably during this period of depression and anxiety Jane knew that she needed to live independently and despite her daily difficulties, pursued this with determination.

Jane moved into a small back-to-back house when Jonny was seven months old. We knew that this would be a testing time for her and Gail increased her support again visiting twice a week allowing time for shopping together for cheap furnishings and electrical goods. Life was stressful and difficult for Jane at this time. She could not furnish the house adequately, had difficulty budgeting and felt lonely and overwhelmed by the responsibility of caring for Jonny who, by now, was often ill with chest infections made worse by a damp house. However, once more, it became clear that despite Jane's appalling living conditions and stressful life she knew what skills she needed to improve to look for work. She began attending classes to improve her literacy skills and then organised a two year work placement through college, which provided a free nursery place for Jonny. She was very committed to the placement and enjoyed working outside the home. During this period she only needed emotional support from Gail as her other difficulties had become more manageable. We were able to offer differing levels of support because our volunteers work flexibly and we recognise that when a family's life is unstable, flexibility may be key to supporting without judging.

When Jonny was three, Jane needed to move house due to its unsuitability for a young child and noise and harassment from neighbours. She was linked with a new volunteer who visited in the evenings to provide company and help her feel less vulnerable. This volunteer helped her tidy up – a constant difficulty for this family, she read to Jonny, cooked meals and invited Jane and Jonny to her own house for meals. At this point, three years from referral, Jane's needs had reverted to her original needs when she was first referred to the scheme. She still needed company, someone to share her pride in Jonny and someone to motivate her to keep herself, Jonny and the house clean.

In the last three years Jane has managed successfully to come off benefits with a part time job. However, common to many single parents, finding adequate child care made this important change impossible to maintain and within a few months Jane had to leave her job. Jane is now back on benefits and attending college. She has moved to a new home and is in regular contact with the Single Parent Support Scheme although she no longer has a volunteer.

Analysis

This example shows that single parent families, like any other families want independence, financial security and a safe and suitable home. Jane wanted to move from the hostel to her own home, she wanted to improve her literacy skills, she wanted workplace experience, she wanted to come off benefits – all of which she managed but all of which were a struggle to achieve on her own and all of which were threatened by the precarious nature of life as a single parent family on benefits. When a family is only just surviving, even taking the smallest risk and making the smallest change can feel impossible and justifiably frightening. It is a credit to families like Jane that they are able to make changes and take control of their lives. Through listening to what Jane said she needed, we were able to change her support appropriately at different stages of her life and could accommodate differing needs.

This case study also shows that many single parents may need low level support for some years but this does not mean that families have not moved on or made changes. Jane has clearly been pro-active in moving her life on, but the basic needs for some single parent families may remain the same because the basic influences impacting on their life remain the same – poverty, poor housing, lack of opportunity and harsh political and social judgement.

Case study 4

Ruth, who had a seven-year-old daughter, Carol, was suffering from an extremely debilitating post-viral syndrome and was referred by her Health Visitor. On a good day she was able to take Carol to school and walk a short distance – on a bad day she could not get out of bed, relied on friends to take Carol to school and was only mobile in a wheelchair. Ruth had no family near by and Carol had limited contact with her father in London, who often let her down by cancelling visits. Ruth was concerned that Carol was losing her childhood and taking on a far more responsible role than she should.

We needed to be highly selective when choosing a volunteer for this family as they had moved frequently and Carol had lost many adults in her life. They needed a reliable, consistent, long term volunteer and Ruth asked for the support to be based on Carol's needs.

We linked them with Jean who had children herself, one the same age as Carol, and who lived locally. Carol was keen to go to Brownies and arrangements were made for her to attend the same Brownie pack that Jean's daughter went to. Jean would pick Carol up from school, take her home for tea, get her to Brownies and give her a bath afterwards, delivering her home in her pyjamas, ready for bed. This fulfilled many needs for the family. After-school activities were almost impossible to organise and Carol spent her evenings watching television and as a result was not tired until 10.00 pm which gave Ruth a long and tiring evening and enforced a routine on the family which neither would have chosen but which the adult was powerless to change. It also gave Carol some normality in her life – she could do what other girls at school did, had something to look forward to and something to talk about the next day. She also arrived home tired and ready for sleep. One afternoon's voluntary work filled three gaps: an after-school activity, a break for Ruth, a suitable bedtime for Carol.

This link continued until the volunteer emigrated. As the link had been so positive, Carol and Ruth were happy to accept another volunteer into their lives. Carol was older now and wanted more activities within the link. This link took the form of baking, reading and board games and the volunteer taught Carol to ride a bike by going to a nearby park. This was much more a link for the family rather than just Carol as the volunteer spent time with Ruth after Carol had gone to bed, talking to her and helping around the house, tidying up, doing the washing and cleaning the fish tank.

After 15 months this volunteer had to move away due to work. Carol and Ruth were again very happy to have another volunteer. The new volunteer's visits overlapped with the moving volunteer to ensure a smooth handover. This volunteer's work is very similar – the focus being on supportive friendship to Carol and Ruth. The weekly support still involves baking, cinema, swimming, helping with homework, tidying up, cleaning, talking to Ruth, and a bedtime routine for Carol.

Analysis

This example shows that when there is long-term illness, a single parent family may be held back from moving on and taking up new challenges. Sometimes the challenge for a scheme like ours is helping a family to keep their lives in one place rather than slipping back. In a family with two partners where there is long term illness there is still some possibility for after-school activities, friends home to play etc. In a single parent family, this becomes severely restricted, if not impossible, as there is no one left to take on this responsibility and both parent and child suffer the consequences.

There has been little change in Ruth's condition over the years and the family's needs are similar to when she was first referred. It is clear that reliability and long-term help has benefited this family. Because the family's experience of receiving help has been positive they have been part of the scheme for four years. Unless there is a change in Ruth's condition, we anticipate that their needs will remain stable and that they will be long-term users of the service.

Case study 5

Julie, a 31-year-old single parent was referred by her Social Worker. She had nine children with baby number ten due any day. Her Social Worker said she needed any support we could give.

Before we even entered her house we knew what she needed! We knew she needed someone to help with shopping, cooking meals, decorating, collecting children from school and nursery, play scheme places, playgroup places, help with older children's homework and someone to talk to. We went to assess her almost immediately as we knew she would be in desperate need and her life must be exhausting and chaotic.

'No thank you' she said. 'I don't need any of that, I just need some help with my eleven-year-old who is struggling at school'. 'But surely' we said, 'you must be overwhelmed and exhausted and we can help you'. 'No, really' she said, 'I just want someone to help my eleven-year-old'.

Analysis

In this example it is clear that we had fallen into the trap of making assumptions about a single parent based on our own selective knowledge. We had perhaps unconsciously not listened to her and to take some control of her life for her. We had under-estimated and patronised her. In our own way we did what the wider world does all the time to her. This experience shocked us and determined us to monitor our own assumptions about a family. A desire to work consistently and anti-oppressively with single parents is not enough. Our own assumptions and prejudices need to be challenged by co-workers and supervisors to prevent us from becoming entrenched in our responses.

Learning from the case studies

What can we learn from these case studies? By reading and understanding the real life situations facing single parents we can begin to build up the basis of good family support practice with single parents:

- Listening to families.
- Accepting diversity of need.
- Low key, long term support is invaluable.
- Working flexibly with the family.
- Providing a reliable service.
- A consistent commitment to the family.

Consumer Feedback

Receiving consumer feedback of any service to families is vital and particularly so on this scheme, as all the work is done in the families' homes beyond the direct supervision of the co-ordinators. In our experience, it is essential that families be given the opportunity to say how they feel about a link and if it is working for them.

We would argue that consumer evaluation of the individual service needs to be carried out privately and confidentially as families who depend on a volunteer's support may be loathe to say anything critical for fear of losing that help or offending the volunteer. Through all of our contact with a family – visiting at their home or speaking to them on the telephone – we encourage them to be honest with us and reassure them that we are here to support them. We also remind them at every stage that their needs are the scheme's priority, and not those of the volunteers. Our experience suggests that by encouraging this open communication from the beginning of our contact with a family we place ourselves in the best position to receive clear and

honest feedback during evaluation. It would be very disempowering not to give single parent families sensitive opportunities to tell us if the support was not right for them and in direct conflict with the aims of our work, which recognises that larger systems and procedures discriminate against single parent families by not allowing them a voice. Our evaluation is carried out privately to make the procedure feel safe and non-threatening for the families.

Although on an informal basis we are constantly assessing links, receiving formal evaluation from the families is appropriate and carried out at six and twelve months into the link. This process is carried out through a self-administered questionnaire, which is sent directly to the volunteer's and family's homes with an explanatory letter. The family can then fill in the form in the comfort of their home.

The evaluation examines what has happened in the last six months and how the link will work in the future, incorporating any changes to type and frequency of support. It needs to re-define the support, if necessary, so that the link remains useful, positive and still within the aims of the scheme.

The completed forms are returned to the co-ordinators. The single parent family and volunteers never see each other's form and the co-ordinators will only act on the information given if it indicates difficulties or problems. We will also help a family complete a form if necessary. We hope that this method allows single parents to feel confident enough to tell us what works and what does not in their link and trust in us to deal with any issue sensitively. However, experience has shown us that if communication and contact between the co-ordinators and the family are open and honest at the outset and throughout the life of the link, there really should not be any unexpected disclosures in the evaluation as difficulties should be identified and dealt with as they arise.

We would suggest that the following points are crucial in considering consumer feedback:

- Evaluation is essential.
- Single parents must be allowed to express their feelings about the link.
- Evaluation must be safe and non-threatening.
- The process should identify problem areas.
- The process should help re-define support if need be.

- Honest communication from the start is vital to positive feedback at evaluation.

Lessons for Practice and Policy Development

In drawing some conclusions about the work of the Single Parent Support Scheme we feel that there are four key areas in our approach to working which determine whether a scheme like this can benefit families – these are:

1. Listening to what single parent families need.
2. Acknowledging that a huge diversity of need exists.
3. Understanding the role of a low key style of support.
4. The importance of open communication.

   Below we address each of these points individually.

1. Listening to single parent families

In our experience single parent families above all else need to be listened to. Single parents tell us that they feel judged for being on their own before anyone takes the time to listen to their concerns and opinions, and that this lowers their self-esteem and their ability to deal with professional bodies that have a deciding role to play in their lives. This is particularly apparent for some parents when dealing with housing officials for example and within education. Many families on our scheme have had difficulty accessing appropriate housing because they have felt that their needs have not been listened to and feel that because they are single parents they will be given unsuitable housing as they perceive themselves to have no voice with which to oppose it. Similarly, within education, parents have told us that they feel anxious about going into school to speak to their children's teacher because they feel that their single parent status will be held against them and used as a reason to explain the child's difficulties. They also feel nervous and vulnerable having to attend these meetings (including parents' evening) without a partner to support them. On our scheme this has led to children not getting the services they need and schools misinterpreting parents' nervous reluctance as lack of interest.

Volunteers on our scheme can help deal with these problems. A very valuable part of any volunteer's role is to take the time to talk and listen to the single parents and their children. Indeed some of our strongest links have been nothing more than a volunteer spending an afternoon every week sitting with a family and talking to them, sharing concerns and ideas thereby placing a value on what the family has to say. Simply talking an issue through with a volunteer can strengthen the parent's resolve to deal with it on their own or it may give them the opportunity to explore other ways of solving problems. If a family has great difficulty dealing with a problem it is quite appropriate for a volunteer to accompany them to a housing office, to a school meeting, a residents' meeting or to hospital to give moral support, to remind them of what they wanted to say and to remember some of the conversation for later. In these ways the scheme can certainly help address the concerns that single parents have of not feeling listened to. Someone to validate their ideas, fears, concerns, etc. can help them feel more confident and more able to take some measure of control over an area of their life. The result is two fold – an adult to hear and recognise what you say and the growing confidence to say it in the right place. However, while we conclude that the scheme can help with one of the biggest challenges that single parent families face, it is right to note that although volunteers can attend meetings etc. with families, our aim is to give them the confidence to do this alone. It is not within the aims of the scheme to make single parent families dependant on volunteers or allow volunteers to speak for them. To permit this would be replicating exactly what single parent families' say they already face – no opportunity to be heard for them.

As co-ordinators we have to take particular care to listen to families. We are their first point of contact with the scheme and how we respond to them initially can make them choose to join the scheme or look elsewhere for help. It is vital that we really listen to what families say they need and not make assumptions based on years of working with single parents. Even small projects can become institutionalised and entrenched in their responses if not careful or open to criticism. If families feel that they are being heard and understood by the co-ordinators they will feel more confident that they will get the help they need from a volunteer and more likely to feel positive about the link. Acknowledging that single parent families do not feel heard has to be attended to by everyone on the scheme, not just volunteers and should be apparent in all our contact. Recognising that single parent families feel disempowered by larger systems and procedures is fundamental to the success of the scheme.

2. Diversity of need

One of the challenges on the scheme is recognising the diversity of need presented by each family. The way in which we face this challenge is by operating as flexibly as we can. This means recruiting from as wide a range of volunteers as is practical so that we access as many life skills and experiences as possible. Working with families who have different levels of need requires different styles of support e.g. a single parent mother at home with two pre-school children may require help with shopping, going to the doctor or an occasional outing whereas a parent with children at school may enjoy the uninterrupted company and conversation from a volunteer.

Recognising need is not just about what the families need but also when they need it. If a family needed some uninterrupted time to talk to a volunteer and that time was in the afternoon when the child was at nursery it would be pointless to insist that we could only offer support in the morning when she was busy with the child. This is why it is essential that our scheme can attract volunteers with varying availability to accommodate the needs of individual families.

It can therefore be argued that a diverse team of volunteers is needed to reflect the diverse needs of the families. This will always mean drawing from and accepting volunteers from a wide variety of backgrounds. With their own life experiences, plus the training offered, they can be helped to understand about the flexibility and the non-judgemental approach needed for this work. The co-ordinators' role in this area is to assess sensitively and carefully to ensure that the level of need from each family is fully understood. Only by working in this flexible way can we ensure that our work is responsive and appropriate.

3. Style of support

After working exclusively with single parents on this scheme for nine years we feel that low key, long-term support has a beneficial role to play in the lives of single parent families. As we indicated in one of the case studies many single parent families know what changes they need to make but stress and anxiety can make them difficult to effect. The regularity and commitment from a volunteer can make these changes easier to sustain, as they are not being faced in isolation. Often a parent will simply need someone to talk to and it is this type of support that over-stretched professionals do not have the time to give. Low key support can play a complementary role to the more focussed and defined support from social workers, health visitors, etc. and give the family the chance to experience a different level of help. The long term nature of this scheme can be valuable in helping families through difficult and changing periods in their lives as the volunteer can provide some continuity and consistency. This can be very important when families have actively made decisions that have changed their lives and may need the reassurance from a volunteer that the support will remain despite the outcome of the decision.

4. Open communication

Open communication is vital in a scheme that operates a three-way relationship between agency, family and volunteer. If lines of communication are blurred, or unclear, families will not know how to ask a volunteer for help, who to go to if the link feels wrong and may feel trapped in a relationship that does not benefit them. Poor communication could make a volunteer feel cut off from support and guidance from co-ordinators and, very seriously, prevent real concerns about how the family is functioning from being passed on, including child protection issues. As part of a social work agency it is a volunteer's responsibility to pass on any concerns and as a scheme it is our responsibility to establish absolutely clear lines of communication about this. We have to ensure, through training and discussion, that volunteers have the confidence to know when to pass on information and to rely on us to handle their concerns appropriately. Without honest and open communication between all three parties, this area of work would be difficult and ultimately disadvantageous to the families' welfare. Families know before they are linked that any concerns will be passed to the co-ordinators. Telling them this in itself is a test of open communication and trust. Families being able to address difficulties face-to-face with us and volunteers being able to pass on concerns are a clear indication in this scheme of a link that operates openly and honestly, as these are the two hardest situations each will deal with.

Conclusion

The scheme has been in existence for nine years and in that time we have been involved with in excess of 200 families at varying levels – almost 100 of these have been actively linked on the scheme. In the future we would like to work more closely with families with newborn babies so that families can access our services before they reach crisis point. Experience has shown us that early intervention can make a family more likely to use our services and better disposed towards receiving help and support. As ever, within the voluntary sector, funding is crucial to this development and we see it as the most appropriate way for this scheme to expand. We would like to be able to take on more than 50% of families referred to us as our figures above indicate; again this is dependant on funding and resources.

We look optimistically to the future with these two aims in mind.

10 Working With Women From Asian and African Communities

Asher John-Baptiste and Tracey Race

Family support is a wide and varied issue, covering many different concepts and theoretical perspectives. Much of the basic work can be seen as similar, but in order to be most effective, the work needs to be culturally sensitive. This chapter discusses these issues when working with women from Asian and African communities.

Introduction

There is a traditional African saying that it takes a village to raise a child. The statement signifies a communal and collective approach to ensuring a healthy and contributing future for children, who are seen very much as the link to both the past and the future (Everett et al., 1991).

However, we live in a society that has grown increasingly fragmented and divided, with many families experiencing breakdown and social exclusion, and many women struggling to raise children in circumstances of isolation and poverty.

Add to this the dynamics of race and culture, and there should be no surprise that many black women experience particular pressures and stresses in seeking to bring up their children with a positive sense of identity, in the context of a Eurocentric society in which many mainstream support services remain inaccessible.

In this chapter we will explore the issues for black women around access to family support services. We will highlight the importance of understanding the experience of black women in the context of their own families and communities, which through the 'ordering' properties of culture, provide black women with a general design for living and patterns for interpreting their lived realities (Ani, 1994); whilst emphasising that a focus on the specificity of black women's experiences enables an accurate understanding of the issues affecting black families (Bernard, 1996).

For this reason we will look at the experience of black women caring for children from Asian and African (Caribbean) communities, providing two case histories of black women's experiences in order to articulate their views as service users. We will then go on to explore the issues for service providers.

Unfortunately limitations of space have made it impossible to address issues around work with young women, asylum seekers and other ethnic groups, although we acknowledge that there are likely to be issues arising out of the chapter which may be transferable to their lives and experiences.

Relevant Government Guidance

Government literature relating to work with black women is generally focused on the needs of children and their families. Further to the studies of Batta, McCulloch and Smith (1975) and Rowe et al. (1989) research has continued to highlight concerns surrounding the links between the over-representation of black children in local authority care systems and the negative ways in which black families are viewed during the application of assessment and intervention procedures (Dominelli, 1988; Macauley Hayes, 1990; Pennie and Best, 1990). There has been a growing recognition of the need to challenge cultural deficit models of black families which focus on Eurocentrically informed 'pathological' factors rather than acknowledging the positive psychological strengths which typify black family life (Robinson, 1995).

After years of neglect of issues of race and racism, gradually government guidance began to emphasise the need for services to provide more effective and appropriate support to black families. The Children Act, 1989, introduced into child care legislation and social welfare practice for the first time, a statutory duty to take account of race, religion, language and culture in the care plans of children for whom welfare agencies had legislative and procedural responsibility. (Children Act, Part III, Section 22(5)). The accompanying guidance and regulations supporting the Act, also acknowledged the impact of racism as a determinant of outcomes with regard to welfare-intervention practices and emphasised the need for practitioners to challenge racism and other forms of discrimination.

However, the Children Act Reports of 1992 and 1993 provide little analysis of the implementation of this new feature of the 1989 legislation. The 1993 Report includes one paragraph, headed 'Taking account of race, culture, language and religion', which states:

> *Further work was needed in all four authorities (studied) to ensure that there is a more systematic and integrated approach to the provision of racially and culturally sensitive services. Authorities should evaluate the effectiveness of existing services given their low take-up by minority communities.*
>
> (SSI, 1993).

Despite the new statutory requirement to take account of issues of race and culture, in reality services were failing to address, let alone meet the needs of black children and their families. *Child Protection: Messages from Research* (1995) provided a unique opportunity to explore the reasons for this failure and to analyse the issues of race and culture pertinent to the delivery of child care services. However, from the Introduction of the document which stated that 'issues of race, gender and rights may not be as salient in the studies as some readers might wish' (1995: p8), it was clear that the document would follow the pattern of previous reports in presenting as another missed opportunity to analyse issues of race and culture as variables in our practice with black families. Nevertheless one finding stands out in the chapter by Farmer and Owen entitled 'Child protection practice: private risks and public remedies':

> *Many black families did not have access to much needed services. Even after registration this situation continued, partly because of a lack of ethnically appropriate resources. Good racial matching was helpful, but there were some occasions when it was done crudely, with the result those workers from very different minority cultures wrongly assumed they understood the family's situation. Where there was successful matching across the dimensions of race, gender and ethnicity, parental satisfaction was higher and the progress of the children correspondingly better.*
>
> (1995: p62).

The emphasis upon culture and cultural sensitivity as the guiding precepts of work with black families,

and the lack of any real acknowledgement or analysis of the impact of racism in government publications has been criticised in the report of the National Commission of Inquiry into the Prevention of Child Abuse:

> *From 'Protecting Children' (1988) to the Children Act, race and culture began to feature in government guidance as specific considerations in working with children and their families, but the perspective is essentially a 'multi cultural' one in which cultural diversity and respect for difference without 'overcompensation' are the main features of social policy in relation to black children and their families. The essential reality of race relations in this country is largely ignored in favour of a more comfortable approach to the issue.*
>
> (1997: p174).

However, *Practice Guidance* (2000) accompanying the *Framework for the Assessment of Children in Need and their Families*, has begun what seems like a long road to addressing the lack of policy and practice focus in this area. The chapter by Dutt and Phillips, 'Assessing black children and their families', provides an excellent analysis of the issues affecting black service users and a clear emphasis on the importance of acknowledging the reality of racism in the experience of black families and of being aware of the possible impact of racism in the assessment process. On this latter point the authors make the following observation:

> *Assessing the developmental needs of children is a complex process which requires all relevant aspects of a child's life experience to be addressed. For black children assessments should address the impact that racism has on a particular child and family and ensure that the assessment process itself does not reinforce racism through racial or cultural stereotyping.*
>
> (2000: p37).

Demographic and Social Information

Evidence suggests that many of Britain's black population are living in situations of economic hardship. Black communities are more likely than the rest of the population to live in poor areas, be unemployed, have low incomes, live in poor housing, have poor health, be the victims of crime and generally have a lower take up of welfare and support services. (Bhat et al., 1988; Luthra, 1997; Social Exclusion Unit, 1998).

Further, research has established the importance, not just in the link between poverty and ill-health, but in the likelihood of ongoing precipitating factors due to the undermining of quality of life and life chances. A study by Nazroo (1997) found that on the whole Pakistani and Bangladeshi communities reported the poorest health during assessments of general health, with Caribbean communities having the next worst state of health. Smaje (1999) identifies a number of studies showing a higher infant mortality rate amongst poorer black communities. Black women are also more likely than white women to be involved in child-rearing, as black households are more likely to include children under 16 and are more likely to have more children than their white counterparts (Haskey, 1997). The important point, noted by Butt and Mizra (1998), is that black communities are at greater risk of experiencing the stresses associated with people who need family support services.

It is also well documented that when black families breakdown under such stress and children are received into the care system, the life chances for black children are particularly poor, compounded by an inability of support services to incorporate issues of race and culture into practitioner and service responses (Maxime, 1993). If black children are to thrive and to reach their full potential it is almost always better for them to remain in their own families, and to this end it is imperative that black women and communities are provided with appropriate support. Understanding the social circumstances of black women and how they experience their roles, is a vital element in the development of services aimed at providing that support.

In order to deliver effective family support services, it is important to understand the situation and the needs of families living in the locality. What follows are two case histories of women who have used family support services in a large Northern city. A brief summary of important facets of the demography of this city helps to provide the context for their stories and highlights the importance of understanding local demography in order to effectively develop culturally relevant services.

Census information indicated that in 1996, the Asian population of this city constituted approximately 16% of the total District population. The majority of the Asian population is of Pakistani origin, many of the Muslim faith. However the Asian community is not a homogenous group. Significant numbers of people have their origins in India and Bangladesh and around 1% of Asian families are of the Sikh religion. Asian communities tend to cluster in certain areas of the city, where they are not an 'ethnic minority', but often a majority group. Those areas are generally characterised by disadvantage, with disproportionately high levels of unemployment, poor housing and ill health. The Asian population of the city is young and growing; almost 50% of school leavers are Asian.

The African (Caribbean) community by contrast is a relatively small community making up less than 2% of the districts population. The majority of the population is of Dominican origin, with smaller numbers of the community having Jamaican and Barbadian origins. A significant number of the community are aged fifty-five and over.

By sharp contrast, the African (Caribbean) community is spread thinly across all peripheral areas of the city centre, although the community continues to come together in areas of the district, which they once populated in significant numbers (Bradford City Council, 1996).

A 1993 report by the City Council, entitled *Areas of Stress within Bradford District*, found that 94% of the areas of multiple deprivation were highly concentrated in ten areas of Bradford. 43% of African (Caribbean), 81% of Bangladeshi, 25% of Pakistani and 14% of white people were living in areas of multiple stress.

Case History 1: Surinder

Surinder was born and brought up in Bradford, a Sikh woman of Indian origin. She has a physical disability, which has deteriorated over recent years. After the birth of her third child, her marriage became increasingly strained. The arrival in this country of her husband's family and their disapproval of Surinder, due to her disability, led to the breakdown of the marriage.

Surinder found herself alone with three small children, her husband's contact quickly becoming infrequent and unreliable. Surinder experienced depression and struggled to cope with the needs and demands of her children, saddened and confused by the loss of their father. Her only family locally was her mother, though her traditional outlook and role in arranging the marriage meant that contact with her added to the pressure on Surinder rather than relieving it.

She felt alienated from local community organisations which she saw as Muslim and male dominated. She began to feel overwhelmed and isolated as a parent and feared she may hit out at her children. She knew she needed help, but was anxious about seeking it, fearing judgement from professionals and possibly the loss of her children into care or into her husband's family. She felt she would be seen as an inadequate mother, lacking the expected extended family network of support and having a disability.

However, rather than take the medication prescribed by her doctor, Surinder decided to confide in her health visitor. She was met with a supportive response; a place was provided for her youngest son in a local nursery and a link made for herself to a centre for people with similar disabilities. However Surinder continued to feel isolated, the centre being used mainly by older, white people. A referral by a centre worker put Surinder in touch with the Family Service Unit, a voluntary organisation providing a range of family support services.

Through the Unit Surinder was able to access the support of a multi-cultural staff team, and began to attend an Asian women's support group. An Asian social worker began to work with the children to enable them to come to terms with the changes in their family, and to support Surinder in her parenting. The children were also able to attend crèches and playschemes. As her confidence grew, Surinder began to attend courses organised by the Unit for Asian women and she gradually built up a network of support for herself and her family. Surinder is now actively involved in voluntary work for the Unit and her children are doing well.

Case History 2: Makare

Makare was born in Bradford, a Jamaican woman of dual heritage parentage – as she described herself. At the time of her seeking family support services from the Community Social Work Unit (CSWU) she had an eleven-year-old daughter by a previous relationship and was in a stable relationship with her partner of several years.

In her previous relationship she had suffered serious sexual abuse, physical and psychological abuse. Unbeknown to Makare, her daughter had also been subjected to serious psychological abuse during the relationship and also during contact visits which had taken place during the earlier stages of the break-up of the relationship. Indeed it was as a consequence of the abuse her daughter had been subjected to, that constituency social service practitioners became involved, in response to a school referral about her daughter's behaviour.

Makare noted the adversarial way in which social workers dealt with the abuse elements of her case in respect of her daughter, and in particular the way in which she was made to feel responsible for allowing the abuse to have taken place. Whilst social workers gave her the impetus she needed to finally end the relationship, this was done by way of giving her the ultimatum of risking her child coming into care.

Makare felt she was led by the hand through the child protection procedures, too afraid to comment and terrified to disagree – particularly in relation to the inferences made about black families and abuse, the sexual behaviours of black men and her loyalties to her ex-partner over and above her duty to protect her daughter. She remembers this had a profound impact on her own 'healing' and in particular the blame she labelled herself with, and consequently her inability to see herself as a victim who had survived an abusive relationship. Further she found it difficult to see herself as someone worthy of meaningful help and support and denied herself that support. Instead she suffered with agoraphobia and developed a fear of people.

Her daughter received counselling and support from welfare services which helped in some way, particularly in relation to being able to maintain a 'normal' school life. However, her daughter suffered with nightmares and mother and daughter developed an intense co-dependent type of relationship with her daughter very much in control of family life.

Close to suicide, Makare finally confided in a friend who was a community worker, who counselled her up to the point where she was able to make a referral to the CSWU in respect of concerns for her daughters' safety.

The CSWU is a Bradford Social Services social work unit catering specifically for communities of African origin who are experiencing social distress. The unit is based in a local African (Caribbean) community centre and its services run by an African female senior social work practitioner – supported by a range of community, voluntary and local authority-based support services and practitioners.

Makare was gradually introduced to culturally-specific counselling which supported her in redefining her identity as a survivor of abuse and her self-worth in terms of her right to a positive and healthy racial identity and quality of life. She was supported in seeking therapeutic input that was personal to her needs, as well as receiving support for her daughter. Her daughter was initially placed on a befriending and support programme which was used as a route to developing trust. After twelve months her daughter moved onto therapeutic sessions aimed at supporting her through the process of disclosing the abuse perpetrated against her and the effect the abuse had on her life.

Makare has gone on to give birth to twins and is actively involved in a number of community programmes involving work with children. She still contacts the unit when she feels the need to 'talk'. Her daughter remains on the therapy programme and continues to work through the abuse issues. Things remain difficult at times but she has been able to attend community-based after-school and play scheme activities for the first time in many years.

Issues Around Access to family Support Services

Lack of information and appropriate services

Many Asian women have little knowledge about the range of services that exist, and are not reached by appropriate information. Many mainstream service providers have no appropriately translated literature publicising their work and few, if any, workers with Asian language skills. Surinder found her way to the Family Service Unit via a circuitous route; many Asian

women in need of support services remain isolated and unsupported.

In their study of the use of Family Centres, Butt and Box (1998) found that 13 out of the 84 centres had no black and minority ethnic users. They concluded:

Our study suggests that black communities do not always have access to family centres and rarely access the full range of services that are available. This is not merely an outcome of black families choosing which service they access (although there is an element of that) but that the services only rarely get black families through the front door and some black users appeared to be unaware of the range of services that were available.

(1998: p105).

There could be no denying that Makare had the opportunity of help from constituency social workers, but the question is – were the practitioners able to communicate with her in an appropriate and relevant way? Did Makare feel understood and were her and her child's experiences and needs interpreted in a way which left her feeling appreciated and recognised?

Apart from the fact that not all African-origined people speak English as a first language, there is a greater issue about how social work and social welfare services are able to relate to service users of African origin when they have not considered the importance of communicating in 'felt and experienced' language. In other words no consideration is given to the consequences of African (Caribbean) clients having to translate their pain and needs from their cultural norms and expressions to white cultural forms of expression which in effect represent the normal language tools for needs assessment.

Social and welfare services which refuse to acknowledge the importance of the issues of language and communication run the risk of offering culturally sympathetic practice responses. Such responses end up inherently promoting existing intervention models which ask black people to mimic white presentations of need and accept models and methods of helping which oftentimes bear no relevance to themselves (Graham, 1999).

Saleebey states that it is clear there can be no remedy to such practice concerns without recognition that:

The orientation of the worker clearly has to be informed, insofar as possible, by an appreciation of the context and meaning system wherein the client dwells otherwise...it is extraordinarily difficult to hear and respect the accounts of clients particularly if they are in socially subordinate positions.

(1994: p355).

Personal and community barriers

For many, being part of their local community, with its particular culture, traditions and religion, will be an integral part of a black identity. Living in the context of a racist society, in some instances has had the effect of intensifying the desire to maintain a cohesive and tightly knit community.

In such settings, the need to protect the honour and reputation of the community may be a deterrent against Asian women for example, seeking help from outside, usually white-led services. Even when a woman is able to acknowledge to herself the need for additional support or expertise around a particular problem, the wish to maintain her sense of resourcefulness as a mother and to ensure the dignity and honour of her family may present insurmountable barriers to her seeking help.

Differing cultural expectations for African-origined people present different personal and community barriers – not least might be the desire to go along with formal social welfare provision whilst simultaneously receiving support from the community. To go public on methods of community support runs the risk of exposing whatever community forms of helping exist to scrutiny by dominant service providers – and as a result, heighten concerns that the community help may not be there next time dominant services let you down.

This was the situation faced by Makare, who felt that making herself known to mainstream social service providers would expose her community helper to interference from outside agencies. For some time she felt responsible for protecting her community helper – an added layer of responsibility which did not help the already difficult situation she was in.

Both case histories highlight the importance of service-providers recognising the possibility of them being seen as oppositional to community based approaches – highlighting the need for family support agencies to look at what they are doing to ensure that those who need their services do not experience their decision to seek help as an either-or choice.

The introduction of practice requirements such as the inclusion of 'Best Value' principles in the provision of family support services, provides a unique opportunity for service providers to take an important step forward in building partnerships with community organisations in order to develop a more integrated and accessible approach to service delivery. At the moment much of the impetus for liasing with community-based services comes at the point when established organisations feel unable to meet the needs of black service users through existing provision. Even when approaches to community organisations are made, the established service provider still tends to hold onto control of the service, with an expectation that what is offered by the community resource will fit in with the policy and practice of the mainstream service.

Being able to offer the kind of servicing choices which would not add to the burden of responsibility experienced by the two women in the case histories could only come when social and welfare support organisations develop healthy, meaningful and respectful partnerships with community organisations on the basis of achieving and reflecting equivalence and parity in the power relationship.

Issues of trust

An Asian woman who decides her situation is so intolerable that she must seek help, may then be faced with dilemmas around where to turn and who she can trust to understand and respond sensitively to her needs. Past experiences of racism, ignorance and stereotyping via contact with white professionals may well deter her from accessing mainstream services. She may fear a breach of confidentiality if she approaches a local worker within her own community. In the case of Surinder, local community organisations may be seen as male dominated or founded on religious values and may raise anxieties about the possibility of condemnation or of judgmental attitudes.

The issues of trust for Makare were similar to those of Surinder – she feared what people in the community would think of her should she come to them with her problems. However, whilst Surinder felt unable to approach a community member for help – for Makare the push towards approaching someone in the community was her belief that a community member would not have the heart or the power to remove her child.

Whilst black communities are homogenised over a range of shared issues and experiences they by no means share all things in common because of the commonality of their experiences of oppression. Makare was happy to approach a community member for support whilst for Surinder this was a choice she did not see as appropriate for her.

We are not suggesting here that their experiences are representative of the choices black communities are likely to make when thinking about approaching support services. However, if service providers' deal with the types of communication issues mentioned earlier, they will establish a much firmer foundation from which to allay concerns around issues of trust and confidentiality wherever they may surface. The priority must be that of enabling black communities to access the support services when they are needed and in the ways that they are needed.

Issues for Providers of Family Support Services

The impact of lack of knowledge and racism

There remain white workers in the field of family support who have had little contact with black people and have scant knowledge of cultural and religious traditions different from their own. Some hold racist and oppressive beliefs. Some organisations fail to monitor the take-up of their services by black families, let alone concern themselves with whether they are providing accessible and appropriate services for the whole community.

Against this backdrop, a request to provide a service for an Asian family is likely to raise anxieties for such organisations and workers, with the likelihood that stereotypical assumptions will be made and effective working partnerships will fail to be achieved. There is growing acknowledgement that the lack of knowledge and understanding of some professionals about the lives and experiences of black women has had a devastating effect in terms of outcomes for black families in contact with child care agencies. Research

undertaken by Barn (1993) indicated that black children entered the care system more quickly than did white children (28% were admitted into care within four weeks of referral, compared with 15% of white children). Also there were qualitative differences in the early stages of referral and admission, in that social workers were less likely to engage black families than white families, in preventative work.

Since the MacPherson Report (1999) however, there has been a growing willingness to recognise the impact of institutional racism upon the delivery of services to black families. However, we are not yet in a position to celebrate the success of social and welfare support services who have yet to take on the recommendations of earlier practice models such as the Barclay Report (1982) – which advocated the maintenance of an open and creative social work and social welfare mind as the best tool for initiating appropriate practice responses for black communities.

The impact of inappropriate models of work

Whether informed by racist beliefs or a failure to understand the impact of racism on black communities, it is clear that some workers and organisations have developed a 'deficit model' in their approach to work with black women and their families. Eurocentric theoretical perspectives, coupled with an understanding of black cultures defined only in terms of difference from white norms, have led to negative stereotyping and pathologising of black families. This has been recently acknowledged in the Practice Guidance published by the Department of Health entitled *Assessing Children in Need and their Families* (2000). The report notes that:

> *Despite the social and economic impact of racism on families and the detrimental impact of the immigration laws and racial violence on families and communities, over many generations black families have demonstrated strengths and resilience in the face of adversity. Unfortunately social work practice with black families has often failed to work with the strengths of black families and has relied instead on a problem oriented approach to black families. A deficit model which views families as dysfunctional can preclude adequate support being provided to families.*

(2000: p64).

Attempts to address these issues and to improve practice with black families have led to increased training around cultural sensitivity. There has been an emphasis on the need for workers to be more aware and respectful of different cultural traditions, religious beliefs and customs and how these affect the lives of women and their children. Whatever the good intentions, the 'cultural sensitivity' approach has serious limitations. For example, it has led to some workers arguing in favour of practices opposed by and oppressive towards Asian women – yet adopted by practitioners because they are supposed to be culturally appropriate. The emphasis on the cultural context fails to give adequate attention to the fact of racism and its impact upon culture. Training around cultural sensitivity has failed to address the impact that racism has on the perceptions, attitudes and practice of workers.

An anti-racist approach, which recognises and explores issues of racism as it impacts upon relationships and service delivery, is a more effective starting point in improving practice with black women and their families. However, anti-racist practice that fails to grapple with the complexities of work with families in situations of extreme stress has been seen to have serious pitfalls.

The report of the inquiry into the death of Tyra Henry (Lambeth, 1987), highlighted the fact that positive stereotyping in relation to the child's African (Caribbean) grandmother and assumptions about her resourcefulness and ability to cope, contributed to workers' failure to provide effective support and protective intervention.

It is evident that stereotypical assumptions and anxieties about addressing 'race issues' can impede the development of effective practice, even where workers and agencies are aware of the need to adopt an anti-racist approach. And, whilst desperately seeking to resolve the tension between the caring and controlling aspects of family support work, and its acute application with black communities – white workers may struggle with feelings of exclusion from activities which black communities and practitioners have redefined as theirs (Dominelli, 1988). The result is confusion and inaction:

> *Yet white social workers will have to create egalitarian relationships with black people if they wish to work according to anti-racist tenets and become involved with black people working in similar directions. The bases on which white people can engage with black people in these processes will be qualitatively different from those currently defining interaction between black people and white people, as power imbalances arising from relations of domination will have to be eliminated from the outset.*

> (Dominelli, 1988: p15).

The responsibility for changing service responses lies with agency practitioners and managers. The question is how much they see such changes as beneficial to white interests. Eradicating racism from institutional practice responses brings with it benefits for all.

The importance of anti-racist practice and black perspectives

It is imperative if agencies are to develop services for black women that provide meaningful support and address the reality of their lived experience, that a commitment is made to work towards an effective anti-racist approach. Such an approach will recognise that racism is a factor in the lives of black women, will acknowledge and wrestle with the pervasive cultural assumptions and racist stereotypes which affect our work with black families and will identify the barriers that impede access to supportive services and seek to overcome them. To refer again to the National Commission of Inquiry into the Prevention of Child Abuse (1997):

> *This should not lead to professionals freezing at the reference to race, but the opposite. An acknowledgement of racism is a freeing process. It allows professionals to face reality without hesitation. It does not hover on the boundaries of people's sensitivity. It confronts reality. Sensitivity harbours blame and hurt feelings; reality allows for acknowledgement, challenge, debate and openness.*

> (1997: p172).

An anti-racist approach will seek to reach out to and address the issues and concerns of black women in the context of their daily lives. It will seek to engage women in a dialogue about their needs and the needs of their communities rather than potentially placing women at odds with their communities and community leaders. It will avoid simplistic assumptions about culture and tradition and recognise the diversity of black women's lives, the impact of multiple oppressions and the strengths of existing support networks and coping mechanisms.

It is well established that agencies seeking to provide supportive services to black women and their families without the input of black workers, preferably at management as well as at grassroots levels, are severely limited in their effectiveness.

Black-led community organisations have achieved much in increasing the recognition and understanding of service providers about the issues affecting black families, and continue to play an important role as both initiators and providers of support services. Farmer and Owen (1995) underline the importance of racial and cultural matching in improving the effectiveness of social work interventions. An exploration of how the task of service development can be shared with community organisations can only strengthen the range of provision on offer to black women and black communities.

In spite of the benefits, however, there are issues for black workers in the delivery of family support services in black communities. Unrealistic expectations may be placed upon them by their agencies which may in turn create conflicts around different approaches to addressing community need. Furthermore, it is unhelpful to assume that black workers 'instinctively' know how to or wish to engage in supportive relationships with their respective communities or that black workers are immune from oppressive or prejudicial attitudes.

Black workers have a right to appropriate support, supervision and training, to enable reflection and where necessary to provoke challenge in order to ensure good practice. And support and welfare services have a responsibility to ensure that it does not become the role or responsibility of black workers to teach everyone else. Ultimately it is the shared responsibility of all workers in the field, black and white, to ensure that appropriate, accessible services are developed that provide meaningful support to black women, their families and their communities.

Black perspectives can bring to the negotiating table a better understanding of the experience of oppression and the processes of challenge and resistance. Indeed Singh (1996) sees black perspectives as having the ability to act as a catalyst for white people to begin to challenge their role and place in supporting the institutions which maintain racism and manage racist outcomes against black people. Black perspectives also supports white people to reconstruct their own sense of history and identity, and can act as a useful basis from which to begin to interact in more meaningful ways with black people. Furthermore Jones and Butt have argued:

> *There is a correlation between the extent to which black workers feel valued and empowered within an agency and the extent to which black people using the service will feel valued and empowered.*
> (1995: p8).

However, whilst there is credence to the usefulness of black perspectives in social and welfare support services we must be careful to ensure that the tendency to make black people the subject of study for a better understanding of the issues, does not detract from the reality that the perspective is located within the same centric thought structures which authored the problems initially. And as such this should not diminish our search for a form of human inquiry which is relative and relevant to the people about whom it is concerned; and which offers them a central and equivalent role of agency in determining the route through their own problems.

Conclusion

Due to a range of complex issues, particularly around access and information, trust and communication, compounded by the dynamics of racism, it is clear that for many black women contact with traditional social welfare organisations has been at times disastrous. (See as far back as the 1960 Family Welfare Association report and as recently as Mekeda Graham's 1999 article).

The white perspective of the world has without a doubt served to standardise the way the world is viewed and the culture and language of engagement at all levels and in all areas of human activity. Deficit models of black family life and stereotypical assumptions have become institutionalised in many aspects of social welfare provision.

In outlining the case histories of Surinder and Makare, not as typical representatives of their communities but as examples of women who have made use of supportive services, the importance of listening to service users and seeking a meaningful engagement in their lived experience has been emphasised. Furthermore, the need to understand the issues and concerns of the various black communities and to develop real partnerships with local grassroots organisations are crucial elements in improving the appropriateness and accessibility of service provision. The importance of training and supporting black workers and ensuring a shared sense of responsibility among all staff for the development of anti-racist policies and practice cannot be over-emphasised. Ultimately, the route to changing the black experience of support services, must be one of ensuring that the power and freedom to use an agency in one's best interest is a principle which is wholeheartedly practised by service providers.

Playing at Home

David Saltiel with Dawn Higgins and Charlotte Jackson

Case studies by Dawn Higgins and Charlotte Jackson

There is an assumption that every parent intuitively knows how to play with their children. This is not necessarily the case. This chapter describes a scheme which encourages parents to develop play and parenting skills with their children.

Introduction

The 'Play at Home' project at West Leeds Family Service Unit began life as a small pilot project in 1996 known as 'Playwork in the Home'. It was extended thanks to a grant from the BBC Children in Need Appeal the following year and is now an established part of the Unit's services, funded by the main grant from Leeds City Council.

Developing the Project

The project has undergone some significant changes in its life so far and in this chapter we will discuss these changes and the project's current work. The intention is to examine, and also to celebrate, a project whose work continues to make an important contribution to offering family support services. This is a very small project but such an examination highlights some important aspects of family support work and the tension that exists between that work and the child protection discourse that still largely dominates statutory social work with families and children.

The original pilot project involved just a few hours of one worker's time. The stated objective was to work with local families with pre-school children who were not using available services with the twin intentions of developing play activities in the home and getting the families more involved in local community services.

A two year grant from BBC Children in Need enabled a substantial development of the project. The aims of the new Play at Home project (henceforward known as PaTH) were: to develop play in the home,

to provide time for parents to explore their relationships with their children, to offer a reliable source of support and to encourage families to join local playgroups, nurseries and other community groups. Referrals of families with children under five would be from social workers, health visitors or the families themselves. PaTH would work with families for up to three months. Funding allowed for two play workers to be employed who would be part of the Unit's multi-disciplinary team that includes social workers, group workers and child care workers.

Referred families were asked to complete a questionnaire. Questions focused on the minutiae of everyday life and were designed to explore the areas of home life the family felt were strengths and areas where they needed some help. If work was undertaken the family and the project worker signed an agreement on how they would work together and at the end of their involvement the family were asked for feedback.

By 1999 the project had undergone some changes and seemed ripe for more. PaTH had been taking on more and more cases with child protection concerns and the focus was steadily shifting towards issues of child safety: workers were being asked to become involved with families with very poor parent-child relationships where there had been maltreatment, often consisting of physical and emotional neglect. With such families PaTH work focused on getting involved with domestic routines – offering practical support and guidance to make meal times, bath times, bed times safer and more pleasurable for parents and children – as well as trying to improve parent-child interactions through play. The complex nature of these families' problems meant that PaTH workers were often involved for much longer than three months.

However, the original name and purpose of the project remained and this had led to a perception in some local social work teams that PaTH was not able and willing to work with families where child protection was an issue. However, there was, amongst the workers some ambivalence about this, not least because it was clear how valuable PaTH could be to families who had maltreated their children. On the other hand, it was not desirable that PaTH changed to become an arm of the child protection agencies and therefore primarily concerned with assessment and monitoring.

Family Support, Child Protection and Play

'Child protection' is a phrase of such ubiquity that it is important to assert that it is a particular conception of how to do social work rather than the 'natural' way to do things. The term arose in the aftermath of the Jasmine Beckford inquiry in 1985 (London Borough of Brent, 1985) and suggested an increased authoritativeness by workers who properly understood their legal mandate, a stronger emphasis on child-centred interventions and a much greater stress on the need to assess the risk potentially dangerous families posed to their children. The increased awareness of the fact that families can be dangerous and distressing places for many children was important but the negative effects of this new turn in social work have been well documented. The Beckford inquiry took place at a time of deep disillusionment with the welfare state, which had nurtured the social work profession, and of central government hostility towards local government which was being attacked ideologically and restricted financially. The new discourse provided a rationale for realigning resource-starved services away from universalist, welfarist notions of need and the 'rehabilitative ideal' (Parton and Parton, 1989: p71) which had held sway since the 1948 Children Act to a more minimalist set of interventions with a narrow focus on risk and family pathology (Dingwall, 1989).

Hill (1990) and Lynch (1992) among others have summarised the consequences of this shift: the focus narrows to abusive acts so that wider considerations of child welfare and family support are lost, interventions become increasingly controlling so that the family, including the children, are not heard properly, assessment takes precedence over treatment, procedures come to dominate professional judgement. Many of these criticisms were echoed in the Department of Health research digest (DoH, 1995) which was influential in reasserting the importance of supporting families in need, although how much practice at the coalface has changed, given resource

restrictions and the fact that 'risk' remains the central principle in child protection work (Wattam, 1996) is questionable.

It might be argued that hard-pressed front line workers, schooled in the new ideology of risk assessment and minimalist intervention, have developed such an impoverished, reductionist conception of the rich complexity of family life that the aims of the PaTH project, with its emphasis on improving play and other activities, came to seem of marginal importance.

So PaTH has been renamed Parenting at Home – which reflects the wider range of interventions the workers now make (and keeps the neat acronym) – with redesigned publicity material to reinforce the change.

Case example

PaTH received a referral from Social Services to assist a family with two young children aged 18 months and two years in developing their play skills.

When the worker visited the family initially it appeared that the mother, Denise, struggled with providing age appropriate activities and also found it difficult to interact positively with the children. Both children appeared to have some developmental delay.

However, after a number of home visits it became apparent that there were many other parenting difficulties. Denise's partner Melvyn, the children's' father, was rarely present during visits. He took very little part in parenting and the majority of the care was left to Denise.

Denise's skills were limited and she seemed unable to take on the responsibilities of parenthood. After lots of discussions with Denise and her social worker the PaTH worker changed the focus of her work, concentrating on a lot of practical parenting issues. Home visits took place at meal times so Denise could be helped to provide a space for the children to eat and to look at the kind of food Denise provided. Denise did not even have a table and chairs and PaTH were able to provide these for her.

One session involved moving the furniture around so that the children had the maximum amount of space to play. It emerged that the children slept on the sofa for long periods of time and Denise was encouraged to put some routines in place to give the children stability and boundaries.

There were lots of sessions looking at play and encouraging positive interactions but the children's development continued to show delay. And despite a great deal of support Denise still failed to meet the children's' basic needs.

After six months involvement concerns about the level of physical and emotional neglect did not lessen and the children were eventually taken into care and placed in foster care where they developed and thrived.

This case shows that the project is not about offering vague unconditional support. Children's needs are paramount and although the ideal end to such support is to keep families together this is not always the best outcome for the children.

Traditionally the voluntary sector, without statutory responsibilities, has been able to provide services to families that are more innovative and holistic and less stigmatising than those of the local authority. We are in the relatively luxurious position, as a specialist agency, of being able to recruit staff with a shared value base, a clear focus on the agency's aims and a high level of skill and motivation (Frost, 1997). We walk a delicate line: a line that tries to avoid offering a service so specialist and restricted that local authority workers do not use it on the one hand, and being too closely associated with child protection work, with its focus on risk assessment, on the other. Families will often work co-operatively with PaTH while remaining hostile to the statutory agencies.

Case example

Alan was a six-month-old boy who had been taken to hospital by his parents with a spiral fracture of his arm. X-ray investigation showed evidence of a previous fracture. His parents could offer no explanation of the injury. Alan was placed on the Child Protection Register but the plan was that he remained at home. PaTH were asked to work with Alan's parents.

They were very young and while apparently co-operating with the agencies involved were still unable to explain the injury. The plan was that PaTH work with both parents but Alan's father got a job and was rarely at home. The work was therefore mainly with Alan's mother Janice. Janice was reluctant to discuss her parenting and claimed that everything was fine and she needed no help. Indeed her parenting of Alan was observed by PaTH and other agencies as being good. The PaTH worker began focusing on Janice's strengths as a parent and building her confidence and a more trusting relationship began to develop.

Janice revealed enough about the marital relationship to suggest that there had been some domestic violence and the PaTH worker suspected that Alan's injuries may have resulted from such incidents. However, there was no firm evidence for this.

After six months Alan was clearly thriving and some of the agencies involved felt his name should be removed from the Child Protection Register. PaTH's involvement was coming to an end. The worker was able to provide a detailed report of her work and of Janice's parenting but stressed that she had not worked with the father or the marital relationship and this could be a basis for further work.

Like many social care agencies PaTH has difficulties trying to engage men. With this family the worker made sure of highlighting this so that the father did not 'disappear' from the case.

One of the problems suggested above has been workers' failure to listen to children – to conceive of them as significant actors rather than passive recipients of 'protection'. The workers on the PaTH project are experienced play workers and from the beginning of their involvement with families they make detailed observation of parents, children and family interactions. These observations are noted on the contact forms that PaTH workers use which are designed so that each session has a clear aim and the methods and strategies that the workers employ are made explicit. These methods are primarily task centred and practical and are worked out in conjunction with parents. They might involve, for example, bringing certain toys along to encourage a particular interaction between parent and child or ensuring the worker is there at teatime to help parents develop better strategies for managing feeding. Parents, children and workers work together to improve the quality of interactions and make children safer and more secure. Supplemented by regular summaries the contact notes are a rich source of detailed and intimate information on the family and have often proved invaluable when such information has been required by the statutory authorities in, for example, child protection conferences, care proceedings and family support meetings. Such intimate work can be highly stressful and workers need to be well supported and supervised: a topic returned to in more detail below.

Case example

Martina was a white single parent in her early twenties when she was referred to PaTH by a local Social Services team. She had three children aged one, two and four years. At the time of referral she was in a refuge following domestic violence from the father, a drug user. She was said to be depressed and unable to cope with the children. They were all on the Child Protection Register due to physical maltreatment and neglect. The youngest showed non-organic failure to thrive.

The PaTH worker worked carefully with Martina to find out how she thought the scheme could help her, if she would be happy for the worker to visit her home and whether she would be prepared to come to the FSU base for play-focused sessions and also to join groups being run at the centre which could offer further support.

Martina felt that she wanted to learn more about doing things with her children, particularly playing with them. Over a period of two years Martina took part in play sessions with the worker from PaTH and attended a parenting group run by FSU. These remained constant supports for Martina during this time while she had three changes of social worker. The worker was able to make detailed observations of the interactions between Martina and her children and tailor her input accordingly so assessment and services were provided simultaneously.

Stevenson (1998a), reflecting on developments in post-war social work, has argued that a crucial advantage of the psychodynamic thinking that informed practice in the fifties and sixties was that it focused attention on attachment and bonding issues and encouraged careful and detailed observations of children and of parent-child interactions. There was a sense that as poverty, apparently, no longer existed compared with the deprivations of the then still relatively recent 1930s, environmental factors were not important in analysing family dysfunctions. The

disillusionment with post-war social progress and the rediscovery of poverty caused such ideas to fall out of fashion as social work developed a more political and sociological agenda. But, as the author suggests (Stevenson, 1998; 1998a) this left social work without a body of child-centred thinking with which to understand the dynamics of maltreating families.

The changes brought about by the Seebohm reorganisation of the early seventies accentuated this process: Westheimer, writing a few years after Seebohm (Westheimer, 1977) describes how an increased emphasis on management and bureaucracy in the big new Social Services Departments was creating a body of practitioners whose work was devalued in status and who increasingly saw career progression in terms of stepping into management rather than developing and refining their practice and its knowledge base. Practice became increasingly proceduralised and controlled by management and the changes in child welfare social work that resulted from the rash of child abuse inquiries of the seventies and eighties further contributed to this trend.

The digest of research on practice published by the DHSS in the eighties (DHSS, 1985) painted a disturbing picture of social workers who did not listen to children or parents. Marsh, a contributor to that research, commented on the Beckford inquiry (LB Brent, 1985) that while that tragedy had resulted from too much focus on parental wishes contemporary research strongly suggested the opposite was more generally the case as families were allowed to drift apart without the wishes of any family members being adequately attended to (Marsh, 1988).

Would it be too bleak to suggest that social workers had been left without the means to listen to and understand either children or their parents?

The recent *Framework for the Assessment of Children in Need and their Families* (DoH, 2000) has attempted to redress the balance. In conjunction with the Looking After Children (LAC) forms it attempts to define the body of knowledge required to attend to the needs of children but also to take a more holistic and ecological perspective that considers the ability of parents or carers to promote good child development and sets families in their social contexts.

For a family support project like PaTH it is essential to get this balance right. The Children Act and the

Department of Health Framework both make it clear that the child's interests must come first and that services to families must be based upon best outcomes for children. But 'putting children first', the mantra of modern social work, is a complex business: much easier to aspire to than to achieve in practice. Too often the concomitant of putting children first has been that parents' needs are ignored or seen as antithetical to those of the children (after all, when we talk of 'child protection' who are we protecting the child from in most cases if not the parents?).

A perspective that gives us a framework for child centred interventions but also for considering family functioning in a wider sense should, it can be argued, be based on attachment. In the light of current research and thinking (for example Howe, 1999; Gilligan in Horwath (Ed.), 2000) an attachment perspective is rooted in child development, considers strengths or protective factors as well as possible risks and also provides a framework for understanding the needs of parents. The interventions of PaTH workers can thus be conceived in terms of carefully observing and assessing the quality of attachments in the family and working alongside parents and children to promote attachment through better interactions.

Howe (1999) argues that attachment is a concept that is useful across the lifespan. It gives workers a framework for understanding children's emotional needs and the kinds of relationships they need to have with their carers for those needs to be promoted. But it also helps them understand why carers may be unresponsive to children's needs. PaTH works with pre-school children, and as Howe (1999) argues the younger the child the more interventions will focus on the carers for it is the quality of that caring relationship that is so vital to children's development. He cites considerable evidence derived from research into maltreating parents' own histories that many have themselves suffered poor attachments. Growing up with the experience of hostile, unreliable, uncaring relationships with parents or carers can impact directly on parenting capacity as such individuals may suffer from many unmet personal needs, low self-esteem and an inability to form stable and nurturing relationships.

Exercises and checklists derived from attachment theory (such as those of Fahlberg, 1994) give workers

practical frameworks for assessing attachments and for devising strategies for improving them. These will involve working alongside parents to help improve everyday activities; feeding children, reading to them, taking them on outings, putting pictures on the wall. As Gilligan states 'Everyday living may be peppered with mundane yet vital opportunities for healing and development for the child in need' (Gilligan in Horwath (Ed.), 2000: p143). An attachment-based perspective, then, is practical, rooted in the every day routines of family life and gives a consistent purpose to workers' interventions.

The question of purposefulness is important. Research suggests that the child protection practices of the 1980s have resulted in initial interventions being more purposeful and authoritative but that practice becomes much vaguer once these are over – once, for example, an initial child protection conference has taken place (Gibbons, Conroy and Bell, 1995) – and is often marked by drift and uncertainty (Corby, 1987; Farmer and Owen, 1995). Family support, if it is to achieve the best outcomes, should never be vague or unclear about what it is doing. As Howe (1992) argues, clear theoretical frameworks are required if practitioners are to give clear answers to the questions: What is the matter? What is going on? What is to be done? How is it to be done? Has it been done?

In this chapter it has been argued that one of the advantages of PaTH working with families in the way it does is that it involves working together with parents and children. Aims and strategies are mutually agreed and there are clear practical objectives which are regularly reviewed. The intention is not to take over peoples' lives but to help them in an empowering way to make decisions that will improve the quality of life in their families. But just as 'putting children first' is not as easy as it sounds in the text books neither are those other buzz phrases about 'empowerment' and 'working in partnership'. Many of the families that we work with seem to have limited potential to change significantly.

Stevenson (1998a), discussing a research project on social work with neglected children, paints a picture of the client families that is similar to those that PaTH works with and familiar to many social care professionals: they are predominantly families headed by single mothers who have a range of social problems such as learning difficulties and mental health problems. These families live in poverty and a degree of social isolation. The children are physically poorly cared for, they are under-stimulated and poorly supervised. The families have a long history of contact with social work agencies. They are, Stevenson argues the old long-term child welfare/family support cases (or as Stevenson calls them 'revolving door clients', 1998a: p2) whose presenting issues have now been reframed by a system using the language of child protection: risk, safety, and time limited intervention and case closure. Such families have long made up social work caseloads, the definitions of their needs and problems changing as the social work discourse changes (Welshman, 1999). It can be difficult to feel positive about such families or to see a way of genuinely empowering them. It can be all too easy for workers to feel they are achieving something by telling them what to do irrespective of whether or not such lecturing actually seems to be working or offering endless amounts of practical assistance.

Following Crittenden (1993), Stevenson (1998a) argues that the constellation of unmet personal needs and lack of social skills in some of these parents has major cognitive implications. The ignoring of a child's urgent need for attention, the interpretation of such a need as being motivated by a desire to annoy the parent, the failure to provide a level of hygiene acceptable for small children, these suggest that the parent finds it difficult to process, interpret and respond to information in a way that will meet children's needs. Instructions or advice will not be enough, it is suggested. What is needed is to observe and assess parental behaviour, attempt to understand the family's meaning frameworks that form the context for this behaviour and suggest strategies that will alter the parent–child dynamic.

It seems to the authors of this chapter that this has some profound implications for practitioners such as PaTH workers who are working alongside such parents. It emphasises the importance of careful observation and assessment but also of assessing parents' capacities to learn and change. Social workers pay far too little attention to the importance of creating the right environment for learning in the families we work with. The adult learning theories espoused by educational theorists (see, for example, Brookfield, 1986) stress the importance of focusing on the strengths and experiences of learners so as to support them and enable them to solve concrete and relevant problems in a climate conducive to learning, a climate that can only exist in an atmosphere of mutual respect.

PaTH workers, working closely with parents on the everyday issues that make up family life are in an ideal position to create the right circumstances for maltreating parents to learn and develop, basing this on a careful assessment of how parents perceive and understand their worlds. It is sometimes a slow process, identifying and building on current strengths and good experiences. It is patient, skilful work and there is no suggestion that it is easy or always possible. But it is a process that we have seen lead to change and empowerment and is surely preferable to 'the endless cycle of advice, practical aid, sending in the dirty squad to clean up' (Stevenson, 1998a: p53) that marks so much family support work.

Recent thinking has stressed the importance of taking an ecological and holistic view of families (see Jack in Horwath (Ed.) 2000). One of the founding principles of Family Service Unit is its commitment to strengthening local communities and reducing social isolation. Since its inception one of PaTH's central aims has been to help families build networks that can support both parents and children. A good knowledge of, and active presence in, the local community has enabled West Leeds FSU to build up integrated services which can if necessary co-ordinate in supporting families. PaTH families can, for example, be invited to join 'Play Space', a group for parents and pre-school children where families are enabled to play together, the children can be offered sessions in the unit's crèche, families can be referred to the unit's volunteer scheme whose work is covered in detail elsewhere in this book. The latter scheme offers families trained volunteer help – what Frost et al. (1997) call 'negotiated friendship' – which can be an invaluable support both in practical and emotional terms.

What has also helped in integrating services has been the moves towards refocusing the statutory child care services in Leeds. As a result of this work one of the social work offices West Leeds FSU works with closely now has regular Family Support Meetings to which families and local statutory and voluntary agencies are invited. Families are empowered to present their own perspective on what services they need. PaTH workers regularly attend these meetings and not only can they offer the project's services but can do so in a co-ordinated way with the representatives of other local services who are also in attendance.

PaTH, then, tries to offer a balanced package of support that is rooted in attachment but with an ecological perspective. Focusing on the internal dynamics of families who are often heavily socially disadvantaged is not enough in itself and neither is offering purely practical support to families whose poor relationships and standards of child care have a more complex origin than just being a response to material disadvantages.

The holistic perspective at the heart of the project's work, and the intimate nature of its work with families, makes PaTH an effective service for working with emotional maltreatment. Influential research (Gibbons, Gallagher, Bell and Gordon, 1995) has suggested that long-term patterns of parenting marked by punitive and 'low warmth' caring have much worse outcomes for children than single instances of physical abuse or neglect. Glaser (1995) also emphasises that it is the 'pervasive and long-lasting nature' (p73) of emotional maltreatment that makes it so damaging: '...it is not a single, or a series, of events but rather a continuing relationship.' (p81). The Department of Health (DoH, 1995) concluded not only that this form of maltreatment was particularly damaging but that child protection systems were particularly poor at picking it up. PaTH workers, working intimately with families over time are ideally placed to assess emotional maltreatment and devise strategies for working with it.

But this close involvement with families sometimes comes with a price.

Case example

Cath was a single parent with learning difficulties with an eleven-month-old son, Aaron. Aaron's father was absent much of the time but returned to Cath's home occasionally. He had a history of violence.

Cath was referred by her social worker because of serious concerns about her parenting. She spent very little time with Aaron, describing him as 'annoying'.

She frequently ignored him, leaving him in bed with a soiled nappy for hours. When she attended to his needs she did so perfunctorily and often aggressively. She never played with him.

At times Cath said that she did not want to keep Aaron but her parents and Aaron's father did not want her to give him up. Cath was prepared to work with PaTH and so, despite the concerns, her social worker did not institute care proceedings.

The PaTH worker spent several months working with Cath trying to encourage improved interactions between Cath and Aaron during domestic routines. The worker also tried to introduce a range of play activities. Cath found working with PaTH much less threatening than with Social Services and usually co-operated. There were some improvements but it became increasingly clear that they were marginal and Cath's care was not good enough. The worker was able to report back to Child Protection conferences in detail on Cath's poor parenting and as a consequence it was decided to make a residential assessment of Cath. The PaTH worker continued to support Cath through this assessment. The decision was finally made to begin care proceedings and Aaron was subsequently removed.

A feature of this case was the distress the worker often felt when faced with Cath's emotional maltreatment of Aaron. This required good support and supervision or she could have been overwhelmed by her feelings.

Studies of child abuse tragedies (for example, Reder et al., 1993) have shown how easy it is for workers' perceptions and judgements to be distorted by the relationships they form with maltreating families. Mattinson and Sinclair (1979) in a classic study of social work with families graphically describe the manipulation, the chaos, the lack of safety that some families create, arousing powerful feelings in those who work with them. As families with many unmet emotional needs oscillate between dependency and hostile rejection so the workers' behaviour can come to mirror that of the family. And yet, as the authors emphasise, without getting close to families, and becoming drawn into such emotional storms, the vital work of enabling them to change won't happen.

The Role of Supervision

Workers involved in such demanding, draining work need good supervision if they are to make sense of their work and stay safe: safe for themselves as well as safe for the families and children they work with. These emotional issues are inadequately dealt with by the more managerial models of supervision that are often found in statutory child protection work. Pressure of work, the imperative to achieve efficient throughputs, a heavily proceduralised and bureaucratic work environment (Howe, 1991) all make it difficult for managers in the statutory sector to enable workers to properly reflect on their work and the feelings and anxieties it engenders. Indeed it has been argued that such reflection is seen as an indulgent irrelevance, getting in the way of achieving the necessary outcomes (Payne, 1998). But, as Reder et al. (1993) have argued unless such feelings are dealt with workers perceptions of the families they work with can become dangerously skewed. Effective supervision, I would suggest, actively takes on the feelings engendered by the work and analyses them as evidence of how the relationship between worker and family is developing (Hughes and Pengelly, 1997).

This kind of supervision will only be useful as a vehicle for professional learning and development if it takes place within a supportive team with a shared value base. As we have suggested earlier, a specialist voluntary agency like ours can build a team with a shared value base within which supervision and support are seen as essential if workers are to do their jobs well. There is a strong commitment to supervision and development in the team and the PaTH project is very much part of this with the workers getting regular supervision as individuals and as a project team.

Conclusion

Family support is not an easy option. It is not something vague and open-ended that keeps families ticking along, dependent on professional help. PaTH work achieves its successes through being purposeful and focused and working to time limits which recognise that for children change must occur within certain timescales. Not all of our cases result in families staying together but that does not mean they are failures. Essential to an effective strategy for family support is the understanding that some families will not change enough or sufficiently quickly for the children's best interests to be met within them.

12 Family Support in Rural Areas
Nicky Ryden

In towns or cities, families live geographically near to each other and there are communities within each conurbation, which can be easily identified. Supporting families in rural areas has its own challenges. This chapter discusses these issues and makes positive suggestions as to how high quality family support can be offered in rural areas.

Introduction

This chapter will examine some of the issues for families with children living in the country. It will consider how services are designed to deliver family support in rural areas and some of the factors which impact on those services. After looking at how we define rural and the influence of the urban majority on our perceptions of family life in the country, it will use a case study to describe one approach to bringing family support to an upland region of England. The case study is based on a recent evaluation of a rural Family Support Project undertaken by the University of Leeds (Frost and Ryden, 2001, see also Frost, 2001 for an extended discussion of some of the issues raised in this chapter).

Defining Rural

The definition is debatable but it is generally agreed that 'rural' is those areas of the country, which have a scattered population, living in communities of less than 10,000, at a distance from larger urban centres and dominated by certain forms of economic activity (Pugh, 2000: p12). The forms of economic activity are expected to be agriculture and forestry, but could as easily be mining or quarrying; increasingly tourism is the major source of employment for people living in the country.

If we ask people to define rural themselves we get more subjective definitions which include notions about social networks and personal identity. As Pugh writes:

...we need to be aware that conventional representations and definitions of rural life may portray the countryside as if it were an integrated and organic entity in which conflict, difference and diversity is absent, or is underplayed.

(2000: p12-3).

One of the consequences of a sparse and scattered population is the trade off between having a lower tax base and the higher costs of provision (Statham and Cameron, 1994; Stone, 1990) the rural premium on service delivery. This has implications for the ways in which services designed to support families are planned and delivered. Instead of facilities being focussed on a building as it might be in an urban area, there will be a need to utilise a range of resources and approaches to overcome the problems of small numbers, distance, lack of appropriately trained staff and resistance to innovation. Any provision needs to be flexible and adaptive to both the needs of parents and the community. The successful involvement of the community can develop multi-functional resources which are more likely to be economically viable and offer the desired flexibility (Palmer, 1991).

The Rural Idyll: Myth and Reality for Children and Families

After centuries of depopulation of the countryside, the developing process of 'counter urbanisation' (Pugh, 2000: p13) is led as much by those families who are moving into the countryside because they are searching for a safer and healthier environment in which to raise their children, as by the older retired people who are seeking a peaceful haven for their old age free from the threats of urban living.

McLaughlin's (1986) study of 876 households in five rural areas in the north, east and west of England showed how the rural population was changing with increasing polarisation between incomers with high income and mobility and low investment in social networks and local people who had lower than national average wages. The local people, 25% of whom were living in poverty suffered from the effects of a high cost of living, poor transport and loss of local services. These trends have intensified over the last two decades; the 'rural idyll' is somewhat tattered when we consider the reality of being other than part of the rural middle class. The SSI report *Care in the Country* comments at the end of its review of the conditions that disadvantage rural populations:

> *The idyll of rural life may be restricted to those who have their own transport to access the facilities of the town for shopping, public services and social activities.*
>
> (Brown, 1999: p6).

The investment made by the urban population in maintaining the ideal of the country as safe, beneficial and stress free has a significant impact on policy for rural areas (James, 1991). Thus in 1994 Statham and Cameron found that only one of twenty-six rural local authorities had rural isolation as an indicator for deciding whether a child was 'in need'.

Needs in rural areas are similar to those in urban areas, but they are experienced differently because of factors such as low pay, the higher incidence of lower incomes, seasonal employment in the tourist industry and agriculture to a lesser extent; to the lack of affordable housing; to poor transport networks and the centralisation of local services away from the village into towns (Palmer, 1991; Williams, 2000). Overall, families living in rural areas will have less choice than families living in urban areas. This may be compounded by isolation, material deprivation, few opportunities to socialise and a changing family profile which means that young parents often lack family support (Statham and Cameron, 1994; Stone, 1990; 1994).

Certainly for the children interviewed in Northamptonshire during a study of how place impacts on children's lives the idyll was tarnished:

> *...many children, especially the least affluent, and teenagers felt dislocated and detached from village life and there was a strong sense of alienation and powerlessness.*
>
> (Matthews et al., 2000).

There is a strong suggestion here that the country childhood experience may be as stressful as the inner city childhood experience, but with the disadvantage that it is not visible and overlaid with a powerful stereotype of country life. Certainly the country child can be well travelled as concerned parents seek out social and leisure opportunities for their children. Palmer (1991) found that children and carers in rural Scotland travelled up to an average of 10 miles to get to playgroups and 17 miles to attend nursery. Some were attending groups in different villages because of the infrequency of sessions, with the travelling time exceeding the time spent at the resource in a few cases. Little surprise then, that those rural families, even though on low incomes, prioritises car ownership.

Family Support in Rural Areas

Hearn offers a comprehensive definition of family support:

> *It...is about the creation and enhancement, with and for families in need, of the locally based (or accessible) activities, facilities and networks, the use of which will have outcomes such as alleviated stress, increased self-esteem, promoted parental/ carer/family competence and behaviour and increased parental/carer capacity to nurture and protect the children.*
>
> (1995: p19).

As already indicated in seeking to implement such provision the rural context for such services is constrained by four major factors:

1. The costs of personal mobility for the service user and the worker.
2. The value placed by society on living in the country, one of the effects of this being that people feel if they choose to live in the country they cannot reasonably demand services regarded as commonplace in the town.
3. The continuation of the trend towards the decline of the community which mitigates against effective informal networks and self help initiative.
4. The implications of government policy for agriculture, (particularly pertinent at the moment as the country struggles with the impact of foot and mouth) and on the role of local government and public services in maintaining local services when the financial support for this is constantly eroded.

> (Francis and Henderson, 1992: p139-41.
> See also Craig and Manthorpe (2000) on this last point).

When considering how workers and organisations are meeting these challenges it seems that there is a heavy reliance on voluntary organisations and existing grass roots activity in the form of playgroups, mother and toddler groups and private provision such as childminders and nurseries. For families struggling to meet the needs of their children such resources are likely to be insufficient and expensive. The budgets for assisting with the costs of such provision are also likely to be under pressure, further limiting opportunity and choice for both family and worker.

There are snapshots of provision around the country from a range of reports and research on rural provision for children and families. Cohen (1994) in a report for the European Commission describes a range of rural provisions throughout the country, from a purpose built nursery in Portree, Isle of Skye, through a private nursery in Market Deeping to a Rural Enterprise Childcare Centre in Warwickshire offering child care while parents train in telecommunications. This organisation also had a mobile resource for more isolated rural communities. These examples are not specifically designed to promote family competence or capacity to nurture and protect children. Mobile resources also feature in Devon, where the Bizzy Bus Play and Community Bus provides play opportunities and after school activities. The Llanelli Community and Family Project has a mobile play scheme which offers bi-lingual play opportunities for pre and school age children, with integrated play sessions for children with special needs during the summer holidays.

Metcalfe (1999) also describes some more specific services in rural areas; Conwy Children and Families Project, a partnership between NCH Action for Children and Conwy Social Services Department, provides outreach services operating in community centres and church halls as well as a play bus. They run a six-week positive parenting programme for the parents of children with behaviour problems, with a crèche and transport if needed. Rural Action with Families in Tynedale, part of the Children North East initiative, uses a play bus to visit six different venues on a 2-4 week schedule, using volunteer drivers and play workers. A toy library is included. In Oxfordshire, as part of the Rural Development Commission Rural Childcare Initiative, a redundant school has been developed as a nursery, after school club, family centre

and IT training centre. This multi-function centre provides a parenting skills course based on the Family Nurturing Network model. The Ormiston Children and Families Trust have 12 projects across East Anglia, with family centres in three towns. It also supports a 'parents supporting parents' scheme in the King Head area of Cambridge. In Cumbria the Howgill Family Centre is a well established resource operating as an independent, registered company, in partnership with the local community and a voluntary trust, to provide a home visiting service based on Homestart principles. There are play sessions, equipment loan and resources for parents, and a mobile resource, the Hippopotobus, which visits communities that lack established groups for parents and pre-school children.

A Family Support Project in a National Park: North England

This case study is based on material from an evaluation undertaken by the University of Leeds in 2000, of a project designed to bring family support to rural families. The project is funded by the local authority and a major children's charity, with additional support from a local voluntary trust. With its office in the area's largest town, the project covers two hundred square miles of upland country. The population density is 0.6 per hectare, compared to 3.2 per hectare for England and Wales as a whole (Cumbria County Council, 1999). Whilst 56% of the area's population lived in more urban areas, 24% lived in rural, small towns and villages; and 20% in deeply rural areas in isolated farms and small hamlets. Roughly one in five (20%) of the children aged 0-14 years live in households claiming some form of income support, although there is obviously significant variation between communities throughout the area (Cumbria County Council, 2000). This is a popular tourist area and much of the employment is associated with tourist and leisure services.

The project has been operating for four years; its original establishment of a project manager, volunteer co-ordinator and two project workers has been supplemented by two temporary posts for one year. The core of the project is its home visiting service and its parenting programmes; the temporary staffs are engaged in piloting projects to introduce play programmes for parents and to promote self-esteem in 7-8-year-olds. The project has been very successful in recruiting volunteers who provide planned practical support to families, participate in the facilitation of parenting programmes and work with the children.

The major social problems for the families that the project works with are isolation (social and geographical), the high cost and low availability of housing, intermittent employment and low wages in the tourist industry, dealing with poor health and disability, domestic violence and drug and alcohol misuse.

Physical and social isolation is a constant factor:

...some communities are very closed...its so difficult for someone in those communities who does feel different...maybe because they are a single parent, or have a disability; or something happened in the family and the whole village won't forget it for twenty years.

(Worker).

...they're very suspicious of organisations coming in. With the Parenting Programme we found people were so worried about what other people might think, it took us ages to recruit a group that was viable.

(Worker).

The distance to be travelled and the consequent cost of travel is a constant for both workers and families:

...things are a long way away, if you haven't got a car things are very difficult, there's nothing just around the corner.

(Parent).

...it's difficult for people get out and about, not everyone has access to a car or a bus route, and even if they do it's only once or twice a day.

(Worker).

One thing I find difficult is the distance to travel to the shops, which it takes practically a whole day just to go and do the shopping.

(Parent).

...it's very hard to make things financially realistic because of the distance, for instance we're here or travelling from 9am to 1pm for a one and a half hour programme.

(Worker).

There is also difficulty of letting people know that there was a service available:

...the size of the area we cover, so many small communities...how we raise the profile of the project within the community where maybe one person uses the service. We have a leafleting campaign through GP surgeries and Health Visitors – it's difficult to get information to people who may need the service most.

(Worker).

Housing is expensive, with very little rented accommodation, most in the private sector is holiday lets and the council housing stock is small, with a waiting list of up to 8 or 9 years. The apparent wealth of the area means that much deprivation is masked and those without feel excluded:

There's a lot of rural poverty masked by quite a lot of rural wealth...There are retired business people, or in the tourist business, people who are comfortably off from it; alongside people who are employed in it and the wages are not good.

(Worker).

Many of the families known to the Project are incomers, having moved to the area for work and so are without the family support that is often vital to young families. Domestic violence is an issue in some families, as is drug and alcohol abuse:

...two of the smaller towns in the area have statistically a worse drug problem than Manchester. This was a surprise to us.

(Worker).

The experience of ill health can mean long journeys to regional centres, and more local services often have long waiting lists, so problems such as childhood behaviour problems can become very entrenched before intervention is possible causing much distress to the child and the family. For such children the risk of exclusion from school is high, and there is often little choice about the school a child can attend.

There are more immediate risks for children:

There's lots of space here which is nice for a child, but he doesn't see many people outside of the family. There are a lot of dangers on a farm, you have to be watching all the time, a child was helping to feed the calves and drowned in a bucket of water.

(Parent).

The project has had considerable success in establishing itself, by targeting its interventions on specific issues and communities, making use of local newsletters and established networks like play group leaders, health visitors and schools to promote its work. The parenting programmes, using the Family Caring Trust package, are now being promoted by word of mouth and personal recommendation from the participants. The parents said:

...someone mentioned it at one of the Baby clubs that we go to, she had been to a previous one...

...my friend who was on the previous course recommended it.

We got a leaflet through at playgroup, and there was a notice on the door, but I think what influenced me more was talking with some friends...

...I talked with other people who had been on the previous programme who said it was really good.

I've said to people, get a leaflet, ring them up, one to one, nobody needs to know you are interested until you actually turn up to the group.

Linked to this are community development initiatives based on work with local children in the schools, asking what would improve their community and trying to stimulate action by the community. The outcome of this stage of the work is yet to be seen, but it will hopefully flourish, if the initial enthusiasm is maintained. Certainly the family play days have been well received, serving to alert people to the fact that the national charity is no longer about orphans:

I went to the Play Day and I think it was the first time I knew that...had changed.
(Parent).

The parenting programmes successfully overcome some of the effects of isolation:

It's the first chance I've had to talk with people with children of the same age.
(Parent).

I just wanted to come in and talk to people!
(Parent).

You worry about sharing your thoughts with other people that you perhaps meet for the first time, but it doesn't worry me now.
(Parent).

I feel much more confident now, than I did before.
(Parent).

If every parent in...had been on this course, what a brilliant place this would be to bring up children!
(Parent).

The parenting programme is a good social opportunity for people who may not know many people in the community very well.
(Worker).

The provision of the crèche was highly valued, and several people felt they would not have been able to come if this had not been provided, although some travelled up to 25 miles to attend a group. Considerable effort was made not to put programmes on at times which would conflict with other resources provided for parents with young children. The venues were community halls and centres in the smaller towns. Project workers and the crèche team put a lot of effort into making sure the rooms were opened up early enough to get heating working and to set up equipment, so that the children entered a welcoming and well set out play space. Parents valued the professional way the crèche was run, so that they could focus on the course, confident that the children were being well looked after. For some children this was their first social experience outside of the family.

The home visiting service is valued for the privacy of having someone come to the house, although given the interest in your neighbour's business this may raise some issues about confidentiality which are not significant in the town (see also Richardson (1995) on demands for home visiting).

...it can be difficult because people see you going from one house to the next, there's no way round it, whereas in town you can whiz from one street to the next and nobody would know.

However for many of the families:

It was a relief not to have to take them all out together, it was more practical and private having...come to the house. That was where the difficulties were and it made it more real somehow. It helped us through a bad time.
(Mother of three all under 30 months).

I did try a parenting programme, but it wasn't a good time for me and I couldn't face being with other people, so we worked through it here. I can be hard on myself as a parent...tells me I'm doing a good job.

For those families where a volunteer was introduced this was valued as:

I looked forward to...coming, it meant I could get out of the house and (daughter) could meet other children.

Families where a parent had a disability, found managing a baby compounded the effects of a disabling society, with the barriers to access exacerbated by limited service provision, and the lack of support meaning that partners had to make difficult choices about continuing employment.

The project has been successful in establishing its parenting programmes and its home visiting service, although there is probably less public awareness of this aspect of the work. When the new initiatives offering play programmes, through workshops and in the home, come on stream there will be another aspect which will hopefully meet individual need and stimulate community action. It is planned to use local providers to lead the workshops, thus publicising what can be available in the area for families to link into. The empowering style and meticulous attention to detail means that a high quality service is being delivered in ways which are responsive to need. Success does bring its own challenges, not least how to continue to meet demand, when resources are not likely to be significantly increased – this may be where the volunteer role will develop further.

Conclusion

There is little published material on the provision of support to families living in rural areas. The needs of families with young children are very similar whether living in the inner city or a small village; all families struggle with the challenges and problems of raising children, sometimes compounded by the impact of unexpected difficulties such as unemployment or disability. In rural areas though, access to services which might make the difference between overcoming those problems or suffering the effects long term can be problematic. The availability of information may be the first hurdle, the distance from resources, the costs of travelling, the inherent conservatism of some isolated communities may all mitigate against seeking help. This lack of a voice will itself have implications for service provision. A lot of research may need to be done to establish the nature of need and the best ways of providing services.

Hearn's requirement for family support delivered through locally based, accessible services will be difficult to satisfy, with high costs attached. It is inevitable that the provision of quality service will mean higher per capita costs when compared with similar provision based in the town or city. There needs to be a willingness to consider the multi-functional use of buildings, the provision of outreach services, transport policies, and the longer lead-in time that may be necessary to overcome suspicion of and resistance to 'outsiders'.

Given those conditions the case study shows what can be achieved in a relatively short period of time, working through existing networks, offering a clearly defined package such as the parenting programmes, supplemented with a more individualised home visiting service, to create a Family Support Service which is responsive to the needs of the rural family.

Recruiting and Supporting Volunteers

13

Jenny Brown

Volunteers are often the best placed people to work with families in a low-key supportive manner. The recruitment and retention of volunteers is a vital part of many organisations' plans. This chapter discusses how best to both attract volunteers and keep them linked to a family support organisation.

Introduction

This chapter is written from the perspective of having been a Home-Start co-ordinator for the past seven years. It is hoped that what follows will have broader relevance and be useful to anyone working with families in the community. The chapter draws on a range of sources and analyses of other peoples' experiences but is written largely from the author's personal experience of the organisation that she works in:

> Home-Start is a voluntary organisation in which volunteers offer regular support, friendship and practical help to young families under stress in their own homes, helping to prevent family crisis and breakdown.
>
> (Home-Start Statement of Principles).

Home-Start is a national organisation set up in 1973 in Leicester when Margaret Harrison, the founder, recognised a need in parents to be befriended and listened to by ordinary parents like themselves, not professionals who were doing it as part of their job. The organisation grew slowly at first, but over the last decade there has been rapid growth until now, in 2001, there are over 300 Home-Start schemes in the UK. In addition there is Home-Start International which supports schemes in countries as diverse as Australia, Russia and Israel. Each scheme is autonomous, bidding for funding locally and run by a management committee made up of members from statutory and voluntary agencies. All Home-Start schemes work to agreed practice standards and are accountable not only to users of the service and to funders but also to the national organisation which

carries out a review with each individual scheme every three years. Each scheme recruits volunteers to support families in their own homes.

The use of volunteers to support families has been, and is, very successful, and volunteers are seen very much as part of the network of support offered to families experiencing difficulties. They do not, and should not, replace the help and support given by statutory services or paid workers but offer something special and unique. Volunteers are not paid a salary but choose to give freely of their time. They may not be given the status of a 'professional' worker but will still be working in a professional manner as part of an organisation and alongside paid workers.

Using volunteers as part of the support for families has great relevance, benefit and validity. Home-Start volunteers could be described as having a 'befriending role'. Volunteers may be parents themselves and will understand some of the stresses and strains of being a parent. Many families seeking support want the support from 'someone like them' – someone who has an understanding of what it is like to have a sleepless night because of a crying baby, someone who is struggling with their child's difficult behaviour, someone who is 'doing it'. And, above all, someone who is there because they want to be. 'Volunteers at Home-Start are there because they are volunteers, they're not there because they are getting paid...'they wouldn't be here if they didn't care'. (mother)' (Frost et al., 1997: p113). However much paid workers care they will nearly always be viewed by the family as being there because they have to be there. Volunteers are perceived to be there because they want to be there and because they want to give of their time and experience.

Who are the Volunteers?

This brings us to the questions: who are the volunteers and what sort of person wants to offer their time freely to support families? There are no easy answers to these questions. Volunteers come from all walks of life and come with varying experience. One of the strengths of having a team of volunteers recruited widely is that they are all different, with different skills, strengths and experiences. This means in practice that families are better supported because the appropriate volunteer can be matched with a family – matched in terms of the needs of the family and the skills of the volunteers, as well as more practical details such as where they live, the time they have for visiting, etc.

The reality is that the majority of volunteers doing this sort of work will be women, and because women tend to be the main carers of children within the family, most of the support will be woman to woman. Women will have common experiences of relationships, childbirth and child-rearing for example, which they can share. The role of men, however, should not be forgotten or ignored. Male volunteers offer their own skills and experience when supporting a family. Some volunteers will see their volunteering as a job, albeit unpaid, and their main occupation. Others will fit their volunteering around their paid job and other activities. Parents who have been supported by the organisation may want to become volunteers, often to give to someone else the kind of support they themselves experienced.

People will volunteer for all sorts of reasons and some of these reasons will not even be clear to them initially. Motivations vary, but there are likely to be some key motivators for those who offer themselves as volunteers to support families. These include: wanting something for themselves (which might include gaining skills and experience to move on to paid work); wanting to help someone else (believing that they have something to offer); making friends. If we have some understanding of what motivates people to volunteer then we will be in a better position to recruit the right volunteers for the job.

Some people who volunteer may be quite needy themselves and perhaps unconsciously believe that involvement in an organisation will give them the support they need. While this is understandable, there has to be a balance – a volunteer who understands what it is to be lonely and need support can give good support to someone in the same situation. A volunteer who is overwhelmed by their own problems is unlikely to be able to offer an adequate level of support to someone else. Just like anyone else volunteers will

experience personal difficulties and this may be while supporting families. This is the point at which some volunteers will leave the organisation. If the support structures within the organisation are good then it is more likely that the volunteers will 'take a break' until their personal crisis is over.

The difficulty faced by anyone working with volunteers is how to recruit them in the first place, and then how to retain them: how to keep them motivated enough so that they will stay.

Recruiting Volunteers

This can be the most difficult and challenging part of the job! In order to recruit volunteers the organisation needs to believe that volunteers can play an important part in the support for families. There needs to be clarity about why volunteers are sought and what they will do once recruited. Volunteers should not be seen merely as a cheap option to paid workers. They should be viewed as valid in their own right and as a positive alternative to other support which might be given. 'I think a voluntary agency can offer a lot more in some ways than we can, because families often see us as a threat' (social worker) (Frost et al., 1997: p22).

When recruiting volunteers thought should be given as to what the needs of the families are – there would be little use in recruiting volunteers who all wanted to help with practical tasks such as gardening or shopping, when what the families want is someone to talk to and to help with the children. Recruitment should be as wide as possible and should reach as many sections of the community as possible. As mentioned earlier, families are all different and will need different kinds of volunteers to support them well. An ideal team of volunteers would reflect the make-up of the community and include people of all ages and classes, different cultures and sexualities, disabled people and both women and men. It would be important therefore to recruit in such a way as to attract this wide range of people. To do this it would first be necessary to know something about the community so as to target advertising and recruitment appropriately.

Some tried and tested methods of recruitment include newspaper articles, advertisements, posters in shop windows, displays in libraries and shopping centres, talks at groups of various sorts, e.g. schools and churches. Leaflets can be left in shops, libraries, schools, colleges. A particularly effective way of recruiting volunteers is by word of mouth. This more personal approach works well. 'The general rule is that the more people you reach through a medium and the less personal the contact, the lower the response rate...is likely to be' (Smith, 1994: p15). Care should be taken, however, as it is likely that we recruit others like ourselves and thus may inadvertently discriminate against those not like us. Successful publicity needs to be trial and error. What works in one area may not work in another; what works one year may not the next. Many people may not respond the first time they see publicity about volunteering. Perhaps they think 'that's not for me'. The second or third time they see something they may begin to say 'maybe I can do that'. It is worth having constant recruitment drives as well as the posters and leaflets in the regular places.

It is important to be sensitive to those whose levels of literacy are not high and who may therefore not be able to respond to the written word. There may also be people whose first language is not English. If representatives from these groups are to be recruited leaflets and posters will need to be produced in the relevant languages. It is important to consult with minority groups before doing this. Coming from the majority culture it is easy to make assumptions, sometimes incorrect, about other communities.

Above all, it is important to be realistic about recruitment. In many areas there is not a culture of volunteering. Many people still equate it with middle class do-gooders who have nothing else to do. This is often far from the reality – volunteers come from a wide range of backgrounds and abilities – but people will need convincing that they have something to offer. A lot of time and energy may be spent with seemingly little gain. A recent recruitment drive in my organisation undertaken by two new and enthusiastic workers resulted in four volunteers – and that with approximately 50 hours given to the task! Worthwhile? It has to be accepted as such in an organisation which relies on volunteers to carry out the function of its work. And each of these volunteers has the potential to support not just one family but possibly dozens during their involvement with the organisation.

As part of the recruitment of volunteers it is important to have clear procedures for interviewing and selection. Going back to an earlier point, the clearer the organisation is about what it wants and needs of the volunteers, the easier it will be to carry out the interview and selection processes. It is useful to have some sort of job description, not only for the use of those carrying out this process, but also to inform potential volunteers of the requirements of the job. This should include information on how much time volunteers will be expected to give to the organisation and what expenses will be paid.

Thought needs to be given to the selection process: who does it, is a written application form necessary (what about those who are not confident of their ability to write and spell well?), where should the interview take place, is there an interview at all? And all the time there should be an awareness of acting appropriately, treating everyone with equal value and respect, and not consciously or unconsciously discriminating against anyone. It is necessary to be particularly aware of the possibility of rejecting anyone who is 'different' and who on the surface may not seem to fit in. This may well be the very person needed to enrich the team.

An equal opportunities policy will act as a useful reference to ensure that the organisation's practice is good and sound. A commitment is needed to recruit volunteers from all backgrounds and to continue to ensure that everyone involved in the organisation is treated with equal value and respect giving due regard to any particular needs they may have. When volunteers are recruited they should receive clear information about the organisation, its ethos and way of working and their induction and on-going training should reflect this. If issues are clarified to begin with it is less likely that problems will arise or if they do they can be more easily dealt with.

Volunteers should be informed at the outset whether they will be subject to police checks and that references will be needed. These volunteers will be working with vulnerable families and the organisation should do everything possible to ensure the quality of support given and the safety of the children within the families.

Retaining Volunteers

Volunteers may of course choose to leave at any time – this is one of the elements of volunteering, that volunteers are not tied to a contract. Volunteers will leave for many reasons; some positive, some negative, and these may be linked to their original motivation for volunteering for the organisation. Retaining volunteers is, however, an important issue for organisations as a great deal of time, energy and resources are spent on recruiting, training and supporting volunteers. As mentioned earlier, some volunteers will take a break from volunteering for personal reasons but if they essentially feel satisfied about their role and the support they are given they are likely to want to return. So, having explored who the volunteers are and how to recruit them, we should have some ideas about how to keep the volunteers we've got! Returning to the motivations for volunteering in the first place will give us some clues.

The majority of volunteers in this Home-Start scheme give their main motivation for volunteering as wanting to help others. This is usually combined with reasons such as having time to spare and wanting to do something worthwhile. A questionnaire was sent recently to volunteers asking the question: what is important to you and what contributes to keeping you as a Home-Start volunteer? They were asked to rate the following from most to least important: satisfaction of helping someone, on-going training, support from staff, making friends, being valued, social events, experience to help future career. The responses indicate overwhelmingly that what is most important to these volunteers is the satisfaction of supporting and helping someone. This is followed closely by being valued and receiving support from staff. One volunteer added 'growing self-awareness.' They were also asked 'what would put you off and make you less enthusiastic?' The responses here linked with the first question with the most common being 'if I felt the family were not benefiting and I was not making a difference', lack of support and not feeling valued.

As stated above, volunteers may choose to leave at any time and it is useful for an organisation to monitor the reasons for volunteers leaving. This will give some idea of the satisfaction levels among volunteers and whether their expectations are being met, as well as highlighting any need for change to the organisation's practice. Reasons for leaving may be linked to the original motivation for becoming a volunteer in the first place. If volunteers want to learn skills and gain experience to further their career they may leave when this has been achieved or when they have gained enough confidence to move on. Some volunteers will look for a natural ending, perhaps when their support to a family ends, and move on to other things. The important thing is to keep in close touch with volunteers and to support and supervise the work they are doing. It will then be more likely that workers will pick up on dissatisfaction, restlessness or lack of fulfilment and be able to manage this appropriately and support the volunteer in whatever decision they make.

Supporting Volunteers

There are a number of different ways in which volunteers can be given support and they will all form part of the support structure of the organisation. The initial induction and the on-going training will be part of this.

Initial training or preparation is vital. Volunteers will usually be joining an organisation about which they know very little and will need information and awareness raising before they embark on the task of supporting families. The importance of such preparation should not be under-estimated. Volunteers will be coming with a lot of skills and experience but will need help to view these in the context of the organisation. They may also come lacking in confidence and having low self-esteem. Home-Start runs courses of preparation for new volunteers. A friendly and informal course gives them the opportunity to share ideas and experiences as well as to receive information about the organisation and its way of working. This should result in well-prepared and motivated volunteers ready for the role of supporting families.

Thought needs to be given to the content of the course – not too intense so as to put people off but not too lightweight so as not to be of any use. This is the opportunity to introduce new volunteers to the way the organisation works, its policies and structures. Home-Start's course typically includes the following: introduction to the organisation, values and attitudes, the role of the volunteer, working with families, confidentiality, child protection, listening skills, commitment, boundaries, support, endings. Even if there is an induction programme rather than a course as such, these are the kind of subjects that need to be covered to prepare volunteers for their role and also to give them confidence in themselves and in the organisation.

Ongoing training is also important. Topics for sessions can be negotiated with volunteers and be a mixture of issues that are related to the work they are doing with families as well as topics aimed more at volunteer's own personal development. Volunteers should be encouraged to attend training sessions but it must be remembered that they are volunteers and cannot be forced to do more than their original commitment. They join the organisation to support families and do not always see training as relevant. Offering sessions that meet their needs is one way of encouraging attendance.

One-to-one support is probably the most important element of support and is invaluable. This need not always be face to face but can be telephone support. Volunteers supporting families, many of whom have difficult and complex issues going on for them, need someone to be there to whom they can offload if necessary. The reassurance that someone is there may be enough. Some volunteers will ask more readily for support than others. It is important to have a structure and procedures for support so that all volunteers get the support they need. It may be a good principle for the worker/volunteer co-ordinator to be in touch with every volunteer at least once a month. In this way it is possible to stay in touch with the issues going on for both volunteer and family. Including volunteers in the reviews and evaluation of the support given to families will play an important part in helping them to recognise the value of what they are doing. Giving good support to volunteers is ultimately about ensuring that families are receiving a quality service. Well-supported, contented volunteers are more likely to give good support to families.

Group support can also play its part. This is an opportunity for volunteers to relax together and to get peer support; a place to share experiences within the policy of confidentiality. Group support will also cater for those volunteers who joined the organisation to make friends and get to know more people. Thought needs to be given to the structure of these sessions, i.e. how formal or informal they should be, and also whether or not there should be a worker present.

Annual appraisals or reviews play an important role in the structure of support given to volunteers. This gives the volunteer and the organisation the opportunity to formally review the volunteer's role, their contribution over the past year and any training or other needs which they might have.

Support and supervision is usually not only about the work that the volunteer is doing for the organisation but may also encompass personal support to the volunteer. Indeed, if the relationship between volunteer and volunteer co-ordinator is good and positive there will inevitably be an element of personal support requested. As mentioned previously, volunteers are as likely as anyone else to experience personal difficulties and will need support if they are to continue as a volunteer as well as deal with their own problems. This may take up a great deal of time but I would argue that it is a valid part of a volunteer co-ordinator's role. In fact it may well be that issues arise for the volunteer as a direct result of supporting a family. Ideally the time given to supporting a volunteer is balanced by the support the volunteer is able to continue to offer the family.

Volunteers should know and understand the support structures of the organisation and the availability of support from the outset and be confident that they are carried out in practice. They should be encouraged to ask for support whether that be one-to-one with the workers, through training or with other volunteers. They should understand that in order to support a family well they themselves will need support.

Difficulties Which May Arise

Volunteers and families need to understand that it takes time to build up relationships and for trust to develop. Nothing ever runs completely smoothly and things are bound to go wrong sometimes. Volunteers will be linked to a family or families and sometimes the initial 'match' may not be right. Usually I work by 'gut' feeling – 'this is the right volunteer for this family.' Sometimes it is necessary to take risks. Sometimes it will go wrong, mostly it will go right! And it is never to be taken lightly – everyone is important and must be treated respectfully, but we are all human and make mistakes.

There may be other reasons why things do not work out, usually to do with the volunteers' or families' expectations, and these not being met. A volunteer who wants to see change and is quite practical may not cope well with a woman suffering from depression and to whom every small step is a major challenge. A family who has been told that the volunteer will help with the housework will not be satisfied if that is not the volunteer's or the organisation's perception of the kind of support offered. A common comment from volunteers is 'I don't think I'm making any difference/doing any good' and this after two or three visits!

Other, more serious mismatches may be the volunteer who is racist and supposed to be supporting a black family, or a homophobic volunteer who supports a young lesbian. A good induction course or programme will raise these issues from the beginning and good support structures will lessen the likelihood of such occurrences. But people are adept at hiding their feelings and prejudices and it may only be when supporting a family that such feelings become apparent. In such situations it is important that the organisation is clear about its ethos and policies and does not tolerate discrimination of any kind. Support should be given to the family. Volunteers should be clear about the organisation's position and extra supervision and training should be provided if necessary.

Conclusion

Volunteers can be a creative and beneficial addition to an organisation giving support to families and are often more acceptable to families than a professional from a statutory agency. They bring their own skills and experience to the team and have much to offer. Volunteers need to be clear about their role from the outset, and clear about how they fit into the organisation. They should be treated with respect, consulted about their needs and given structured and constant support. To use volunteers effectively, organisations will need to have clear procedures for recruitment, selection, training and support as well as an equal opportunities policy and policies on confidentiality and child protection. Organisations should be committed to using volunteers effectively as part of the 'jigsaw' of support to families.

The relationship, between volunteer and family, seems to offer a method of support which carries less stigma than the 'statutory' friendship offered by the professional agencies. This is because the mothers and fathers make a connection between 'friendship' and Home-Start. Because receiving a visit from a Home-Start volunteer is 'like a friend calling in', it seems to be largely free from stigma (Frost et al., 1997: p212).

14 Parenting Within the Youth Justice System
John Clark

The behaviour of young people can be troublesome and sometimes illegal. Working with the parents of these children requires a particular approach, not least since the introduction of the Parenting Order. This chapter discusses issues raised by this difficult and often controversial issue.

Introduction

We have all been young and many of us will become parents, relatives or friends to young people. As such, we all run a high risk of coming into contact with offending behaviour and (if caught) with the criminal justice system. This system lays down the steps which may be taken should we transgress the criminal code. In recent years there has been an increasing focus on the links between youth justice and the issues of parenting. This link is the topic of this chapter.

In England and Wales there is a separate process reserved for young people between the ages of ten and seventeen years, which is referred to as the Youth Justice System. We attain adulthood in the United Kingdom at the age of eighteen years and can only enter the criminal systems when we reach the age of criminal responsibility, which in England and Wales is ten years. This entry age compares unfavourably with most Council of Europe countries, where it is often higher (House of Lords, Hansard, 1995).

The system has within it a number of stages beginning with arrest and finishing with delivery of a formal reprimand, warning or with the administration of a court sentence should the case go to court. Whether or not we enter the system at all or the degree to which we enter it can be determined not just by the offence but by other accidents of time and space. The law is not constant and determinant factors can include our parent's education, where we live, which school we attend and what public attitudes and moral panics are abroad at a particular time. All this is in spite of repeated government attempts through criminal justice legislation to introduce some consistency into ways in which society responds to actions which break its laws.

The Crime and Disorder Act (1998) places all those working in the Youth Justice System under a statutory duty to have regard for a principal aim of preventing offending by children and young people (Crime and Disorder Act 1998 – Home Office Guidance.) This legislation also seeks to introduce practices which will help to avoid justice by geography and creates by statute multi-agency Youth Offending Teams – 154 in number throughout England and Wales.

Against the Law

There exists in this country a large body of codified law to enable society to deal with crimes committed by children and young people and an unedifying flurry of law making can be observed as general elections loom on the political horizon. The present Government has sought to embody in its current (Crime and Disorder Act, 1998) the enactment of legislation dating from previous decades in 1994, 1993, 1991, 1988, 1982, 1969 and so on. Much of the content, however, is 'new' provision as the legislation seeks to reform the system, tackle delays and introduce new concepts such as restorative justice and reinforces the responsibilities of parents.

'Poor parenting', the Government found, is one of the key influences in the likelihood of a young person offending (Home Office, 1998). This is why there is an important link between youth justice and the topic of this book – family support.

This reinforcement of parenting was provided for in the provision of support and encouragement in the form of a Parenting Order and built on the 'binding over' of parents for their child's good behaviour to be found in the Criminal Justice Act, 1991, which in turn followed the trend of encouraging parental responsibility as it is defined in the Children Act, 1989.

Crime has always been high on the public agenda and if we believe what is presented as public opinion in some sectors of the media and press, then we could be forgiven for thinking that crime is also high on the agendas of most young people.

Received wisdom among many youth justice professionals has it that most young people offend at one time or another but that the vast majority do not go on to commit more than one or two crimes and do not continue to offend into adulthood. And yet the majority are not subject to any intervention other than a warning of a formal or informal nature. *Misspent Youth*, a report by the Audit Commission (1996), drawing on results from Youth Lifestyles Survey estimates that half of all young men admit to having offended at some time. Most such surveys are based upon self reported crime by young people rather than official statistics, which are based upon the proportion of known offenders, who are aged between ten and seventeen years (British Crime Survey, 1998).

The above survey estimates 11% of recorded crime to have been committed by this age group. It also assumes this to be an underestimate. Suffice to say, it is commonly accepted by professionals that trivial offending is not uncommon among teenagers and that most teenagers stop offending without formal responses from the courts. It is also probable that the public constantly overestimates the overall proportion of crime committed by youth and that this in turn informs media and official (government) responses (British Crime Survey, 1998). What emerges then is a picture of a large and costly Youth Justice System, which is to be judged by public and professionals alike, to have serious limitations in its success in dealing with crime and preventing further offending by children and young people.

The System Responds

In 1994 the Government commissioned the Public Audit Office to examine the Youth Justice Services. As a result, the Audit Commission Report, *Misspent Youth*, was published in 1996. The report for the first time identified costs attached to the administration of the system and made some wide ranging recommendations, many of which were embodied in the subsequent white papers, *No More Excuses, Tackling Delay in the Youth Justice System* and *Reforming the Youth Justice System*. These were subsequently to emerge in the 1998 Crime and Disorder Act and the 1999 Youth Justice and Criminal Evidence Act.

Misspent Youth, as well as identifying costs and recommending reform, concerned itself with some of the causes of crime and it may be remembered what the Labour Government in waiting had made one of their pre-election calls. 'Tough on crime, tough on the causes of crime' (Tony Blair, when Shadow Home Secretary).

The reforms of the 1998 Act now determined entry into the Youth Justice System. A first offence, subject to seriousness, will now be responded to by a Reprimand in the Police Station. A second offence, if within two years, will evoke a Final Warning, which will in turn trigger a referral to the local multi-agency Youth Offending Team. Any further offending will result in prosecution, in the Youth Court. Very serious offences may subsequently be committed to the Crown Court, which has greater powers in relation to length of custodial sentence.

All offences are subject to gravity scoring and the final score, as well as whether it be first or second offence, determines at what level the system responds. For the purpose of this chapter we will focus on the implications for family support – a critique of the system can be found in Goldson (2000).

Referral to the Youth Offending Team elicits a response in the form of a visit and assessment for intervention from a Youth Offending Team member, usually a police officer, who will then devise a change or rehabilitation programme, with the consent of the child or young person and their parents (Crime and Disorder Act 1998 – Sec. 65, 66).

Any further offending will, as indicated above, result in being charged and an appearance in court, should there be sufficient evidence. When a child or young person appears in court for the first offence (or first offence following a warning) the court has three options open to it by way of sentence, presuming an admission of guilt:

1. Absolute discharge (usually where the offence is very trivial or involvement minimal).

2. A Referral Order of three to twelve months involving appearing before a panel, in the community, which will determine the content of the order, if possible taking into account the wishes of the victim (see Referral Order Guidance HO, 2001).

3. A custodial sentence, where the courts judge the offence to be so serious as to merit it (up to two years in the Youth Court.).

For young people aged twelve to seventeen years this will be in the form of a Detention and Training Order of up to two years, half of which is served in the custodial institution and half in the community under the supervision of a Youth Offending Team Officer.

A custodial sentence being dispensed on the occasion of a first offence in court is not common and most first convictions will be dealt with by way of a Referral Order. Any subsequent offending can be dealt with by the court from a menu of court orders:

● Reparation Orders

● Action Plan Orders

● Attendance Centre Orders

● Curfew Orders

● Supervision Orders

● Supervision Orders with Requirements

● Community Rehabilitation Orders

● Community Punishment Orders

● Combination Order

● Detention and Training Order

These interventions can measure from hours – Attendance Centre, Reparation or Action Plan Orders through to years in the case of Supervision Orders for which the maximum period is three years. The content of some orders is determined by Youth Offending Team Officers and Courts according to a young person's age, maturity, living circumstances and the nature of the offence. Such areas as work, addressing anger control, examining consequences of actions, inappropriate sexual behaviour or victim awareness might all be included. The intensity of such orders will again be determined by the nature and seriousness of the offence.

Frequency of contact, however, is generally governed by standards, which have been set out by the Youth Justice Board (a non-departmental body established by the Government to set standards and monitor the performance of Youth Offending Teams), in a set of standards relating to all interventions within the Youth Justice system (National Standards for Youth Justice, April 2000)

Further detail relating to court ordered interventions can be obtained from the above standards as well as from a variety of guidance documents produced by associations such as NACRO and local Youth Offending Teams.

Parental Responsibility

One of the connections between family support and youth justice is to be found in the concept of parental responsibility. Parental responsibility is defined as all the rights, duties, powers, responsibilities and authority, which by law a parent of a child has in relation to a child and their property (Children Act, 1989 S.3.).

This definition may also include the local authority and under the Children Act more than one person may have parental responsibility. The purposes of this chapter, however, are concerned with duties in relation to children and young people who offend and what might be expected of a parent.

The law distinguishes between parents of young people above or below the age of sixteen years and appearing in court. If under sixteen the court must require a parent to be present. Over sixteen the court may impose such a requirement (Children and Young Persons Act, 1993 s.34A).

Such distinctions are also reflected in the law when a person aged sixteen or under is arrested. The Police and Criminal Evidence (PACE) Act, 1984, requires the police to notify parents or carers in such circumstances and also provides for the attendance at interview of an 'appropriate adult' (PACE, 1984 Code of Practice Code C).

This practice is based, in this case, on an assumption of vulnerability due to age. Vulnerability might also be on grounds of mental ill-health or learning difficulties. In most cases it is the parent who fulfils the function of safeguarding the welfare of their child.

There may be circumstances where the parent or carer is unable to fulfil this role, for example, when they have been the victim or the witness to the alleged offence or where they might have colluded in the offence. In these cases another 'appropriate adult' may be identified by the child or their parent, but should this not be possible then a trained volunteer or social worker from the Youth Offending Team or

Social Services can be requested (by the police) to attend and fulfil the role.

This is likely to be the first formal contact that a parent of a young person who has offended will have with the formal criminal justice system, and one of the rights that parents can exercise is a right to free legal advice on the child's behalf whilst at the police station.

The process following the interview will be determined by a number of considerations, such as whether there is sufficient evidence and whether the child admits or denies the alleged offence.

As indicated above, should the offence be admitted and there is other corroboration evidence, then in the case of a first offence (not of sufficient seriousness to warrant Warning or Charge) a Reprimand will be administered at the police station. This process is carried out in the presence of the parent, whose responsibility it is to reinforce the message and thus reduce risk of re-offending.

A second offence within two years will, subject to seriousness, illicit a Final Warning from the police, once again delivered in the presence of the parent. This Final Warning is accompanied by a referral to and intervention from the Youth Offending Team in whose area the child lives. Subsequent assessment and interventions would be expected to involve the parent.

After being questioned, it is probable that a delay will occur before the next intervention, be that reprimand, warning or charge, and court. During this period the child will be placed on bail (PACE, 1984 s.47:5), which may be unconditional, the only requirement being the imposition of a duty to surrender to custody or return to the police station or court at a pre-determined time.

A significant number of young people fail to answer bail at the appointed time and a major contributory factor in such cases is a lack of parental support or oversight. To fail to answer bail is an offence and can place the young person at risk of arrest and in some cases, overnight detention.

Amendments to PACE and to the Bail Act were introduced by the Criminal Justice and Public Order Act 1994. These extended the powers of the police to impose conditions of bail such as a residence requirement, observation of a curfew, to stay away from certain locations or a requirement not to associate with co-accused or interfere with witnesses. Once again parents or carers will be involved in ensuring that their child observes whatever conditions are imposed.

Should a child commit a third offence and should there be sufficient evidence, then prosecution results and a parent will need to accompany their child to court.

Clearly, there will be circumstances where parents might be unable to attend; severe illness or incapacity might be an acceptable reason to the court for non-attendance of a parent. Grandparents or other close relatives may in these cases take the parents place, although this can at times limit the courts ability to impose financial penalties.

Fines, if imposed on children or young people less than sixteen years of age, must be enforced against the parent or guardian unless it would be unreasonable in the circumstances of the case to do so (Criminal Justice Act, 1991).

Should the young person be sixteen or seventeen years of age then the court still has the power to require the parents to pay, but is not bound by a duty to do so. In cases where a parent is judged to have the opportunity to attend court, but has failed to do so, then a fine can be imposed in their absence.

In any event, most parents would wish to accompany their child to court in order to support and possibly protect them. This, however, is not necessarily as straightforward as it may seem and even first time offences are not always dealt with on a first appearance. This is in spite of the Government pledge to reduce the time it takes to deal with matters that come before the Youth Court.

Thus a parent might find themselves attending court on a number of occasions for the same offence. This might present difficulties in relation to child care responsibilities, where there are younger siblings or in the work place should both parents be in employment.

There exist two other court ordered interventions, which may be imposed on a parent or parents, where their child has been convicted of an offence. The power to 'bind over' parents for their child's good behaviour was legislated for in the Criminal Justice and Public Order Act, 1994. This is similar to a common law bind over except that in this case the parent can be bound over not for their good behaviour, but for their child's. Such bind overs are commonly imposed for one year and a sum of money may be forfeit should the bind over be broken by further offending by the child.

There have been wide variations in the way in which the parental bind over has been used by the Youth courts throughout England and Wales. When the legislation came into force some courts clearly took the view that they had a duty to impose these bind overs, unless it could be demonstrated to them that another was in loco parentis at the time the offence was committed i.e. the child was resident at a school.

The implementation of the Crime and Disorder Act, 1998, has brought with it a potentially more intrusive method of ensuring that parents of young people who offend are enabled to fulfil their parental duties. The 'Parenting Order' will offer parents training and help to change the offending behaviour of their children and contain a requirement that they exercise control over their children's behaviour (see Gibson, 2000).

A 'Parenting Order' may be imposed on a parent or other adult with parental responsibility for a maximum period of three months and require attendance at weekly sessions, the aim of which is to provide training or guidance.

As indicated earlier in this chapter the Government have taken indicators from earlier research and from the audit of Youth Justice Services and identified 'poor' or inadequate parenting as a significant predictor of offending behaviour in the children subject to such parenting (see Audit Commission, 1996).

Accordingly, they concluded that providing lessons in parenting could go some way to addressing this. Thus, should a child find themselves in Youth Court and be convicted, and should a report be requested from the Youth Offending Team that report will be expected to make comment about the suitability or otherwise of a Parenting Order.

The increase of provision of parenting support programmes is something which most social care agencies working with children and families would welcome. The question over whether access to such support should come in the form of an order in the Criminal Court is one which has been debated extensively. Unease and resistance from many of the professions involved in dealing with young people, who offend has borne witness to this.

The parent, usually the mother, who is made subject to an order, is not entitled to separate legal representation at the time the order is imposed. Failure to comply with the order can result in the imposition of a fine of up to £1,000. Non-payment of fines can of course result in imprisonment.

A programme evaluating the success of parenting programmes on the basis of reconviction rates is due to report back to the Youth Justice Board in summer 2002.

This chapter has outlined the shape of the present Youth Justice System and draws particular attention to the areas concerned with parents, parental responsibilities and interventions to which parents can become subject. All of the above therefore will only be of relevance to a parent should the child offend, be caught and should the law enforcement agencies become involved.

Whether or not to involve the police following some misbehaviour might appear to present the self-evident answer – whenever the law has been broken.

The issue is however more complex than it would appear. How many of us can judge when adolescent carelessness might become an offence of criminal damage or high spirits reach a point when an offence is committed under the Public Order Act, 1976. Clearly, the degree of damage or upset as perceived by the victim rather than by others needs to be a determinant factor in such considerations. It might be helpful at this stage to distinguish between behaviours displayed within the family and those displayed beyond the family home. As cited at the beginning of this chapter a family's tolerance of challenging or thoughtless behaviour being displayed by its adolescent off-spring can be determined by a number of significant influences. Attitudes to possessions, their own and those of others, what the social norms are for the area in which they live and is the child or young person loved and valued.

So a window or a piece of furniture broken within the home in temper or as a result of carelessness could arguably be best dealt with by the family rather than by the law enforcement agencies. For it is in families in most cases where the strongest controls operate. It is fear of a parent's displeasure or distress that prevents most children from repeating wrongdoing.

Where a family is dysfunctional or abusive then there is a far more complex set of circumstances operating and in such circumstances behavioural boundaries may well have become distorted. Where this is so then some form of help from outside the family may be needed. Even so the extended family may well be best placed to offer it and the introduction of Family Group Conferencing into Child Protection and Youth Justice arenas has sought to harness the strengths of a family in addressing the difficulties being experienced by other family members.

Self evidently, children and young people require guidance and correction when they do wrong. How otherwise can they learn to do what is right, but it is also true, however, that learning to make choices and to make them in a way which does not bring harm to others is a lesson best started in early years rather than beginning in the eleventh or twelfth year.

There exists a range of agencies that have built up experience in dealing with children's behavioural difficulties. Few are accessed until a crisis occurs and sometimes this crisis is in the form of offending behaviour. It is through schools that most early assistance might be accessed but once again, the expertise of Social Services, the NSPCC, Barnardo's, Family Service Units and others are seen to be agencies whose services can be called upon when issues of 'Child Protection' are identified.

Conclusion

A change of culture which enabled advice and assistance to be obtained without stigma attaching to it would arguably go some way to obviating the need for such interventions as Parenting Orders when a child has reached adolescence. Healthy adolescent development will always display some challenging and risk taking behaviour and self-report surveys indicate that significant numbers of young people report having committed an offence during their teenage years. It is fair to say that most of these do not enter the formal criminal justice systems, nor do they indulge in repeat offending or continue into adulthood.

These young people then cease to offend through a natural fear of being caught, through family influences and through change and self-development. The youth justice system is far from perfect, as well as being over stretched as a result of the large numbers of young people who are precipitated into it unnecessarily, assisted by a low age of criminal responsibility.

It is Family Courts and the civil processes that are those best placed to help parents to manage when courts do have to become involved. The criminal processes and the Youth Court are best reserved for those for whom there are no alternatives. I would also submit that this is true of parenting assistance when it comes into contact with youth offending. Family support has a crucial role to play in assisting parents under pressure.

Undertaking Assessments
Rosie Jakob and Kevant Coates

There are times when, despite other offers of support, there are still serious concerns about the welfare of children living in families. On such occasions, a full assessment of the child's needs is necessary in order to promote their welfare. This chapter discusses this process and shows that even at what may be seen as a crisis point, the family support agenda can still be pursued:

> The first comprehensive assessment I did, I had no idea how complex and challenging the whole experience would be – it was a big learning experience and one that has informed all of my social work practice.

Introduction

A key task of all social work and family support practice is assessment. Assessment may be very brief in terms of one interview or may span many months. Within child protection and family support work, it is often the first stage in understanding a child and their family's needs and how best to move forward in addressing those needs.

In this chapter we intend to concentrate on an assessment as a specific piece of work. Within this remit we have to be guided by the Department of Health publication, *Framework for the Assessment of Children in Need and their Families*, DoH (2000). This guidance uses as its basis an assessment triangle (see Figure 1), encompassing three domains and twenty dimensions. It draws on a wealth of research about the needs of children and good practices, aims to have a holistic and balanced approach ensuring that its central theme is safeguarding the child and promoting their welfare.

A major theme of the Assessment Framework guidance is that the assessment process should be grounded in evidence:

> Practice is expected to be evidence based, by which it is meant that practitioners:
> Use knowledge critically from research and practice about the needs of children and families and the

outcomes of services and interventions to inform their assessment and planning.
> Record and update information systematically, distinguishing sources of information, for example direct observation, other agency records or interviews with family members.
> Learn from the views of users and services i.e. children and families.
> Evaluate continuously whether the intervention is effective in responding to the needs of an individual child and family and modifying their interventions accordingly.
> Evaluate rigorously the information, processes and outcomes from the practitioner's own interventions to develop practice wisdom.
> The combination of evidence-based practice grounded in knowledge with finally balanced professional judgement is the foundation for effective practice with children and families.
> (DoH, 2000: p16, 1.58-59).

Preparation for Assessment

Preparation is essential in all assessments in order for the process to be as thorough, reliable and effective as possible. Following are some important elements of preparation.

Gathering information

> If we hadn't known about the family history before going in there, we would never have been able to persuade them to discuss it.

Before any direct assessment work can be undertaken it is important for the workers to gather as much information with respect to the family as possible. This may include reading any social work files (past and current), meeting with relevant professionals and looking at any relevant papers before the court. We have found this process itself time consuming, especially if the family has moved from one local authority area to another. Sometimes it has taken months just to travel to different towns and cities in order to interview relevant professionals. It is, however,

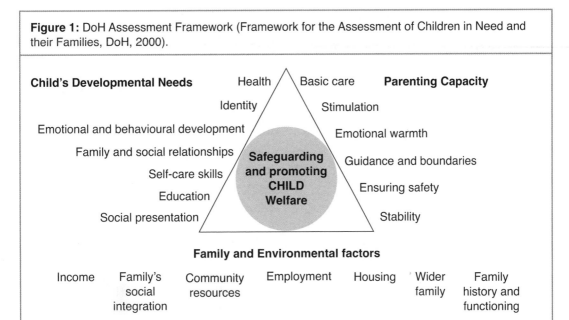

Figure 1: DoH Assessment Framework (Framework for the Assessment of Children in Need and their Families, DoH, 2000).

Child's Developmental Needs

Health
Identity
Emotional and behavioural development
Family and social relationships
Self-care skills
Education
Social presentation

Safeguarding and promoting CHILD Welfare

Parenting Capacity

Basic care
Stimulation
Emotional warmth
Guidance and boundaries
Ensuring safety
Stability

Family and Environmental factors

Income | Family's social integration | Community resources | Employment | Housing | Wider family | Family history and functioning

---

a valuable exercise because of the overview that can be acquired by drawing all of this information together. It is important to note that it may also be necessary to obtain the leave of the court to access certain records, such as medical information or prison records.

Once the information has been gathered the compilation of a chronology can help workers to make sense of events. Such a chronology enables information to be accessed more readily, aids cross-referencing and helps in establishing factual evidence.

Practical details

I forgot to tell them that it would be a session with just them – it was a nightmare trying to get all the other family members to leave the room so that we could talk to them in private!

Prior to commencing the assessment it is important to ensure all necessary practical arrangements are considered. These will include identifying a suitable venue. In our experience a neutral venue has been useful initially – because the nature of assessment can be experienced by families as intrusive. A neutral venue offers them an opportunity to develop a relationship with the workers before allowing them into their own home. In such a venue it is important to take into account whether this will ensure

confidentiality, offer ease of access, smoking facilities (if applicable), minimal interruption and noise pollution, child care arrangements – nursery facilities or other family members or staff available to care for the children if still in the care of the family. Consideration needs to be given to any other special needs of the family, for example, is an interpreter required? Does an advocate need to be identified? Are there gender issues that need to be considered? Is literacy an issue?

We have learnt from our own mistakes that time is a very important factor in assessments. If this work is only part of a workload, then it is very easy to allow other work to take priority. As detailed assessments are often part of care proceedings, there will be deadlines and it is important that the assessment is not 'crammed in' at the last moment, increasing the likelihood of errors of judgement being made. Enough time should be allowed for preparation prior to the session, the sessions themselves, supervision of the assessment and writing up sessions. It is important to offer the service user the opportunity to look at the recorded sessions each time – everything that has been written down is about them and their lives and it is better to make the assumption that they will want to see what you have written about them and to plan accordingly. This is an important element of partnership working. The amount of time an assessment takes is almost always underestimated. Working with people can often mean taking into account such things as illness, emergencies, annual leave; even a reluctance to participate can get in the way. It is important to allow some leeway at the end should you require further sessions.

Co-working relationship

It has been so important to me to be able to safely bounce ideas and thoughts off my co-worker without fear of looking or sounding stupid.

As with all social work, assessment workers are in a position of power in the lives of families. The need for accuracy and lack of bias makes it important for the assessments to be jointly undertaken by two workers, one of whom needs to be a qualified social worker. We have found it helpful to identify which of us will be taking down a written record of the session and which one will take the lead in asking questions during the session. It is useful to decide this before each session – often workers will take turns or, if one of you has had a tiring week or difficult day it might be easier to be the note taker that session.

Having said this, it is essential that the workers have an effective working relationship with each other. Assessments can at times be emotionally demanding, challenging and require clarity of thought. With this in mind workers need to be able to support each other, work honestly and openly with each other, and have faith in their co-workers professional competence. Co-working needs to be viewed as a partnership and without the above qualities it can become detrimental to the assessment process and get in the way of the task in hand. An example of this experienced by one of us was when our co-worker over-identified with a service user to the point of taking inaccurate records, relaying what he thought the service user would say instead of what she did say. Such over-identification can be recognised and dealt with only if there is a trusting professional relationship between co-workers.

Supervision

If we hadn't had our supervisor to discuss this with, we would have worried that we were barking up the wrong tree – especially as everyone else was disagreeing with us.

During the course of these assessments the workers are engaging in quite intensive relationships with service users. Apart from co-working, another safeguard to avoiding subjectivity is the use of supervision. An appropriate supervisor needs to be identified. The supervisor could be an experienced worker from within your own organisation, or alternatively someone who is independent of the agency. Again it is important that the workers feel able to explore their feelings and views openly with the supervisor in order to ensure a fair and well-balanced assessment is undertaken. At all times the workers must not lose sight of the power they have in the assessment process and of the fact that the decisions they make will possibly have a life-changing impact on the members of the family being assessed. Making good use of supervision is about recognising this and respecting the service user within the process.

In addition to supervision, in some circumstances it may also be important to obtain a specialist worker to act as a consultant during the assessment process. This may be necessary, for example, when the workers are not familiar with the cultural or religious background of the family being assessed.

Agreement

Having an agreement with the family always helps to make it a two-way process – in my experience most families like to have something in writing about what they are expected to do.

Once all the preparation has been completed a written agreement needs to be drawn up (with prior consideration of literacy and language issues). The purpose of this is to explain to the family the purpose, nature and content of the assessment. It will outline the timescale, venue and expectations of both workers and family. It may include requesting permission from a family to speak with other family members, GPs or other identified professionals. The agreement is an important tool in working together with families, as it clearly includes them as an integral part of the assessment process and sets out in writing what will be required.

It is important to be clear from the outset of any assessment about the issue of confidentiality. The family need to be made well aware that information discussed within the assessment will not remain confidential to the workers only. It is easy to forget to make this clear with families and we have both found ourselves in situations where the family has expressed surprise or anger that information has been shared with other agencies such as the police. Again this is about being honest and open with families about the assessment agenda.

On the other hand there is flexibility about the confidential process and families need to be assured that information will not go beyond the professional remit. An example of this is when a father shared information with us about his childhood but was anxious that his mother was not told that he had spoken about it. In situations like this we can reassure the service user that we will not be discussing their account of their history with extended family, unless they are party to care proceedings.

Process

Sometimes I can get so absorbed by the parents' own story, that I find it difficult to keep the focus on the child or children. It's at times like this that I find it important to return to the experiences the child, or previous child, might have had in the care of these parents. Maintaining a balanced perspective is crucial.

The agreement, once written, is a useful tool in facilitating the introduction of the assessment workers to the family. Again, it is important to allow enough time for the family members to consider the proposed agreement, ask any questions, and receive clarification of any of the points. The language used must be user-friendly and jargon-free. If literacy is an issue then alternative ways of enabling the family members to clearly understand the details of the agreement must be sought. This may include reading out the agreement on more than one occasion or offering a taped version of the agreement to the service user, so that they are still afforded the opportunity to take the agreement away with them to consider before signing and to show to their legal representative if they wish.

This first meeting with the family is crucial in establishing a positive working relationship. If the workers are from an organisation independent of Social Services then this can assist in establishing rapport

and trust with the family. Families being assessed are often at a point at which they feel overwhelmed by the power of Social Services and have little hope of being treated fairly. The smaller of independent organisations, such as Family Service Units, can be seen as less intimidating and therefore less threatening. There are, however, inherent tensions due to the nature of the work, often involving care proceedings and the more extreme interventions found in child protection work. Moreover, the organisation may be viewed historically as one that offers family support in order to maintain the family unit. This can create some tension if the outcome of an assessment recommends the removal of the children or no rehabilitation.

Effective use of inter-personal skills throughout the course of the assessment is essential in enabling the service users to feel valued, listened to, and respected. This should include good eye contact, active listening, and open body language. There are always opportunities to begin positively engaging with families, for example, offering a lift to the venue to a heavily pregnant mother. It is important for the workers to consider how they may come across to the family – for example language may need to be adjusted in order to be understandable and accessible. Hopefully these kinds of changes can be made within minutes of meeting the family. Be aware of the family's previous experience of social work input – for example, if a parent has had previous children removed from her care she may well have a valid degree of hostility towards social workers.

It is useful to begin the detailed assessment work by covering material which is hopefully not too threatening and factual, such as a family tree (although this can never be guaranteed – with one family we worked with, the parent became very distressed because of the isolation she felt in relation to her family). This is helpful in enabling quite a lot of information to be gathered in a diagrammatic form and can also be completed in a relaxed and informal style, such as with a worker drawing the genogram onto a large piece of paper on the floor or table.

Once a positive relationship has begun to be developed between the workers and family members, each session can focus on specific areas in relation to the domains and dimensions of the Assessment Framework.

The way information is elicited from families can make a significant difference in terms of the quality of such information. It is therefore important to make use of a variety of social work tools. The Department of Health have produced a *Family Pack of Questionnaires and Scales* (Department of Health, Cox and Bentovim, 2000) to assist in the gathering of information. Although questionnaires can only provide limited information, they are often useful in serving as a starting point with people. Often if you ask people to describe their personalities, for example, they struggle to do this. We probably would too – a questionnaire that provides examples of different personality traits (for instance City of Salford, 2000) can assist in this and can be completed in the service users' own time.

Alongside this numerous other tools exist. In the past we have used self-esteem scales, such as the one constructed by Rosenburg and others found in *Conducting Family Assessments* (City of Salford, 2000). These scales are useful as the family members can take copies away and complete them after some consideration, which is often preferable to expecting them to be completed within the time scale of the session. The scales can also provide further insight into areas that the workers may have otherwise missed. There are always questions we might forget to ask or where we may have made assumptions. An example of this we recently experienced was when a service user ticked a box saying that he was aggressive. As violence and aggression had never been an issue with this family to our knowledge and because of the service user's demeanour, we had not considered discussing this area in any depth until he highlighted it himself. There are also materials available for use with people with learning difficulties, which are a combination of pictures and questions (see McGaw et al., 1998).

Another important aspect of the assessment process is observation. This will include observing the parental relationship, parent-child and sibling relationship and interactions. Observation is a crucial and often underused skill within social work assessments, offering a different perspective on family functioning than just discussion. It also acts as a useful reminder that the assessment has the child's well being at its centre. Observation requires practice and time and the use of relevant publications to assist in

developing this skill further, such as *Learning Through Observation* (Fawcett, 1996) can be helpful. If the child is in a nursery or school, observing them in this environment can provide an excellent insight. The use of tools based on assessing attachments within relationships are helpful, such as those found in the book *Neglected Children: Issues and Dilemmas* (Stevenson, 1998b) and the siblings' checklist found in *Patterns and Outcomes in Child Placements* (HMSO, 1991), can also be helpful.

Depending on the child's age and stage of development, direct work is also an important aspect of the assessment process that can often get lost. A decision needs to be made at the outset of the assessment as to who is the best person to undertake this work. It may be felt appropriate for the family's key worker to do this rather than introducing another person into the child's life. Direct work can include non-directive or structured play. The degree to which any discussion can be of a more formal nature will depend on the age and understanding of the child. Some tools which may assist in this regard are the *All About Me* game (Barnardo's, 1991), constructing an Ecomap, using toys, art, imaginative play or games and story telling.

Analysis

So much information – how do we make sense of it?

The key purpose of any social work assessment is to identify the needs of the child and consider whether the parents have demonstrated an ability to change and move on sufficiently in order to provide 'good enough' parenting. This will be based on evidence gathered throughout the assessment.

Once the information has been gathered in as much detail as possible the task of organising this into the three domains (child's developmental needs, parental capacity and family and environmental factors) should be undertaken.

It is important that the analysis of this information is systematic, thorough and balanced. In order to facilitate this, use of a variety of theoretical perspectives and models is helpful. In our practice we have used aspects of attachment systems, cognitive-behavioural and psychodynamic theories. These have been applied by using models such as Prochaska and Di Clemente's

Comprehensive Model of Change (1982), David Howe et al's (1999) publications on attachment theory and practice and Gerrilyn Smith's (1994) model for assessing a non-abusing parent's capacity to protect.

We found the Gerrilyn Smith model extremely helpful in assessing one young mother's ability to protect. This was a particularly intensive assessment in which the parent had disclosed her own sexual abuse for the first time. Using the pointers in Smith's model as a baseline we were able to guide the content of the assessment in order to consider her responses to each area. This enabled us to make clear judgements about the parent's ability to protect without becoming too enmeshed in their own emotional needs.

The use of theoretical perspectives and models can also assist the workers in being more objective in their analysis, helping to safeguard against personal bias. Moreover, it is also useful in keeping the assessment focused and offering a structure in which the information can be measured.

Within any family there will be both strengths and difficulties. It is our job, within social work assessments, to make informed judgements about these factors. Within child protection work there has often been a tendency to focus on the difficulties a family has in caring for their child whilst minimising any strengths that may exist. It is important, particularly to avoid alienating the family, that these strengths are recognised and acknowledged. Strengths can be found in any family. If a parent has been able to ensure that their child has had enough food to eat, toys to play with, or a clean environment, these are all positive factors in their parenting abilities. At times it has been important to look at parenting practices in the context of how the parents were parented. An example of this was an assessment we undertook in which the family home was dirty, with ashtrays overflowing onto all surfaces and the floor, and bags and bags of rubbish were left festering in the kitchen. Although their home was not in an acceptable condition for a child to live in, when looking at the parents' own histories we found that they had lived in far worse squalor with dog and cat faeces spread everywhere and no carpets, meagre furnishings and rats living in their furniture. In this context these parents felt they had made vast improvements in maintaining a home and they clearly had. It is the

recognition and acknowledgement of these factors that ensure the assessors maintain a positive relationship with the family.

When making final decisions about parental abilities, one of the key indicators for a positive outcome will be the parents own understanding and acceptance of the expressed concerns, coupled with a willingness and ability to change. Tony Morrison has adapted Prochaska and Di Clemente's *Comprehensive Model of Change* for use in assessing the level of motivation to change. We have found this useful in many different circumstances. In completing an assessment of a woman whose previous child had died, we found this model extremely helpful in not only assessing her level of motivation to change, but also keeping the strong emotions we had about the circumstances of the child's death in perspective. We have also used this model in assessing families in which one of the parents has committed sexual offences against children. Although a perpetrator may be required to undergo a specialist assessment in relation to their offences, their offending behaviour will inevitably need to be addressed within a social work assessment as well. In one example the perpetrator refused to discuss his offences at all and laid the blame on his young age at the time. His refusal to engage with workers on this matter or to see it as in any way posing a problem would place him at the stage of pre-contemplation on the Model of Change. This is then useful to refer to when making any decisions or recommendations.

The use of supervision or consultancy is critical at this stage. It provides an opportunity for the workers to have space to reflect on the information and to discuss, with an impartial colleague, the intricacies of the assessment. The supervisor can assist the workers in considering each of the relevant factors in terms of the risks involved, using the concept of significant harm as a baseline, and assessing the likelihood of change.

Sometimes, making the final analysis can be extremely difficult and the balancing of strengths and difficulties very challenging. Being conscious of the power inherent in any recommendations made should make the worker even more cautious about their decision. In one assessment we conducted, the issues were so finally balanced that we were having to consider whether a parent should have the care of one child or all her children, and if one child, which one? These decisions often occur during the time the assessment report is being written. The impact of deadlines ensures a sharp focus on the outcome/report. This is a time when all the paperwork and note taking is brought together.

Possible Outcomes

It was so sad, leaving the mother with bad news, knowing we would not be likely to see her again, except in court, and having opened up so many old wounds.

An assessment can produce a broad range of outcomes, from no further intervention required to permanent separation of the child from their parents. Having said this, the outcome of an assessment may not be as conclusive as this, and may recommend further pieces of work to be undertaken, such as offering support services, therapeutic work, more specialist assessments or respite care. Alternatively it may be suggested that extended family members are considered suitable to provide a permanent home for the child.

Whatever the outcome of the assessment, it is likely that the assessment workers will no longer be involved with the family. Disengaging from the family can be difficult for both workers and family members. The assessment process is, by its very nature, an intimate experience. Often it will be the family's first opportunity to talk about their own experiences to someone who is attentive and demonstrating concern. As such the process can be somewhat cathartic. It is important therefore that the workers remain sensitive to the possibility that issues raised within the assessment may well have unearthed hitherto well-buried feelings and memories for parents. The workers need to be conscious of the fact that they are not therapists and are not there for the purpose of helping parents work through issues or to problem-solve. When conducting an assessment our role is not as that of the family social workers and this can often lead to an internal struggle for workers whose role in other cases might be to become involved in other aspects of the family's needs.

Conclusion

In ending the assessment workers' involvement with the family, the family may well miss the regular opportunity they have had to talk. This needs to be acknowledged with the family and handled with sensitivity. It may be appropriate to suggest alternative agencies for the family to refer themselves to if certain issues have arisen, for example After Adoption Services. It is also important for the workers to have a final assessment supervision in which they are able to openly acknowledge any feelings the assessment outcome may have left them with. We have at times grown to like a family, but still had to make a decision that their children do not remain with them. It is important to use each other and the supervision process to own and deal with these ambivalent feelings before moving on.

Appendix 1

Framework for the Assessment of Children in Need and their Families. Department of Health, 2000: p19-23.

Dimensions of a Child's Developmental Needs

Health

Includes growth and development as well as physical and mental well-being. The impact of genetic factors and of any impairment should be considered. Involves receiving appropriate health care when ill, an adequate and nutritious diet, exercise, immunisations where appropriate and developmental checks, dental and optical care and, for older children, appropriate advice and information on issues that have an impact on health, including sex education and substance misuse.

Education

Covers all areas of a child's cognitive development which begins from birth. Includes opportunities: for play and interaction with other children; to have access to books; to acquire a range of skills and interests; to experience success and achievement. Involves an adult interested in educational activities, progress and achievements, who takes account of the child's starting point and any special educational needs.

Emotional and behavioural development

Concerns the appropriateness of response demonstrated in feelings and actions by a child, initially to parents and caregivers and, as the child grows older, to others beyond the family. Includes nature and quality of early attachments, characteristics of temperament, adaptation to change, response to stress and degree of appropriate self-control.

Identity

Concerns the child's growing sense of self as a separate and valued person. Includes the child's view of self and abilities, self-image and self-esteem, and having a positive sense of individuality. Race, religion, age, gender, sexuality and disability may all contribute to this. Feelings of belonging and acceptance by family, peer group and wider society, including other cultural groups.

Family and social relationships

Development of empathy and the capacity to place self in someone else's shoes. Includes a stable and affectionate relationship with parents and caregivers, good relationships with siblings, increasing importance of age appropriate friendships with peers and other significant persons in the child's life and response of family to these relationships.

Social presentation

Concerns child's growing understanding of the way in which appearance, behaviour, and any impairment are perceived by the outside world and the impression being created. Includes appropriateness of dress for age, gender, culture and religion; cleanliness and personal hygiene; and availability of advice from parents or caregivers about presentation in different settings.

Self-care skills

Concerns the acquisition by a child of practical, emotional and communication competencies required for increasing independence. Includes early practical skills of dressing and feeding, opportunities to gain confidence and practical skills to undertake activities away from the family and independent living skills as older children. Includes encouragement to acquire social problem solving approaches. Special attention should be given to the impact of a child's impairment and other vulnerabilities, and on social circumstances affecting these and the development of self-care skills

Dimensions of Parenting Capacity

Basic care

Providing for the child's physical needs, and appropriate medical and dental care. Includes provision of food, drink, warmth, shelter, clean and appropriate clothing and adequate personal hygiene.

Ensuring safety

Ensuring the child is adequately protected from harm or danger. Includes protection from significant harm or danger, and from contact with unsafe adults or other children and from self-harm. Recognition of hazards and dangers both in the home and elsewhere.

Emotional warmth

Ensuring the child's emotional needs are met and giving a child a sense of being specially valued and a positive sense of own racial and cultural identity. Includes ensuring the child's requirements for secure, stable, and affectionate relationships with significant adults, with appropriate sensitivity and responsiveness to the child's needs. Appropriate physical contact, comfort and cuddling sufficient to demonstrate warm regard, praise and encouragement.

Stimulation

Promoting child's learning and intellectual development through encouragement and cognitive stimulation and promoting social opportunities. Includes facilitating the child's cognitive development and potential through interaction, communication, talking and responding to the child's language and questions, encouraging and joining the child's, and promoting educational opportunities. Enabling the child to experience success and ensuring school attendance or equivalent opportunity. Facilitating child to meet challenges of life.

Guidance and boundaries

Enabling the child to regulate their own emotions and behaviour. The key parental tasks are demonstrating and modelling appropriate behaviour and control of emotions and interactions with others, and guidance which involves setting boundaries, so that the child is able to develop an internal model of moral values and conscience, and social behaviour appropriate for the society with which they will grow up. The aim is to enable the child to grow into an autonomous adult, holding their own values, and able to demonstrate appropriate behaviour with others rather than having to be dependent on rules outside themselves. This includes not over-protecting children from exploratory and learning experiences. Includes social problem solving, anger management, consideration for others and effective discipline and shaping of behaviour.

Stability

Providing a sufficient stable family environment to enable a child to develop and maintain a secure attachment to the primary caregivers in order to ensure optimal development. Includes: ensuring secure attachments are not disrupted, providing consistency of emotional warmth over time and responding in a similar manner to the same behaviour. Parental responses change and develop according to child's developmental progress. In addition, ensuring children keep in contact with important family members and significant others.

Family and Environmental Factors
Family history and functioning

Family history includes both genetic and psycho-social factors. Family functioning is influenced by who is living in the household and how they are related to the child; significant changes in family/household composition; history childhood experiences of parents; chronology of significant life events and their meaning to family members; nature of family functioning, including sibling relationships and its impact on the child; parental strengths and difficulties, including those of an absent parent; the relationship between separated parents.

Wider family

Who are considered to be members of the wider family by the child and the parents? Includes related and non-related persons and absent wider family. What is their role and importance to the child and parents and in precisely what way?

Housing

Does the accommodation have basic amenities and facilities appropriate to the age and development of the child and other resident members? Is the housing accessible and suitable to the needs of disabled family members? Includes the interior and exterior of the accommodation's immediate surroundings. Basic amenities include water, heating, sanitation, cooking facilities, sleeping arrangements and cleanliness, hygiene and safety and their impact on the child's upbringing.

Employment

Who is working in the household, their pattern of work and any changes? What impact does this have on the child? How is work or absence of work viewed by family members? How does it affect their relationship with the child? Includes children's experience of work and its impact on them.

Income

Income available over a sustained period of time. Is the family in receipt of all its benefit entitlements? Sufficiency of income to meet the family's needs. The way resources available to the family are used. Are there financial difficulties which affect the child?

Family's social integration

Exploration of the wider context of the local neighbourhood and community and its impact on the child and parents. Includes the degree of the family's integration or isolation, their peer groups, friendship and social networks and the importance attached to them.

Community resources

Describes all facilities and services in a neighbourhood, including universal services of primary health care, day care and schools, places of worship, transport, shops and leisure activities. Includes availability, accessibility and standard of resources and impact on the family, including disabled members.

16 Working With Children Whose Parent or Carer Has Died

Warwick Turnbull

Children who have experienced bereavement have very specific needs. Often, the family grief can cause those needs to be lost. This chapter demonstrates how valuable support for bereaved children can be – not just for the child but also for the wider family.

Introduction

The death of the carer of a child is unlike many of the other issues we face in family work. Usually it happens not because of harmful intention or neglect where we may blame a perpetrator or because of inequality and injustice where we may blame society. Most often it comes in an arbitrary way: it is bad luck that the victim was driving on that night or that their body chemistry devised a cocktail leading to the growth of a tumour. We would always try to treat medically and psychologically the child who suffers physical abuse, or provide welfare benefits for the family of a child who would otherwise be hungry. Yet we so often just hope for the best in the case of bereaved children or those we expect to be bereaved.

The evidence suggests, however, that we cannot afford to ignore the matter. Black in Parkes et al. (1998) shows that psychiatric disorder can be five times more likely amongst bereaved children. She concludes that children are less likely to become mentally ill if they are prepared for a parent's death or have opportunities afterwards to share their grief with others. Worden's research (2002) indicates the importance of children having clear information so that they understand they cannot catch cancer and they are not responsible for their parent's illness. He demonstrates that one third of bereaved children experience serious emotional and behavioural difficulties within two years. Sheldon (1998) indicates that the risk of a poor bereavement outcome is increased if the death is unexpected or the deceased person is young.

Help so often means affirming the strengths that we find in families facing bereavement. A relatively small amount of assistance can often provide a catalyst. The parents in one large family had already explained to the children that their mother, Sharon, would die from her illness. They had many memories to share such as how they met and the mischief in which the mother was involved as a child. With support they met to record these essentials of their history, completing it while Sharon was well enough to fully participate. Barnes and her colleagues (2000) show that it is too huge a task for many mothers to talk to their children about their breast cancer at the time when they themselves are coming to terms with the disease. Few are offered help and many would like it. For some, having the one-to-one opportunity to address their own loss of themselves, their partners and their children is enough to enable them to embark on preparing the children for bereavement. Hence, sometimes those of us working in family bereavement do not need to meet the children in some of the families.

Silverman (2000) notes some of the contemporary features of our society that can make it more difficult for families facing loss. What she calls the culture of individualism can increase the likelihood that adults will interpret passive behaviour in a child as indicating that all is well, whereas they may seek help in correcting overt behaviour problems. The child can be construed as the problem when, in fact, the problem is the tragic loss that the whole family is enduring. An approach that capitalises on the intrinsic benefits that the family already brings to the child reinforces collective responsibility. For example, ten-year-old Alan's surviving carers became concerned by his mood swings and requested that he be seen individually. During a therapeutic session in which he addressed some of his fears, Alan identified how the women and men in his life offered him different forms of support. He could then let a relative know this so that she could tell the rest of the family. In this way he contributed to adjustments that the whole family was making. Sometimes there is more disparity between the individual child and the carers. Far from accommodating each other's grieving, some hide their own grief so as not to add to the pain faced by themselves or others. In such cases, family group work can help people to understand such superficially callous reactions and to improve communication. Alternatively, through individual work, a child can be helped to grieve more effectively.

Sometimes features that promote good grief are inherent in the family's culture. Children from Muslim families have told me of the sense of purpose they find in offering regular prayers at a graveside, not only for their own parent who has died but also for the occupant of every grave in the cemetery. Some such children have presented with an already learned conviction that grieving is an essential and healing part of their lives. For other children, making meaning from their unwanted situation is more of a do-it-yourself exercise. Alan found his own way of connecting with his mother who had died. He expressed his helplessness at having been unable to save her and then attached himself to her in his dreams and drawings as the fun-loving centre of his family with whom he could continue to have a different kind of relationship. Others have found techniques such as writing letters to the deceased or talking to them as if they were sitting in an empty chair to be good ways of connecting. The theoretical and research-based rationale for supporting children in finding new meanings and in 'reconstructing' their lost parents can be found by reading Nadeau and Silverman whose works are mentioned in the bibliography. When bereaved children are invited to draw an 'ecomap' of their network most of them, unprompted, seem to include the dead person very close to themselves. Some children may be facing a changed family because the illness or death may have caused distant relatives to become more involved or, conversely, closed down contacts with one side of the family.

By drawing an ecomap a child can reflect on the support available in their social network. The child writes their own name in the centre and surrounds it with the names of significant people from the family, peer group and school. Those individuals who are most significant are placed closest to the child. Some children find concentric circles useful for defining categories of attachment.

The work involving Sharon, her partner and children coming together to recall old stories from their history not only created a memory bank but also enabled the family to celebrate itself. Family group work can also provide a setting for showing what is possible in everyday life: children being listened to, sharing of information about the illness, the validity of distraction to relieve stress, family members being able to consider what attributes they hold in common. There are constraints: children often want to 'do', whereas adults may want to talk; families have their 'pecking orders' and hierarchies that may be threatened by the structure of a session promoting equality; the parent who is ill may have limited mobility or energy-level. However, we can work in ways that offer children choices and give them control at a time when bereavement is denying them ultimate choice. In doing so we can help to restore some of the self-esteem that went as a result of the prospect of the loss of a parent or carer. Sessions facilitated jointly by workers of different genders and professional backgrounds can widen the possibilities of family group work.

Meetings between the worker and brothers and sisters can provide opportunities for children to acknowledge and develop ways of supporting each other in a common crisis. In time it may feel right to offer separate sessions so that work appropriate to the needs, developmental level and personality of each sibling can take place. It is often in one-to-one settings that young people can feel safe enough to broach their most serious issues. All of the following are real examples: 'Am I to blame for the illness by bringing on that pain when she was bouncing me on her knee?', 'Will I get cancer from my Mum?', 'How can I talk about how I feel when I will upset my Dad?', 'Isn't there more treatment to save her life?', 'I can't stand the way my brother is behaving but I feel I'm supposed to be nice to everyone at home', 'I want to go away to university eventually but how can I leave the family?', 'I'm gay but I feel compelled to keep quiet about it – especially now', 'I don't want to worry them about the bullying'.

Kurtz and Ketcham (1992: p89) claim that 'Only in telling another the truth about ourselves do we discover the truth about ourselves. We can 'tell' only what we know, but we come to 'know' only in the telling'. In recounting significant events through talking, play and drawing, children and young people both acknowledge what has happened and discover new things about themselves. They become their own audience. Ball (1998) says that the medium of drawing allows children to frame and distance potentially overwhelming experiences. Alan, who was mentioned earlier, expressed the irrevocable nature of death as he drew his family at his mother's bedside. In doing so he confronted his own desolation that this had occurred and his sense of solidarity with those who had been with him. He seemed to find proof of her value in talking about the large number of people who attended her funeral and the distances some of them had travelled. Silverman (2000) suggests that by exploring changes in this way children are making new meanings to their lives.

Silverman describes meaning making as 'arising out of the interaction between the child's developmental stage, the events in which the child is participant, and the behaviour of those around him or her' (2000: p43). As workers we are required to establish a safe setting and empathic responses. We may have our own questions about motivation and about interpreting what the child is doing or saying, but our role is not to impose our insights on the child. Instead we should create a climate whereby the child can find their own meanings. Of course, we should not necessarily expect them to articulate those meanings. Seven years later Alan may be able to abstract from his reflections a summary of his position along the lines of, 'I experience isolation by the loss of the person with whom I have had the closest attachment. However, I can value her and I know that my family are there for me as we share our grief together.' At the age of ten he can only live his life with that meaning, which is what counts.

Many of us have been inclined to treat a child's grief rather like an illness from which, given the right treatment, the child would 'recover' and start to live 'normally' again. However, recent research is making us think again. In her study of bereaved children living in Massachusetts, Silverman (2000) found that most children did not experience an emotional detachment from the deceased. Instead the children reported that they identified a special place to remember the dead person, that they kept up contact through dreams, felt watched over, sensed their presence and talked to them. Similarly, Tonkin's research with adults in New Zealand (1996) found that subjects did not report a diminishing of grief, but felt instead that their grief

remained, as it were, the same size, whilst they grew round it. The implications are that what we can expect from a good grief process is that a child will retain an attachment and, with maturity, develop a deeper understanding of the person who has died, just as they will develop deeper understandings of significant people who remain alive. The process will equip them for future crises. Encouraging children to find their own ways of connecting with the deceased may be a healthier approach than providing metaphors to 'soften the blow'. Often adults will explain death to a child by describing the dead person as having a new state of being as a star or an angel. Such analogies can alarm children because they imply that, although they cannot see the deceased in a recognisable form, the deceased can see them just as they are.

An excellent cartoon video called *Grief in the Family* (Leeds Animation Workshop, 2002) illustrates grieving children's need for distraction by showing a girl carrying a box, representing the range of feelings that comprise her grief, which she puts down before performing a cartwheel and then picking up the box again. Children achieve a sense of balance in their lives by finding things that are constant and familiar at times when it feels like their world has fallen apart. The distraction may take the form of a television programme, a conversation or an activity. It may only last for a few minutes or less, but it serves the purpose of reassuring the child that some things remain constant at a time of otherwise swamping change. Carers can assist in this process by retaining some of the constants in the child's life such as the expectation that the child will fulfil everyday responsibilities. Workers can keep to familiar routines by good time keeping and promote continuity by remembering minor details from a previous session which they may recall at the next.

The 'box of grief' that is being carried may include a wide range of feelings: shock, anger, despair, isolation, anxiety and relief. Physical symptoms may be experienced. The child's mind and body could be reacting to the fear that not only this source of love has been lost but also love itself, struggling to make real something that up until now has been unthinkable. Anger may arise from a sense of injustice: 'why has this loss happened to me when some of the nastiest kids at school have healthy parents?' for example. Anxiety may be directed at the surviving parent who is suddenly seen as mortal and more vulnerable, even to the point of needing to be kept constantly close. Efforts made by the child to preserve an even keel at home by being especially good may not be sustainable at school. Relief may come because the stress in the family resulting from a long or difficult illness has gone or, in some cases, because a perpetrator of abuse has died. However, the relief is likely to be mixed with other conflicting emotions. The overwhelming nature of some of these feelings can produce reactions belonging to an earlier phase in the child's development, before they had learned to reason: this is fitting because what has happened defies reason. I remember a nurse explaining to the twelve-year-old daughter of a patient who was near to death how her mother's cancer had spread. The girl sunk her head into her carer's lap and proceeded to speak in a cross baby voice using baby language. We told her that her behaviour showed us how angry and sad she felt and we validated those feelings. In instances of regression like this the child is behaving normally. Regressive behaviour should not be interpreted as a problem that must be cured. The problem is the bereavement: regressive behaviour is one of several normal reactions to it.

Funerals are important to people of all ages because they help us to acknowledge that someone has died, assist us in the early stages of grief, allow us to affirm the person and help us mark the death according to our own religion or philosophy. Children are no exceptions. They too need the opportunity to say goodbye and receive support. However, many children will not know what to expect from a funeral and may need to be aware of what will happen and that people attending will express a range of emotions in tears or solemnity or laughter. A child might join in the planning of the funeral or make a contribution to the proceedings. Children have shorter time spans for expressing feelings, so they may change from grief to play or other distractions during the proceedings. It helps if adults do not regard such behaviour as disrespectful, but rather as a child's way of coming through. Making the free choice of seeing and perhaps touching the body alongside a supportive adult can be a significant way of a child understanding the change from life to death and making a parting.

Practical Work

We will now consider a range of activities and approaches that may be of use in helping children and sometimes their carers. I would rarely use them in direct work with pre-school children. In such cases the focus is more often on helping the carer to assist the child. Older teenagers may prefer a talking and listening approach to some of the methods involving play. In thinking about 5-15s we are dealing with a large age span and very different levels of development. Younger children in this age range may only just be grasping the idea that death is for all and is permanent. They may need repeated explanations that the dead person will not return. Older children may be developing their own philosophies influenced by the experience of loss and may gain confidence in exploring possible ways in which they can help themselves. However, the principles remain the same:

- Children will share and trust if they feel safe and if they can exercise choice and have some control.
- Because of some of the constraints in families, schools and peer groups children may need opportunities to express feelings knowing that they will be accepted.
- Children may need information to make sense of change and support in reaching their own solutions.
- Distractions from serious issues provide relief and balance.
- Remembering a significant person in the child's past can help the child to retain attachments and can validate both the child and the deceased.

Getting Started

Who is this 'helping person' whom the child is meeting for the first time? There may be similarities with other helpers in the child's life, but this person is not one of the more familiar people such as a teacher or a doctor or a relative or a friend. Therefore commitment is needed to acclimatising to the new relationship and to exploring some of its possibilities. Ground rules, devised and agreed by all participants, can help clarify expectations. I always establish how long sessions will last (usually an hour) and explain that our work is confidential. The exception is if I learn that someone may be harmed, then we will need to decide about involving others to prevent the harm. Some children seem to welcome a plan for a first session with an indication as to how long each part might take. Within the first two sessions we decide how many more sessions there will be and at what intervals.

Self-disclosure and Ritual

Early on I may introduce a game in which we take turns to pull phrases out of a hat such as 'favourite music' and 'worst food'. This gives us opportunities to talk about some of the best and worst things in our lives. An alternative and more zany game (thought 'too daft' by some children) is where the worker takes a collection of hats, invites the child to add household hats and then child, worker and any others present choose and wear a particular hat for a while after saying why they have chosen it. That game signals that permission giving, listening; choice by the child and valid distraction will be on the agenda in future sessions. Another game which facilitates safe self-disclosure is' When the big wind blows' which is suitable for family group work. At least three (but preferably more) people sit in a circle. One other stands in the middle and says 'The big wind blows on anyone who...' To complete the sentence the player adds something about her, e.g. is wearing green, likes crisps, and sometimes has sad dreams. Any of the other players to whom the statement applies must move to another seat. Meanwhile the middle player tries to find a seat, leaving another occupying the middle, who says, 'The big wind...' At any point the middle player can simply say, 'Hurricane!' In that case all the players have to move. Participants can take minimal risks (items of clothing) or bigger ones (owned emotions). The players themselves have that control. Children sometimes use it to raise a significant matter that can be taken up later, but its important to keep the game flowing and not to interrupt for discussion.

Learning about children's support networks by the use of ecomaps or family trees in the early stages helps the worker to have a broad picture of the family history and current context and allows the child to take stock of their supports.

As we support children and their families through loss and change, we need to be sensitive to the 'little losses and partings' in our work. The affirmation pyramid game has worked well in some family group work. Participants stand in a circle close together. One person puts their hand out at arms length and says something affirmative about the person on their left. Another does the same, placing their hand on top of the first player's hand. This goes on until all have had their turn. Then the pyramid of hands moves about according to the will of the group, up and down and from side to side until it finally comes to rest on the floor. As a tension release some of us will sometimes leap into the air, Jack-in-the-box fashion, and shout at that point. The affirmation, physical contact and pyramid gyration in this game all seem to help bond group members. Grief is often lonely, but this game says that we are not alone. Some families have chosen to use this game regularly at the end of their sessions, so it has become a ritual. Alternatives to affirming the person next to you are to say something positive about yourself or about what has been good for you about the session.

Affirming Feelings

All of the above activities provide opportunities for children to disclose information about themselves. The next section looks at strategies to help children face their feelings and have them affirmed. As many children in this age range are at a stage of development when they are more familiar with expressing themselves through material things rather than abstract ideas, objects are used as tactile and visual stimuli. In the first activity of this type, family members and facilitators bring different sorts of stones to the session. Some are rough, some unattractive, others smooth to touch, others shiny gem stones, others have interesting markings. The stones are pooled and are used to describe recent experiences, such as the best thing that happened during the week or something which has been uncomfortable recently. In group work, the focus of the listeners on an object can be especially helpful to children who get embarrassed when they feel that all eyes are on them.

The next activity normalises and validates anger. The facilitator provides clay and a large board. Participants make a list of people and things that they feel angry about (e.g. cancer, my mum, hospitals). They then throw clay at a board, shouting out the source of the anger at the point of throwing. When all the throwing is completed the clay is used to make symbolic objects, which gives a hopeful second half to the activity, making the point that the energy which anger gives us can be turned to good use. In this exercise as in most others it is important that adults are not bystanders. If they are present they (workers included) should join in rather than spectate. If anyone prefers not to participate they should perhaps be doing something else rather than watching an emotionally charged activity so as not to inhibit others. The objects which are made do not have to be fired, though of course, like some of our real hopes, they can be quite fragile if they are not.

When I have used masks it has usually been at the request of the children themselves. In one session they make the mask, often depicting a fearful character and then in a subsequent session the mask is worn to make an improvised play. Very often this play has had a first half of terror, wrongdoing or death and a second half in which things are made better. We too join in the plays as directed by the children. Other routes into role-play are through the use of puppets or playmobile characters. Children can use these objects to carry their feelings and wishes in their own stories which often depict efforts to prevent disaster happening. In some cases the story has been enacted several times before ultimately reaching a tragic ending. This playing with happy and sad conclusions reflects the reality of the child's situation: a dreaded outcome has happened or is expected to happen despite people's best endeavours. However, in the process of dealing with the situation people can learn new strengths and find new meanings. We let the masks and plays speak for themselves rather than attempt interpretation. If, like me, you start to feel out of your depth in the midst of the strong emotions which can be generated by such activities, try remembering back to the vividness of your own imaginative play in childhood. Remind yourself that play often has connections with reality and that your job is not to analyse but to facilitate play and believe in its healing properties.

Making Sense of Events

Playmobile people in a toy hospital setting can also be useful for explaining treatment and de-mystifying what is involved in being in hospital. Sometimes a child will develop a session that began as information giving to explore fears. Often they need to express their own understanding of the disease and treatment. Some of this may come as a surprise to the parent and some of it may be unlike a medical explanation. Perhaps what matters most is that the child is making sense of what is happening. Some children will require logical descriptions. For this, three dimensional anatomy books for children can be used to show what treatment does or how the development of the disease has changed. I often find co-work helpful here because sometimes I can ask naïve questions and a nurse or doctor (as well as the family) can respond. *My book about...* produced by St Christopher's Hospice is a workbook for younger children to complete at a time when they are learning more about the life-limiting illness. As well as pages devoted to the illness there are sections which enable children to look at their supports and at what they can do to help.

Finding Solutions

Asking a child to list those factors in life which are currently hurtful and those which are helping can be a useful way of acknowledging what is difficult and indicating the solutions which already exist. The 'hurts' and 'helps' can feature as prompts in a snakes and ladders game, precipitating changes of fortune. As well as providing a distraction, the game can give an opportunity for hurts and helps to be revisited and for emphasising that sometimes changes occur beyond our responsibility – or, as it were, on the throw of a dice. Sometimes children have used drawing to depict themselves in the middle of a maze. We have identified the things in their lives that prevent them from moving on and the considered strategies for dealing with each one. Using post-it stickers with a 'problem' on each, the child has identified changes in the significance of each problem session by session. Problems emerging are not always related to illness and loss, indicating that the individual session with the worker may sometimes be the only opportunity a child has to solve other matters when the household is preoccupied with grief. If older children appear swamped by problems they can be asked to imagine themselves as over eighty years old looking back on their lives. They may then develop a wider perspective, recognising the potential that remains in their lives and examining what they will need to plan to do in order to achieve it.

Remembering

Writing a poem about a bus worker with kidney disease, Roger McGough has the man asking himself if the sky was ever as blue. In his famous last television interview shortly before he died Dennis Potter spoke of seeing 'the blossomiest blossom' that ever was. Helping children and their carers to construct memory boxes is a way of catching similar precious elements in the relationship. In sessions with children happening soon after the death of a parent I sometimes ask them to bring me a meaningful object associated with that person. Usually that object has been something which has been frequently held by the parent, as if the aura has been deeply imprinted and still remains. Perhaps such objects do not belong in boxes like corpses but deserve to hang around and continue to be used. In writing memory books children can record particular special features about the person, details of their funeral and specific memories. This work can enable children to remember the person in a rounded way, defying 'beatifications' which sometimes happens when parents die young. Memory boxes and books can be begun with child and parent before the death. Both Barnardo's and Winston's Wish (details at the end) provide very helpful resources for such work. Some children enjoy making candles to light in remembrance. Simple kits of wicks and coloured wax can be obtained. The wax can be moulded to represent significant objects.

Groupwork

Groupwork for bereaved children from different families can be aimed at helping children feel less isolated and stigmatised. Like other approaches it can improve self-esteem and demonstrate the validity of fun and distraction. Christ's research (2000) suggests that 9-11 year-old boys may be less likely than girls of that age to express sad and depressed feelings. Facilitators may feel that single gender groups for such children are warranted as girls and boys may feel more comfortable with gender-specific modes of interacting. Groups specifically for children bereaved of mothers and for those bereaved of fathers may also be indicated. When we have organised such groups we have found that children have been more able to explore similarities and differences both in terms of their parents' characteristics and in terms of the loss that they have experienced than when the groups have comprised some children bereaved of mothers and some of fathers. However, these factors may be outweighed by practical considerations made when forming groups such as the numbers of children available. Some families have received most help by being put in touch with other bereaved families. Carers have sometimes reported that understanding is greatest when it comes to those who have experienced similar loss and confronted similar issues in the care of children.

Many of us who work with family bereavement have ourselves experienced the death of significant people. McMillan (1997), proposes that our own experience may enhance empathy if we can use it as part of our general understanding of loss. It may bring to us an enthusiasm for the rights of bereaved people to construct their own new meanings, make their own choices and keep the attachments which make them whole when others may expect them to have 'got over it'. Like the researchers and practitioners cited here we also need to be prepared for the families with whom we work to be our teachers. If we can bring good intention to our work we will be forgiven our mistakes. As those of us who have watched recordings of their own practice can testify, those who use our services may continue to accept our sometimes-unskilled efforts so long as they trust our intentions. Finally, we need boldness because, as we have seen, strong feelings are frightening. It can be helpful to remember that to sense being alongside someone in a dark cellar is a privilege and that just because there is no light at that moment does not mean that all light is forever inaccessible.

Useful Resources

Barnardo's (tel. 01268 520224) for a game called *All about me*, useful for early self-disclosure and for memory books and memory boxes as well as information booklets.

Cancerlink (tel. 020 7833 2818) for a booklet to give to carers called *Talking to children when an adult has cancer.*

Child Bereavement Trust (www.childbereavement.org.uk) for information for workers and carers including booklets and videos based on evidence from families.

Leeds Animation Workshop
(www.leedsanimation.demon.co.uk) for *Grief in the Family* a video film for use with families.

St Christopher's Hospice, Department of Social Work, 51-59 Lawrie Park Road, Sydenham, SE26 6DZ for *My book about...*

Winston's Wish (ww.winstonswish.org.uk) for services for families facing bereavement and training for workers.

Part Three

Resources for Working
in Family Support

Using Information in Family Support
Mike Sells

Introduction

Service provision for supporting individuals and families continues to develop and diversify and is probably more varied now than ever before. Getting to grips with the array of local statutory, voluntary and private sector's provision as they evolve, re-organise, find and lose lottery and other grants can be a difficult and time-consuming task for staff and professionals from any organisation.

For the potential service user, with a problem to solve, most of the kaleidoscopic changes of re-organisations are of little interest. But that little chink of colour near the edge of the changing pattern – the Health Visitor's New Mums Group on the local estate, or whatever – may perhaps be just the extra boost that the family needed to nudge them through a really difficult time. It might enable the mother to cope a little better when all might have been lost. But how difficult is it for the family to find out what is available?

Knowing what is there and getting the right information at the time its needed, in the right format, can be desperately important – enabling the worker to survey what is there and select a possible service, or empowering the service user directly to find their own support.

This chapter is about how people get to find out about what services may be available in any one area and how we, as workers, also go about locating those essential guides and directories. It includes a very practical section on how to approach the task of creating an information resource from scratch if it is found that there is no existing resource.

The chapter is in four sections:

1. How people get the information they need.
2. How to get all the (local) information you as a worker need.
3. Creating an information resource.
4. Case studies.

How People Get the Information They Need

I wish I'd known that before.

Verbal information from friends and family

Studies have shown that many people prefer to get the information they need by simply talking to people they already know. Verbal information, often passed on from friends or family is therefore very important, and often the preferred, way to receive information (Frost, 2001).

However, there may well be circumstances where this is either impossible, or far from ideal, and there may be difficulties with verbal information passed on in this way:

● Individuals may need specialist support which their friends or everyday contacts may be unlikely to know about. (e.g. mental health carers support group) or they find it difficult to talk about (e.g. counselling following sexual abuse).

● The verbal version may be coloured by the perceptions of the friend passing it on, incomplete or inaccurate.

● After information has been passed on by talking to a helpful friend, there may be a variety of reasons why the individual may find it difficult to accept: 'It's not for people like me', 'I wouldn't fit in' or 'I'm past all that stuff'.

● Verbal information can be easily forgotten and it may not be easy to go back and ask the person again.

● There may be real or perceived practical problems in accessing information, such as problems with child care, finance, getting to the place where the information is located and so on.

Hence, although verbal information from friends and existing contacts may be ideal in some ways it may be ineffective in terms of actually getting the individual to the service they may need.

Verbal information via staff or workers

It may be possible to improve the situation if a skilled worker, armed with all the correct information, is the one communicating it. The worker may be able to correct misunderstandings, re-interpret the person's situation so as to allow the 'fit' to look better, or simply persuade them to give it try. The worker may be able to suggest solutions for, or directly help with, any apparent practical problems of finance, transport or child care, for example.

Written information – printed or through electronic or web media

Individuals may be able to search out their own support by looking through appropriate listings – such as in directories and leaflets. Information from written sources accessed directly by the service user concerned has some advantages:

- It should be accurate and complete.
- It can be read at any time – and re-read later.
- It is private and need not involve anyone else knowing about it.
- The individual can make their own independent selection.

  However, there are disadvantages:

- It may be difficult to find the material at the exact time it is needed.
- The format may make it difficult to use, for example, they may not have the required literacy levels, or

it may not be in their first language of the person. Sometimes they may not have the means or the necessary skills to access electronic media.

- The information may not be orientated towards the needs of a particular individual.

Where information from written sources is accessed by the worker – for example, when a worker looks through a booklet or uses a web reference and passes the copy or print out to the service user – many of the details may well have changed or be out of date There is also clearly less independence as the worker has done the work of locating, selecting and maybe 'selling' the idea to the person. The worker interprets the information and can effectively control the situation – if they make a good selection that may be useful – but they may not be so accurate. The person may be able to reject the suggestions or advice but may simply accept it and may learn additional dependent behaviour into the bargain.

Working together

In practice the person may be involved with the worker in considering other possible services. The degree of guidance involved will relate to how much independence the worker gives or the person takes. It may be a first step for a service user to select what sort of support they need. Although the ideal may be to get towards independence for the user, many families need support and involvement and it is necessary to work at lower levels, in the beginning at least. The diagram illustrates the point:

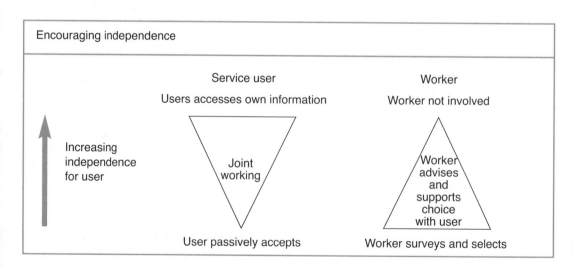

However this dilemma is resolved for each situation, we still need to obtain the set of information, to enable the family, or the worker to use it.

How to Get All the (Local) Information You Need – the Worker's Perspective

As a worker involved in supporting a family you are likely to be in a much stronger position to be effective if you have a good knowledge of as many as possible of the organisations and services existing around that area of need. If the situation changes or if your understanding of the situation alters you may be able to consider involving another organisation or recommend or refer the family or individual somewhere, perhaps to carry out some joint work. You may be able to suggest a useful direction for the family to look at, pass on an appropriate collection of information to them and leave them to make the next move.

In this section it is assumed that you have recently taken up a new post, perhaps in an area you are not entirely familiar with. If this is not the case you may like to use this as a checklist of places and people to check whether they have anything to help you locate useful sources of information.

Your own organisation

Colleagues in your own organisation may already have a good knowledge together with staff from other agencies. This has to be the first priority and if they are not able to help directly they are likely to be able to point you towards useful information sources. If you feel that you are not getting the whole picture you may need to look further afield.

Other organisations

Amongst the plethora of service providers and organisations there is little consistency about whom or which one organisation will have good sets of social care information across different parts of the country.

Social services departments have some duties in law to provide information in several areas of need, but across the country there is a great deal of variation as to how many resources are provided to do this and

therefore how well it is done. Services to older people in particular should however be well provided with information. The recent National Service Frameworks highlight publicity and should result in more attention being given to information about service provision over the next few years. Social services should have a well-developed presence on the local authority's web site.

Social service departments are therefore a good place to start and should be able to provide good, up to date, sets of information in some areas. They may in addition have access to or may provide listings of other organisation's information production. If you do not get anywhere at a local office try the central or head office and find out if someone there has the responsibility for information to the public.

Voluntary organisations

There may be an aspect of the local voluntary organisations that is particularly orientated towards information aspects especially if there is an umbrella organisation.

There may be information-specific organisations such as a DIAL (Disability Information and Advice Line) or other similar organisations in the area. Search these out – they may have their own information products or good collections of other organisation's work. They may have a database to enable a precise search to be made for a particular service or a set of information around one idea or geographic area. Staff running these organisations are generally very pleased that they are able to use their resource for an appreciative user.

Local libraries

The traditional guardians of information – local authority libraries may have excellent social care information resources. This may vary considerably between libraries as it may be either the responsibility of each individual library or there may be authority-wide encouragement to make this kind of provision. Libraries often hold these sorts of booklets, directories and leaflets in their reference section only but this may enable you to see what is available and then order it or get it from the source. Librarians are obviously trained in this sort of work and are often keen to help and to join with you in locating other sources of information. Their expertise is not always well used or appreciated – many of the staff really enjoy being able to use their skills and knowledge and will happily give of their time.

Health

Some Health Trusts are developing excellent web sites and may have public information well represented on their sites. The developing Health information Telephone Centres (NHS Direct) may have good information listings and may already send information out directly to the public.

Community Health Councils (CHCs)

Community Health Councils have always needed to use and to provide information to the public and others and may have good collections. Citizen Advice Bureaux (CABs) likewise may be a good source.

National sources – especially if you are looking within a recognised specialist area, such as HIV/AIDS

There may be excellent national information services who also know a lot about local services. In summary then if you can locate good sets of information – use them! (and maybe tell the editor or collector that they were useful – people in roles like mine rarely get this sort of feedback!)

If you cannot find what you are looking for, or if you know that there is no existing collection of information in that area of need, you may begin to see how useful it could be and to consider how such a collection could be brought together. If so…read on.

Creating an Information Resource: How to Write the Book

This section assumes that you have been unable to find what you think is needed and you are considering creating your own information resource/initiative. Information is needed in many different forms:

seminars, training for staff, radio, newspaper or TV advertising, community festivals, information days, poster campaigns, information kiosks, videos and many others. This section focuses mainly on the production of a resource in the most common format – a set of printed information e.g. a booklet, guide etc. However, much of what is here applies in some respects also to the creation of other resources, especially sets of information for use on the web.

At the outset it is not always clear how useful a particular resource may be – but often once created and in daily use it is likely everyone will agree it was essential. It is not impossible for a well organised individual or preferably a small group of determined people to produce a really useful resource – a local directory of services maybe. An information resource is often a useful product that a new interest or pressure group may attempt – to collect together all of their combined information and make it available to others. It may well help in establishing a new group.

If an information resource in the field existed previously that may be really helpful – people can express opinions about it and you can learn from their pioneering work. If it is an entirely new initiative then you have the advantage of a blank sheet and all the ideas can be new. Either way it is possible to see several distinct stages in the process:

- Plan it – there are many crucial but obscure aspects to resolve.
- Collect all the information – a considerable amount of work.
- Organise and store it – maybe a database?
- Create a format – decide how to present your information.
- Print, launch and distribute.
- Audit and feedback – Did it all work?

Planning

Make as many of the decisions about the whole project at the very start, if you possibly can, before you begin to collect the information. Sometimes you may be inheriting someone else's half begun work but it's equally important to check that it's been thought through.

Steal ideas

No-one wants to re-invent the wheel...but can you improve it?

Look at what other people have produced – maybe other subject areas within your geographic area or have people elsewhere in the country done anything similar? Do you have colleagues or friends living where some of this work has already been done? There are also national organisations whose members can help track down or connect people working on similar information projects. You may be able to find your local member. There is also the Social Services Information Network (SSIN – see the end of this chapter).

Either way, there are some essentially important questions that must be answered before the detailed work is begun:

Who is it for? – The answer to this may not be simple but it will help when you have to make so many decisions about the initiative.

What is its main purpose? – Also unlikely to be straightforward.

Coverage

Decide on a realistic coverage. It is often tempting to try to include everything you find but there must be some well-defined edges to what you can do. Is the range geographic or specialist or a combination of the two?

Is the need for it proven and documented or has it ever been attempted or done before? Is it clear what people want? It is likely different groups would like to see different things from it.

Can you find the resources to do it?

Access?

Can you produce it in other formats as well? Can you organise it so that it is not just a one-off? The resource will soon need updating or developing. Who is it for? – the target audience. The target group may well be a mix of both 'professionals' staff and the public or service users. Nearly all directories, guides or web sites designed primarily for service users are also used extensively by professionals, (although the reverse is rarely true). So if you are designing it for the public bear in mind that staff in many agencies will use it as well.

Consultation

The ideal is to try to involve some of the people who might be using the publication from the very start of the planning if you possibly can. However this can often be difficult, especially if it is a small or very local directory. It may be difficult for some people to imagine the whole thing – something concrete that demonstrates the reality may be easier to criticise – especially if you can provide a series of options, or better still mock ups, or try to borrow a range of other interesting directories. However you do it, it is essential to try your ideas and initial plans out on a few users before you go too far. They may see things very differently.

Getting the support – finance and people

There is a lot that can be done on a very limited budget if you have access to a photocopier or web access and time that you can dedicate to the task (yours or somebody else's). If however, you can find some funds, then the essential work of planning, researching, collating, organising and publishing an information resource can be used to much greater effect and a number of useful products might be possible at the end. So how can you find the money and the people to help?

Possible sources of support:

- Your own organisation (if you work for one). Many organisations may like the idea of the kudos and recognition; it may help establish them in this field of work.

- A shared project. Can you locate some other organisation, which might be interested in making it a joint project: sharing the work and the finances? See below for possibilities.

- Local or national grants. Get advice on what may be available.

- Local statutory organisations. They may be able to help directly with funding or may be able to redirect you, for example, the new local forms of the Health Authority – Primary Care Trusts may be keen to join with initiatives to produce localised information. Or you may want to try different departments of the local authority.

- Voluntary organisations (including grant making organisations).
- Financial support from a local councillor or one who has a specialist interest.
- Commercial sponsorship.

What can you get for the money?

Below is a practical guide to the finances of producing helpful information:

How much have you got?	Notes	What you can expect to get for the money
Very limited budget or nothing.	Assuming some dedicated time and you have access to someone's photocopier.	A small black and white booklet of local services that still looks professional. 10-100 copies? A simple web site.
£100	You may be able to pay for some of the above.	As above.
£500	This would properly cover the reproduction costs (photocopying). Or you could pay for a simple printing job and get many more copies (Digital direct printing).	As above but the booklet could begin to look better – smart cover? more pages? more copies? Still black and white only. Web design services could be bought for better site.
£1,000	Traditional (litho) print possible for larger numbers. May be possible to buy some simple but professional design? Colour cover? Or professional web site built.	Large number (1,000+) of printed copies possible for smaller booklet. 20-30 pages. Still black and white or black + one other colour?
£10,000	Professional design work, two colour or full colour, 'perfect binding' (i.e. not just stapled). You could do other formats. Full web site.	Very large numbers possible. 50 pages. 5-10,000 copies possible for simple booklet.
£20,000	The whole project could be paid for, including paid staff to do the work, with an excellent product as above. You could look at other expensive formats e.g. video.	As above plus expensive production – larger size – fold out sections, pockets special finishes? Some staff time to distribute, support or research?

Note: All figures are approximate and based on 2002 prices.

The planning is essential to ensure that you make as many of the decisions about the whole project before you begin persuading people to give you all they ever knew about X or Y. You need to avoid getting to the end and finding that there are important things missing or you have a lot of information that you cannot finally use. Knowing the final formats will help you ask for exactly what you need.

Collecting the Information

Does any of the information you want to include already exist in parts of other existing collections or better still in electronic format? If so, can you use it, with permissions and acknowledgements by agreement? If not you will have to contact people. Writing has many advantages but it is slow and you are likely to have to phone some anyway. e-mail is ideal if everyone is on it and you have many e-mail addresses – but all this is unlikely. You will probably have to write.

Providing information for others is unlikely to be high on everyone's agenda and some people may put off replying if they can, so make it as easy as possible for them and efficient for you:

- Do not ask for any more than you are going to use and do not ask for things you already know. Use a standard letter but personalise as much as you can – no one likes circulars.

- Provide a format for each item of information and give it to them, preferably as a printed form to complete. Ask for exactly what you need and avoid having to go back and ask them if they have a Minicom number etc.

- Ask them to supply their information in very simple, ordinary language and give them an exact word limit – so that you don't have to write it out again and then go back and ask them if it's still accurate.

- Give them a precise response time. A reply in 10 days to 3 weeks is about right for a simple request, longer if they will have to consult others.

- Say exactly what you are going to do with the information – how you will keep it and what else you are planning to do with it and whom you are going to pass it on to. For example, might someone want to include it on their web site later on? (You need to say all this to comply with the Data Protection Act – see the Act for more details). Include a statement to be signed from someone in authority in their organisation to say that permission has been given for the information to be used for these purposes.

Storing and Checking the Information

Unless you are also teaching a calligraphy evening class and have access to a set of scribes willing to write and re-write, your storage system has to be electronic! Any word processing package will do, on any computer. However, it is useful if it is compatible with other people's and generally that means a PC Windows product – Word or maybe WordPerfect. These can be made to do some of the work of organising for you –

at least into alphabetical order – but you need to know how to put it in so you can manipulate it afterwards.

It is much better however if you can store the information in a database or spreadsheet. These will allow you to endlessly re-order, select, or re-arrange your information. Again you have to have thought carefully about how you have recorded the information and separated the various pieces of data within each record. You may be able to find one ready written and set-up, this is a very common and simple job for a database.

Updating and later development

It is easy to concentrate on your immediate production, but thinking ahead to later on, how might it be updated? Might someone else or you be able to extend and develop the idea in years ahead? Make this possible by ensuring that you store the electronic version somewhere accessible or best of all make it into a 'live database or listing', and encourage or arrange for someone to update it as things change.

Checking the information

Saying 'Yes, please go ahead and print me 12,000 copies' of this work that you have produced is always a moment of mixed emotion – it is a positive end of a project...but have you got it right?

There are always bound to be some small errors or omissions but you need to get it as good as you can and there are ways of working that make this easier:

- Involve methodical well-organised people on the project if you possibly can – especially if this is not your own strength. Stick to strict organisational methods and make sure everyone else does too.

- Double check all the hard factual data against any other sources you can find. If an address is slightly inaccurate then a letter may get redirected or delivered by a keen postman but if a telephone number is wrong it is completely useless. The telephone is also most likely to be the contact method chosen. However this is the one piece of information where it is easy for an error to occur in passing on and recording the number. It is obviously not possible to go back and read and check all the entries against their original source, but you can check telephone numbers and I suggest that this is well worth doing. It is a straightforward job that can be simply split up and given to any number of people. You may also pickup some other last minute changes at the same time.

- Try to ask someone who has not been involved with data gathering to proof read it – at least for typos and errors that spell-check cannot find.

- Show it to as many people as you can – have you forgotten a really central service or missed anyone really important?

Formats – How to Present the Information

If you gather a group of people together there often seems to be as many ideas about the best way of organising the information as people present. There are some excellent, well thought out sophisticated formats but a simple design often works best. If you watch people using a reference book (try it in Argos!) of any type, one very common way of finding the right part is simply to pick it up and flick through it with the thumb until they hit a likely looking page or word. Or people may use an index if they are getting nowhere.

Although you may see the perfect logic of your system, others may fail to recognise the beauty of it and will see it differently. Unless you have a good reason for doing it in a particular way I suggest that a straightforward A-Z type with redirects ('Children' – see 'Youth' and so on) as necessary, with a good index at the back, has a lot to recommend it.

There is a lot of general advice around about how to present information in terms of text size and layout, but generally keep the font size as big as you can and keep the graphics simple. If the booklet is aimed at people who may reasonably be expected to have sight problems then 14 point text minimum is often recommended. The type of font and the other spacing measures are however equally important. You may have to offer a large print version but this can be simply done from an electronic file.

Other formats

Not everyone will be able to access the ordinary English language version and you may need to think about whether it is possible to produce any other versions. This will depend very much on the area you are working in, both in geographic terms and the nature of the work. Possibilities would include:

- Large print, which is easy, using a word processor.
- Web based version of the original, relatively simple as a PDF version.
- Tape or compact disc versions, which can be expensive to produce.
- Translations into local community languages.

Graphics

If you are to have any graphics or illustrations work out who can produce them. Remember that some people are delighted to have their drawings or other illustrations reproduced. If you use photographs of people be very careful – get their full permission and signatures as required by the Data Protection Act.

More copies

Say clearly in the directory or guide who has produced it and where people can get more copies from.

Acknowledgements

Do acknowledge people who helped and maybe their organisation – it is fair and it also may help next time when you may need their support again.

Dates

Put a date clearly on the front so people can clearly see once it starts to become doubtful information. Three years seems about the absolute limit in these changing times. After that you need to do it all again!

Getting it Printed and Distributed

Economies of scale – how many dare you print?

Keep it small? There may be an advantage to keeping the production run small and cheap with photocopying as the method of reproduction – you can easily develop and improve it. If you forget that very important councillor's favourite group or find a good cartoon too late you can always change it and copy some more off. More seriously if you get some useful feedback and want to develop the whole idea you can do that more easily. You can anticipate problems and announce that the first version is merely a draft for consultation to sound out the idea. If you only produce limited numbers, this may in effect be an excellent way of consulting users (see Feedback below).

Large print runs

However, in many situations, if you are going to a full print job, there are enormous savings to be made once you get into large numbers of copies. If you want less than about 500 copies most printers, using traditional printing techniques, will give quotes where the costs seem very high. However, if you are able to consider a print-run in the order of thousands then the process becomes much more efficient and the price per copy falls dramatically. When getting quotes, ask for 'run-on' costs, for example, 2,000 copies with run-ons of 500 up to 3,500. The difference becomes very apparent. Basically once they have done all the work of setting up the job and sorting all the paperwork it costs very little to keep the presses rolling.

Difficult numbers

Many jobs may fall into the awkward gap where you really only need a few hundred copies. This can be a large number for photocopying (especially if there is colour), but it's a very small traditional print run. Developing technology has raced to our aid here with digital printing. This is basically a process where everything is done electronically, without using traditional photographic plates and all the associated work. It can present an ideal answer for local booklet production, undercutting photocopying and traditional printing.

If you are using a designer they can do the 'print buying' for you if you ask – but it is very useful to have an idea of what is possible.

Launch event

It is an excellent idea to launch your initiative. Even if only a handful of people are there it allows you to create a media story which gives you free publicity –

make sure you write part of the account yourself so its right and people know who to contact for more information.

Distribution

Work out how you are going to do the initial distribution – you may be able to combine it with your launch if you can, but more importantly think about how you are going to get it out to people on an on-going basis. Use places where they will get back to you if they run out or even give you feedback about what people think to it.

Feedback and Audit – Did It Work?

After all your hard work you should get lots of praise and thanks – but you might not. People tend to accept these things as something that is just there. Many people also find it very difficult to see how improvements could be made – they are just satisfied that something is there. So you may have to work out a way of getting some feedback if you are thinking of improving it. Possible ways of doing this could include:

- Join a regular meeting with a group of people involved in the particular area of work. Arrange to ask their opinion (get copies to them beforehand).
- A feedback form can be included with the original directory – but very few people complete these.
- A one off advertised event, to look critically at the production and to discuss a new initiative.
- A simple evaluation form sent out to a known group of users or selection of workers or organisations known to use it. Or get a slot at one of the meetings of such groups.

Some Case Studies

This final section gives some brief outlines of a few very different information initiatives that the author is familiar with. They have been chosen to illustrate different aspects of developing a resource and different final products rather than being the best produced or the biggest.

Each account begins with a short overview of the principal outline facts about that particular information theory.

Case study 1: The Bereavement Directory

Subject: Support and help available in Leeds following bereavement and loss.

Type: A-Z booklet. 40 pages. 70 organisations. Double indexed.

Number of copies: 5,000.

Costs: Design £1300, Printing £ 4,800.

Produced by: Joint voluntary/statutory partnership.

This is a less common subject for a directory but it has proved very successful. One of the local hospices had already produced a small and simple booklet about bereavement support. The idea to build on this and develop it into a directory came out of a series of cross agency workshops on supporting people through grief and loss. A sum of money was found from mental health funds for the printing and some design work, social services agreed to organise the work jointly with a newly created Bereavement Forum and the Hospice.

How the work was done. We had enough money to employ a designer for a simple design and to print a professional looking mini-directory. We had a list of a few dozen organisations that needed to be in from the old booklet but not all the details about them. Several people had ideas about other organisations that ought to be in but we really did not know how many entries we would end up with.

We realised that there would have to be a lot of typing to get all the data in and organised, and one of the secretaries at the Hospice was able to help and sent out enquiries to everyone and keying in the replies.

We decided to use a simple database (we used Cardbox) to enable us to order the information simply. We agreed on a simple format that could be used for the database, and it formed the basis of both the enquiry form and the final print out. We agreed several standard facts for each entry, although not all were relevant for every organisation. Where there was no data we skipped that line in the final print out altogether. Once agreed this worked very well. The database was able to produce a text output that the designer could use without too much work.

We used the database to produce a draft mock-up of the booklet and showed it to groups of other professionals and to a few of our most targeted users – GPs. In general they liked it very much although we changed our ideas about how to arrange the booklet and went for a total A-Z format that included a few important national organisations mixed in amongst the local and regional ones. They also suggested a few other organisations that could be included.

The designer came up with a simple and clean layout based on the one we had mocked up. We calculated that we could afford a two-colour inside (usually black plus one colour but we used dark blue and dark red – it worked very well).

The booklet was fairly simple to design and it was done in record time as we were trying to hit the launch event date already set for it. We made the date with a day or two to spare. It was very well received and we are looking at how we can now produce a PDF version to go onto one or two web sites, this should be a simple task and will enable us to update and correct the few entries that need it. As it is now in database form it should be relatively easy for us – or anyone else to update it in a year or two.

Case study 2: Black and Minority Ethnic Communities

Subject: Support and help available especially for people from black and minority ethnic communities.

Type: A4 Ordinary paper but coloured, plastic spiral spine, card cover. A-Z booklet. 40 pages. 70 organisations. Three sections, indexes.

Number of copies: 200 approximately.

Costs: Printing was minimal – about £220 for photocopying. The design was undertaken by my organisation and we paid for a part-time, dedicated worker to research and collect data over a six month service.

Produced by: Joint Health/Social Services partnership.

Nothing like this had been attempted in the city before and it was produced in recognition of the difficulties that many people from black and minority ethnic communities have in finding and using organisations which understand and can address their needs. It was difficult identifying who or even which organisation might have a particular responsibility for producing something like this. We were however encouraged by obtaining a one-off grant from Health funds. As we had nothing to start from and we were very unsure which organisations should or would like to be in it or what forms it should take, we decided to spend it on a worker to look in detail at these issues. They were guided by a small steering group who in practice, found setting and keeping to a steady course, difficult.

It was not easy for the worker to consider all the issues, start the considerable task of collecting the information and to have a realistic vision of what the final directory could look like.

As a result, we asked for what turned out to be far too much information from each organisation and this made it difficult for them to respond to us and when they did, difficult for us to handle. It was difficult to know who to send the enquiry form to as we were unsure what people would say in their replies. There were so many possible ways to organise it that we spent too long trying to decide how to do it. The best decision we made was to store all the information on a database so that we could re-organise the information or search it easily. The various possibilities of how to organise it depended heavily on what could be practically extracted from the database, but few people understood this.

Despite a lot of problems we did eventually produce a useful and practical directory which was 'reprinted' (by photocopying) several times because of demand. It had a unique way of indexing where it was possible to approach the information by several different methods (in some ways similar to the way a database might be searched):

● by title – the main alphabetical listing
● by type of service provider – translators/benefits advice/legal etc.
● by ethnic minority group

In the directory itself the organisation was helped by using coloured pages for the different sections.

Unfortunately, as the original was funded from a one-off grant we have not at the time of writing been able to find funds or anyone's time to dedicate to updating it.

Case study 3: Feeling Good in Chapeltown – A Local Directory About Mental Health Services

Subject: Support and help available for people living in one particular area of Leeds who may need mental health services.

Type: A5 booklet. 96 pages. 150+ organisations. Two colours inside. Divided into 12 'Themes' but with full A-Z index at the back .

Number of copies: 1,500 approximately.

Costs: Funding came mainly from local health (Primary Care Trust) funds. We paid for a professional design and the printing was relatively expensive as it was a local directory and we did not need huge numbers: £1,200 for design (including some research) + £3,400 printing (included 20+ scans).

Produced by: local health worker in partnership with other social care organisations.

We have an excellent organisation pulling together information about mental health in Leeds (Information for Mental Health) and they were able to select and supply much of the information needed for the book. This set of information was taken as the basis and was then added to and commented on by local workers and users.

One of the most remarkable aspects of the book was the speed of its production – the whole exercise was started and completed in a matter of months as there was a pre-arranged date for the ideal launch event. It was excellent having such a target to hit, although many decisions had to be taken very quickly.

It was also produced on a CD and translated into ethnic minority languages. It has been very successful, and is being mirrored in other Primary Care Trust areas in Leeds.

Case study 4: Directory of Voluntary Organisations, Clubs and Societies in Leeds

Subject: Major listing of voluntary organisations, clubs and societies in Leeds.

Type: Large A-Z directory over 270 pages. Listing over 1,400 organisations.

Number of copies: 2,500 initially.

Costs: Printing was around £5,100 and design was £500 (reduced because of re-using existing style and technique). A worker was employed to collect and research the massive amount of data for this impressive directory.

Produced by: Mainly voluntary organisation, but some joint input from the local authority.

The idea for this had been around for a time and was a vast extension of a smaller database collection of social care information pulled together by a cross agency group of information workers.

Initially the project won a substantial lottery grant but last year it went 'self-funding' and the directory is now sold to users. The information is also available via a web site and on a CD. The searching possibilities are enormous and it is very professionally produced. The book sells normally for £20 but there are big reductions for voluntary groups or bulk buys. It is well used and appreciated across the city.

It is an excellent example of a project growing into a major and impressive initiative.

Case study 5: Community Resources for Parents and Social Care Staff

Subject: Support and help available for parents living in the Harehills area of Leeds.

Type: A5 booklet. 56 pages. 200+ organisations. Simple black and white photocopying with paper cover. Divided into about 20 sections.

Number of copies: In batches of about 100.

Costs: There were few direct production costs above the photocopying.

Produced by: Local area children's workers from 'Re-Focussing' project and education worker. It built on a previous 'Family of Schools' publication.

This has been a very successful publication completed with practically no production costs. The photocopying was done within the departments. There was a simple but effective design all completed by one of the workers involved, using 'Publisher' software. (A particularly useful programme as it is also possible to send material to print from it).

The collection was built up from a previous set of information, and it was added to by contacting as many of the workers in the area as possible, and by researching other information booklets, listings etc. It did not follow a strictly identical format for each item but simply printed what was known. The names of the service or organisation plus telephone number were the only absolute constants.

It has been much used and appreciated and there are now plans to do a much bigger version that could be used on the web and across the city.

Conclusion

This chapter has attempted to illustrate in a very practical way how information can be used to support and enhance family support practice. The information contained in this chapter can hopefully be used in conjunction with the material in Chapters 8-16 to support and enhance practice in each of those areas.

Those wishing to initiate projects may wish to consult the Social Services Information Network.

The Social Services Information Network (SSIN) is an organisation bringing together all those who work with information in social care. Locate your nearest contact from the web www.ssin.org.uk

Social Services Information Network: 'Promoting good practice in social care public information throughout the UK'

Useful Resources and Web Sites

Publications

Butt, J. and Box, L. (1998). *Family Centred: A Study of the Use of Family Centres by Black Families.* London: REU.

A useful study focusing on the particular experiences of black families in using family centres.

Colto, M., Drury, C. and Williams, M. (1995). *Children in Need: Family Support Under The Children Act 1989.* Aldershot: Gower.

One of the first studies to assess the impact of the Children Act, 1989 on family support.

Department of Health (1995). *Child Protection: Messages from Research.* London: TSO.

Probably the most influential contribution to the re-focusing debate

Department of Health (2001). *The Children Act Now: Messages from Research.* London: The Stationery Office.

An account of the impact of the Children Act drawing on a wide-range of interesting research studies.

Gardner, R. (1998). *Family Support – Practitioners Guide.* Birmingham: Venture Press.

A brief handbook of use to all practitioners.

Glass, N. (1999). Sure Start: The Development of an Early Intervention Programme for Young Children in the United Kingdom. *Children and Society,* 13: 257-64.

The definitive account of the development of Sure Start from a civil service perspective.

Hardiker, P., Exton, K. and Barker, M. (1999). Children Still in Need, Indeed: Prevention Across Five Decades. In Stevenson, O. (Ed.). *Childhood Welfare in the UK.* Oxford: Blackwell.

The Hardiker et al. framework is probably the most significant in understanding family support. Useful as a theoretical framework and a policy tool.

Hearn, B. (1995). *Child and Family Support and Protection. A Practical Approach.* London: National Children's Bureau.

An accessible guide to family support - with useful exercises.

Office of National Statistics (2002). *Social Trends.* London: TSO.

The annual report which is always a useful source of facts and figures – including data on household structure and income.

Parton, N. (Ed.) (1997). *Child Protection and Family Support: Tensions, Contradictions and Possibilities.* London: Routledge.

A very useful edited collection covering a wide range of issues and concerns.

Social Services Inspectorate (1999). *Getting Family Support Right.* London: Department of Health.

One of the more accessible SSI studies which provides a useful steer in planning family support services.

Tunstill, J. and Aldgate, J. (2000). *Services for Children in Need: From Policy to Practice.* London: TSO.

An interesting study assessing whether services for children in need have delivered.

Waldfogel, J. (1999). *Early Childhood Interventions and Outcomes, CASE Paper 21.* London: London School of Economics.

A brief report which summarises a wide range of studies.

Organisations

Organisation	Address	Telephone	Website
Barnardo's	Tanner's Lane, Barkingside, Ilford, IG6 1QG	020 8850 8822	www.barnardos.com
Child Poverty Action Group	94, White Lion Street, London, N1 9PF	020 7837 7979	www.cpag.org.uk
The Children's Society	94, White Lion Street, London, N1 9PF	020 7837 4299/ 4422	www.the-childrens-society.org.uk
Daycare Trust	21, St George's Road, London, SE1 6EZ	020 7840 3350	www.daycaretrust.org.uk
Family Rights Group	The Print House 18, Ashwin Street, London, E8 3DL	020 7923 2628	www.frg.org.uk
Family Service Units	207, Marylebone Road, London, NW1 5QP	020 7402 5175	www.fsu.org.uk
Home-Start UK	2, Salisbury Road, Leicester, LE7 7QR	0116 233 9955	www.home-start.org.uk
National Children's Bureau	8, Wakley Street, London, EC1U 7QE	020 7843 6000	www.ncb.org.uk
National Council of Voluntary Child Care Organisations	Unit 4, Pride Court, 80-82, White Lion St., London, N1 9PF	020 7833 3319	www.ncvcco.org.uk
National Family and Parenting Institute	520, Highgate Studios, 53-79, Highgate Road, London, NW5 1TL	020 7424 3460	www.nfpi.org.uk
NCH Action for Children	85, Highbury Park, London, N5 1UD	020 7226 2033	www.nch.org.uk
Parentline Plus	520, Highgate Studios, 53-79, Highgate Road, London, NW5 1TL	020 7284 5500	www.parentlineplus.org.uk

Web sites

These web sites are very useful. For those new to using web sites the Department of Health web site is a useful starting point. It is comprehensive and has many useful links to voluntary sector web sites.

www.cypu.gov.uk A useful web site with some interactive material aimed at young people.	The Department for Education and Skills, Children and Young Persons Unit.
www.doh.gov.uk A good starting point with useful links.	The Department of Health
www.doh.gov.uk/scg/socialc.htm The specialist social care web site - with much useful material on family support. Useful for keeping up to date with policy developments.	The Department of Health, Social Care Group
www.statistics.gov.uk A self explanatory site!	The Office of National Statistics
www.surestart.gov.uk A very interesting and comprehensive site.	Sure Start
www.tsonline.co.uk The source for all official publications.	The Stationery Office

Bibliography

Aldgate, J. and Bradley, M. (1999). *Supporting Families Through Short-Term Fostering.* London: The Stationery Office.

Ames, J. (1991). *Just Deserts or Just Growing Up.* London: National Children's Bureau.

Ani, M. (1994). *Yurugu: An African Centred Critique of European Thought and Behaviour.* New Jersey: African World Press.

Argyris, C., Schon, D. (1996). *Organizational Learning II.* Reading, MA: Addison Wesley.

Audit Commission (1994). *Seen But Not Heard: Co-ordinating Community Child Health and Social Services for Children in Need.* London: HMSO.

Audit Commission (1996). *Misspent Youth: Young People and Crime.* London: HMSO.

Badham, B. and Eadie, T., (2002). A Changing Relationship? *Community Care*, 28 February–6 March, pp34–6.

Ball, B. (1998). I, You and the Art: The Interactive Space in Art Therapy with Children. *Dissertation Abstracts International: Sec. B: The Sciences and Engineering*, 59: Nov. p2411.

Barclay, P. (1982). *Social Workers: Their Roles and Tasks.* London: Bedford Square Press.

Barlow, J. (1996). *HIV and Children – A Training Manual.* London: HMSO.

Barn, R. (1993). *Black Children in the Public Care System.* London: Batsford.

Barnardo's (1991). *All About Me.* Barkingside: Barnardo's.

Barnes, J., Kroll, L., Burke, O., Lee, J., Jones, A. and Stein, A. (2000). Qualitative Interview Study of Communication Between Parents and Children About Maternal Breast Cancer. *British Medical Journal*, 321: pp19-26.

Batchelor, J., Gould, N., and Wright, N. (1999). Family Centres: A Focus for the Children in Need Debate. *Child and Family Social Work*, 4(3): pp197-208.

Batta, I., McCulloch, J., Smith, N. (1979). Colour as a Variable in Children's Sections of Local Authority Social Services Departments. *New Community*, July: pp78-84.

Bean, P., Melville, J. (1990). *Lost Children of the Empire.* London: Unwin Hyman.

Beishon, S., Modood, T., Virdee, S. (1998). *Ethnic Minority Families.* London: Policy Studies Institute.

Bernard, C. (1996). *Black Feminist Perspectives on Child Sexual Abuse.* London: University of London.

Bernardes, J. (1997). *Family Studies: An Introduction.* London: Routledge.

Besharov D.J. (Ed.) (1999). *When Addicts Have Children.* Wahington DC: Child Welfare League of America.

Bhat, A., Carr-Hill, R. and Ohri, S. (1988). *Britain's Black Population: A New Perspective.* Aldershot: Gower.

Boyd, C.J. (1994). The Antecedents of Women's Crack Cocaine Abuse, Depression and Illicit Drug Use. *Journal of Substance Abuse Treatment*, 10: pp433-8.

Bradford City Council (1996). *Areas of Stress Within Bradford District.* Bradford: Bradford City Council.

Bradford City Council (1996). *Bradford in Brief.* Bradford: Bradford City Council.

Bradshaw, J. (Ed.) (2001). *Poverty: The Outcomes for Children.* London: FPSC.

Brandon, M., Thoburn, J., Lewis, A. and Way, A. (1999). *Safeguarding Children with The Children Act 1989.* London: The Stationery Office.

Brookfield, S. (1986). *Understanding and Facilitating Adult Learning.* New York: Jossey Bass.

Brown, D. (1999). *Care in the Community. Inspection*

of Community Care in Rural Communities. London: Department of Health.

Brown, M. (1998). The Unheard Cries. *Connections*, Summer: pp8-9.

Bruce, M. (1968). *The Coming of the Welfare State.* London: Batsford.

Butler-Sloss, E. (1988). *Report into Events in Cleveland in 1987.* London: HMSO.

Burton, S. (1997). *When There's a Will There's a Way.* London: NCB.

Butt, J. and Box, L. (1998). *Family Centred: A Study of the Use of Family Centres by Black Families.* London: REU.

Butt, J. and Mizra, K. (1996). *Social Care and Black Communities: A Review of Recent Research Studies.* London: HMSO.

Campbell, B. (1988) *Unofficial Secrets: Child Sexual Abuse – The Cleveland Case.* London: Virago.

Canavan, J., Dolan, P. and Pinkerton, J. (2000). *Family Support: Direction from Diversity.* London: Jessica Kingsley.

Chapman, P., Phimister, E., Shucksmith, M., Upward, R. and Vera-Toscano, E. (1998). *Poverty and Rural Exclusion in Rural Britain.* York: Joseph Rowntree Foundation.

Cheetam, J., Fuller, R., Petch, A. and McIvor, G. (1992). *Evaluating Social Work Effectiveness.* Buckinghamshire: Open University Press.

Children Act Advisory Committee (1993). *Annual Report.* London: NCB.

Children and Young People's Unit (2001). *Children's Fund Guidance (Part 1).* London: TSO.

Children and Young People's Unit (2001). *Building a Strategy for Children and Young People.* London: TSO.

Christ, G.H. (2000). *Healing Children's Grief.* New York: Oxford University Press.

Cohen, B. (1994). *Childcare Services for Rural Families. Improving Provision in the European Union.* Brussels: European Commission Network on Childcare and Other Measures to Reconcile Work and Family Responsibilities.

Colton, M., Drury, C. and Williams, M. (1995). *Children in Need: Family Support Under The Children Act 1989.* Aldershot: Gower.

Conway, L. (1994). *Working With Volunteers: Support.* London: Volunteer Centre.

Conway, L. (1994). *Working With Volunteers: Training.* London: Volunteer Centre.

Coontz, S. (2000). Historical Perspectives on Family Studies. *Journal of Marriage and the Family,* pp283-97.

Corby, B. (1987). Working with Child Abuse. Buckingham: Open University Press.

Cox, T. and Bentovim, A. (2000). *The Family Pack of Questionnaires and Scales.* Department of Health.

Craig, G. and Manthorpe, J. (2000). *Fresh Fields: Rural Social Care, Research, Policy and Practice Agendas.* York: Joseph Rowntree Foundation.

Crittenden, P. (1993). An Information Processing Perspective on the Behaviour of Neglectful Parents. *Criminal Justice and Behaviour,* 20: p1.

Cumbria County Council (1999). *Trends Affecting the Demand for Childcare: Findings from the Early Years Development and Childcare Partnership's Childcare Audit 1998.* Cumbria County Council.

Cumbria County Council (2000). *Households with Children Claiming some Form of Income Support – 1998/99.* Cumbria County Council.

Daniel, B. et al. (1999). *Child Development for Child Care and Protection Workers.* London: Jessica Kingsley.

Dartington Research Unit (1995). *Child Protection: Messages From Research.* London: HMSO.

Davidoff, L., Doolittle, M., Fink, J. and Holden, K. (1999). *The Family Story: Blood, Contract and Intimacy, 1830-1960.* London: Longman.

Davis, H. and Hester, P. (1996). *An Independent Evaluation of Parent Link: A Parenting Education Programme.* London: Parent Network.

Dean, M. (2002). Society. *The Guardian,* 3.7.02.

DfEE (1998). *Meeting the Childcare Challenge.* London: DfEE.

DoH (1991). *The Children Act 1989 Guidance and Regulations Vol 2: Family Support, Day Care and Educational Provision for Young Children.* London: HMSO.

DoH (1995). *Child Protection: Messages from Research.* London: TSO.

DoH and SSI (1995). *The Challenge of Child Protection: Practice Guide.* London: HMSO.

DoH (1996). *Refocusing Children's Services.* London: DoH.

DoH (1996). *Children's Services Planning Guidance.* London: HMSO.

DoH (1998). *Tackling Drugs to Make a Better Britain.* London: DoH.

DoH (1999). *Modernising Social Services: Cm 4169.* London: TSO.

DoH, Home Office and DfEE (1999). *Working Together to Safeguard Children: A Guide to Inter-Agency Working to Safeguard and Promote the Welfare of Children.* London: TSO.

DoH (2000). *Framework for the Assessment of Children in Need and Their Families.* London: TSO.

DoH (2000). *Working Together to Protect Children.* London: DoH.

DoH (2000). *Assessing Children in Need and their Families: Practice Guidance.* London: HMSO.

DoH (2001). *The Children Act Now: Messages from Research.* London: TSO.

DHSS (1998). *Working Together: A Guide to Inter-Agency Co-operation for the Protection of Children from Abuse.* London: HMSO.

DHSS (1974). *Non-Accidental Injury to Children.* LASSL 74/3.

DHSS (1980). *Child Abuse Central Register Systems.* LASSL 80/4.

DHSS (1985). *Social Work Decisions in Child Care.* London: HMSO.

Dingwall, R. (1989). Some Problems about Predicting Child Abuse and Neglect. In Stevenson, O. (Ed.). *Child Abuse: Professional Practice and Public Policy.* London: Harvester and Wheatsheaf.

Dominelli, L. (1988). *Anti-Racist Social Work.* Hampshire: Macmillan.

Dore, M., Doris, J. and Wright, P. (1995). Identifying Substance Abuse in Maltreating Families. *Child Abuse and Neglect,* 19(5): pp531-43.

Etzioni, A. (1993a). *The Parenting Deficit.* London: Demos.

Etzioni, A. (1993b). *The Spirit of Community.* New York: Touchstone.

Everett, J., Chipungu, S. and Leashore, B. (1991). *Child Welfare: An Africentric Perspective.* New Jersey: Rutgers University Press.

Exploring Parenthood (1997). *Moyenda: Black Families Talking.* London: Exploring Families.

Fahlberg, V. (1994). *A Child's Journey Through Placement.* London: BAAF.

Family Welfare Association (1960). *The West Indian Comes to London.* London: Routledge and Keegan Paul.

Famularo, R., Kindscherff, R. and Fenton, T. (1992). Parental Substance Abuse and the Nature of Child Maltreatment. *Child Abuse and Neglect,* 16: pp475-83.

Farmer, E. and Owen, M. (1995). *Child Protection Practice: Private Risks and Public Remedies.* London: HMSO.

Fawcett, M. (1996). *Learning Through Child Observation.* London: Jessica Kingsley.

Featherstone, B. and Frost, N. (2003). Families, Social Change and Diversity. In Bell, M. and Wilson, K. (Eds.). *The Practitioner's Guide to Working with Families.* Basingstoke: Palgrave.

Ford, R. and Millar, J. (1997). *Private Lives and Public Responses: Lone Parenthood and Future Policy.* York: Joseph Rowntree Foundation.

Fox-Harding, L. (1996). *Family, State and Social Policy.* London: Macmillan.

Francis, D. and Henderson, P. (1992). *Working with Rural Communities.* Basingstoke: Macmillan.

Fraser, D. (1973). *The Evolution of the British Welfare State.* London: Macmillan.

Freeman, C., Henderson, P. and Kettle, J. (1999). *Planning with Children for Better Communities.* London: The Policy Press.

Frost, N. and Stein, M. (1989). *The Politics of Child Welfare.* Brighton: Harvester Wheatsheaf.

Frost, N. et al. (2000). *Leeds Refocusing Evaluation.* Leeds: Leeds University.

Frost, N. (1990). Official Intervention and Child Protection: The Relationship between State and Family in Contemporary Britain. In *The Violence*

Against Children Study Group Taking Child Abuse Seriously. London: Routledge.

Frost, N. (1992). Implementing the Children Act, 1989. In Carter et al. (Eds.). *Changing Social Work and Social Welfare*. Milton Keynes: Open University.

Frost, N. (1997). Delivering Family Support: Issues and Themes in Service Development. In Parton, N. (Ed.). *Child Protection and Family Support: Tensions, Contradictions and Possibilities*. London: Routledge.

Frost, N. (2001). *Family Support in Rural Communities*. Barkingside: Barnardos.

Frost, N., Johnston, E., Stein, M. and Wallis, L. (1997). *Negotiated Friendship*. Leicester: Home Start

Frost, N., Johnson, E., Stein, M. and Wallis, L. (2000). Home-Start and the Delivery of Family Support. *Children and Society*, 14: pp328-42.

Frost, N., Mills, S. and Stein, M. (1999). *Understanding Residential Child Care*. Aldershot: Ashgate.

Frost, N. and Ryden, N. (2001). *An Independent Evaluation of the South Lakeland Family Support Service*. Barkingside: Barnardo's.

Frost, N., Johnson, E., Stein, M. and Wallis, L. (1996). *Negotiating Friendship: Home-Start and the Delivery of Family Support*. Leicester: Home-Start.

Gardner, R. (1998). *Family Support*. Birmingham: Venture Press.

Gibbons, J., Conroy, S. and Bell, C. (1995). *Operating The Child Protection System*. London: HMSO.

Gibbons, J., Gallagher, B., Bell, C. and Gordon, D. (1995). *Development After Physical Abuse in Early Childhood*. London: HMSO.

Gibson, B. (Ed.) (1998). *Introduction to Youth Justice*. Winchester: Waterside Press.

Giddens, A. (1998). *Sociology*. Cambridge: Polity.

Giddens, A. (1999). *Runaway World*. London: Profile.

Gilligan, R. (2000). Promoting Positive Outcomes for Children in Need: The Assessment of Protective Factors. In Horwath, J. (Ed.). *The Child's World: Assessing Children in Need*. NSPCC/DoH/ University of Sheffield.

Glaser, D. (1995). Emotionally Abusive Experiences.

In Reder, P. and Lucey, C. (Eds.). *Assessment of Parenting*. London: Routledge.

Glass, N. (1999). Sure Start: The Development of an Early Intervention Programme for Young Children in the United Kingdom. *Children and Society*, 13: pp257-64.

Goldson, B. (2000). *The New Youth Justice*. Lyme Regis: Russell House Publishing.

Gomby, D., Culross, P. and Behrman, R. (1999). Home Visiting: Recent Programme Evaluations – Analysis and Recommendations. *The Future of Children*, 9(1): pp19-26.

Gordon, L. (1985). *Heroes of Their Own Lives*. London: Virago.

Graham, M. (1999). The African Centred Worldview: Developing a Paradigm in Social Work. *British Journal of Social Work*, 29(4): pp251-76.

Grimshaw, R. and McGuire, C. (1998). *Evaluating Parenting Programmes – A study of Stakeholders' Views*. London: National Children's Bureau.

Gutch, R. (2002). *The Guardian*, June 2002.

Hardiker, P., Exton, K. and Barker, M. (1991). *Policies and Practice in Preventative Child Care*. Aldershot: Avebury.

Hardiker, P., Exton, K. and Barker, M. (1999). Children Still in Need, Indeed: Prevention across Five Decades. In Stevenson, O. (Ed.). *Childhood Welfare in the UK*. Oxford: Blackwell.

Haskey, J. (1997). *Population Review (8): The Ethnic Minority and Overseas Born Population of Great Britain*. London: Office of National Statistics.

Hearn, B. (1995). *Child and Family Support and Protection. A Practical Approach*. London: NCB.

Hearn, B. (1997). Putting Child and Family Support and Protection into Practice. In Parton, N. (Ed.). *Child Protection and Family Support*. London: Routledge.

Hearn, B. (1991). *Setting up a Family Group Project*. Harlow: Longman.

Hemings, P. (1991). *All About Me*. Barkingside: Barnardo's.

Heywood, J. (1978). *Children in Care*. London: Routledge.

Hill, M. (1990). The Manifest and Latent Lessons of

Child Abuse Inquiries. *British Journal of Social Work*, 20.

Hill, M. and Jenkins, S. (1999). *Poverty Among British Children: Chronic or Transitory?* Colchester: University of Essex.

HM Treasury (2000). *Tackling Poverty and Making Work Pay: Tax Credits for the 21st Century.* London: HM Treasury.

HMSO (1991). *Patterns and Outcomes in Child Placements.* London: HMSO.

Hoffman, J.P. and Su, S.S. (1998). Parental Substance Use Disorder, Mediating Variables and Adolescent Drug Use: A Non-Recursive Model. *Addiction*, 93: pp1351-64.

Hogan, D. (1997). *The Social and Psychological Needs of Children of Drug Users: Report on Exploratory Study.* Dublin: The Children's Research Centre.

Hogan, D.M. (1998). Annotation: The Psychological Development and Welfare of Children of Opiate and Cocaine Users. Review and Research Needs. *Journal of Child Psychology and Psychiatry*, 39: pp609-19.

Holman, B. (1988). *Putting Families First.* Basingstoke: MacMillan.

Home Office (1991). *Criminal Justice Act.* London: HMSO.

Home Office (1998). *Supporting Families.* London: TSO.

Home Office (1998). *Crime and Disorder Act.* London: TSO.

Home Office (1998). *British Crime Survey.* London: TSO.

Home Office (2000). *Attitudes to Crime and Criminal Justice.* London: TSO.

Home-Start. *UK Policy and Practice Guide.* Leicester: Home-Start UK.

Howe, D. (1991). Knowledge, Power and the Shape of Social Work Practice. In Davies, M. (Ed.). *The Sociology of Social Work.* London: Routledge.

Howe, D. (1992). *An Introduction to Social Work Theory.* London: Ashgate.

Howe, D. et al. (1999). *Attachment Theory, Child Maltreatment and Family Support.* London: Macmillan.

Howland Thompson, S. (1998). Working with Children of Substance-Abusing Parents. *Young Children*, 53(1): pp26-42.

Hughes, L. and Pengelly, P. (1997). *Staff Supervision in a Turbulent Environment.* London: Jessica Kingsley.

Jack, G. (2001). Ecological Perspectives in Assessing Children and Families. In Horwath, J. (Ed.). *The Child's World: Assessing Children in Need.* London: Jessica Kingsley.

James, S. (1991). *The Urban Rural Myth or Reality. Geographical Paper 7.* Reading: University of Reading.

Jones, A. and Butt, J. (1995). *Taking the Initiative: The Report of a National Study Assessing Service Provision to Black Children and Families.* London: NSPCC, REU.

Kamerman, S.B. and Kahn, A.J. (Eds.) (1978). *Family Policy: Government and Families in Fourteen Countries.* New York: Columbia University Press.

Kandel, D.B. (1990). Parenting Styles, Drug Use and Children's Adjustment in Families of Young Adults. *Journal of Marriage and the Family*, 52: pp183-96.

Kaplan-Sanoff, M. and Rice, K.F. (1992). Working with Addicted Women in Recovery and their Children: Lessons Learned in Boston City Hospital's Women and Infants Clinic. *Zero to three*, 13(1): pp17-23.

Kirkcaldy, A. and Crispin, A. (1999). *Home-Start in Scotland: An Evaluation.* Home-Start UK.

Kumpfer, K.L. and De March, J. (1986). Family Environmental and Genetic Influences on Children's Future Chemical Dependence. In Griswold, et al. (Eds.). *Childhood and Chemical Abuse: Prevention and Intervention.* New York: Haworth Press.

Kurtz, E. and Ketcham, K. (1992). *The Spirituality of Imperfection: Storytelling and the Journey to Wholeness.* New York: Bantam.

Lloyd, E. (1998). Introducing Evidence-based Social Welfare Practice in a National Child Care Agency. In Buchanan, A. and Hudson, B.L. (Eds.). *Parenting, Schooling and Children's Behaviour.* Aldershot: Ashgate.

Lloyd, E. (1999). *Parenting Matters: What Works in Parenting Education.* Barkingside: Barnardo's.

Lloyd, E. (2000). Changing Policy in Early Years Provision and Family Support. In White, K.J. (Ed.). *Children and Social Exclusion.* London: NCVCCO.

Local Government Drugs Forum and Standing Conference on Drug Abuse (1997). *Drug Using Parents: Policy Guidelines for Inter Agency Working.* LGA.

London Borough of Brent (1985). *A Child in Trust: The Report of the Panel of Inquiry into the Circumstances Surrounding the Death of Jasmine Beckford.* London Borough of Brent.

London Borough of Lambeth (1987). *Whose Child? A Report of the Public Inquiry into the Death of Tyra Henry.* London Borough of Lambeth.

Luthra, M. (1997). *Britain's Black Population: Social Change, Public Policy and Agenda.* Aldershot: Arena.

Lynch, M. (1992). Child Protection: Have We Lost Our Way? *Adoption and Fostering*, 16: p4.

Macauley Hayes, M. (1990). *Placing Black Children.* London: ABSWAP.

MacDonald, G. and Roberts, H. (1995). *What Works in the Early Years.* Barkingside: Barnardo's.

MacPherson, Sir W. (1990). *The Stephen Lawrence Inquiry.* London: HMSO.

Marsh, P. (1988). *In Whose Trust?* London: National Foster Care Association.

Matthews, H., Taylor, M., Sherwood, K., Tucker, F. and Limb, M. (2000). Growing up in the Countryside: Children and the Rural Idyll. *Journal of Rural Studies*, 16(2): pp141-53.

Mattinson, J. and Sinclair, I. (1979). *Mate and Stalemate.* Oxford: Blackwell.

Mauss, M. (1969). *The Gift.* London: Unwin Hyman.

Maxime, J. (1993). The Therapeutic Importance of Racial Identity in Working with Black Children who Hate. In Varma, V. (Ed.). *How and Why Children Hate.* London: Jessica Kingsley.

McCudden, J. (1998). *What Makes a Committed Volunteer?* An unpublished dissertation.

McGaw, W. et al. (1998). *Parent Assessment Manual.* Trecare National Health Trust.

McGough, R. (1967). My Bus Conductor. In Henri A., McGough, R. and Patten, B. *The Mersey Sound.* Harmondsworth: Penguin.

McKegoney, C. (1999). *Pre-teen Drug Use in Scotland.* Edinburgh: Addiction Research.

McLaughlin, B.P. (1986). *Rural England in the 1980s. Rural Deprivation Study. Summary of Findings.* Chelmsford: Department of Environment Development Commission/Essex Institute of Higher Education.

McMillan, M. (1997). The Experiencing of Empathy: What is Involved in Achieving The 'As If' Condition? *Counselling*, 8(3): pp205-9.

Metcalfe, R. (1999). *Family Support Solutions. A Database of Family Support Methodologies.* East Riding: NCH Action for Children/East Riding Health Authority/East Riding of Yorkshire Council Social Services.

Moore and Wilkinson (1994). *Youth Court: A Guide to the Law and Practice.* Longman.

Morgan, D. (1999). Risk and Family Practices: Accounting for Change and Fluidity in Family Life. In Silva, E. and Smart, C. (Eds.). *The New Family.* London: Sage.

Morrison, T. (1998). Adaptation of Model of Change. In Howard, J. (Ed.) (2000). *The Child's World.* DoH, NSPCC and University of Sheffield.

Moss, P. and Sharpe, D. (1979). Family Policy in Britain. In Brown, M. and Baldwin, S. (Eds.) (1979). *The Yearbook of Social Policy in Britain.* London: RKP.

Mullins, A., McCluskey, J. and Taylor-Browne, J. (2001). *Challenging the Rural Idyll: Children and Families Speak Out about Life in Rural England in the 21st Century.* London: The Countryside Agency/NCH: Action for Children.

Myers, B. (1996). *Raising Responsible Teenagers.* London: Jessica Kingsley.

Nadeau, J.W. (1998). *Families Making Sense of Death.* California: Sage.

National Commission of Inquiry into the Prevention of Child Abuse (1997). *Childhood Matters.* London: HMSO.

National Family and Parenting Institute (2001). *Four Principles of Family Support.* www.nfpi.org.uk.

Nazroo, J.Y. (1997). *The Health of Britain's Ethnic Minorities.* London: Policy Study Institute.

New Policy Institute (1998). *Monitoring Poverty and Social Exclusion.* York: Joseph Rowntree Foundation.

Office of National Statistics (2000). *Social Inequalities.* London: TSO.

Office of National Statistics (2000). *Social Trends.* London: TSO.

O'Neill, O. (2002). *A Question of Trust.* Reith Lecture 3, BBC.

Owen, D. (1964). *English Philanthropy.* Cambridge, MA: Belknap Press.

Palmer, J. (1991). *Childcare in Rural Communities.* Edinburgh: HMSO.

Parkes, C.M. and Markus, A. (Eds.) (1998). *Coping with Loss: Helping Patients and Their Families.* London: BMJ.

Parker, R. (1980). *Caring for Separated Children.* London: MacMillan.

Parker, R. (1990). *Away From Home: A History of Child Care.* Barkingside: Barnardo's.

Parton, C. and Parton, N. (1989). Child Protection, The Law and Dangerousness. In Stevenson, O. (Ed.). *Child Abuse: Professional Practice and Public Policy.* Harvester Wheatsheaf.

Parton, N. (1985). *The Politics of Child Abuse.* London: MacMillan.

Parton, N., Thorpe, D. and Wattam, C. (1997). *Child Protection: Risk and the Moral Order.* Basingstoke and London: Macmillan.

Parton, N. (Ed.) (1997). *Child Protection and Family Support: Tensions, Contradictions and Possibilities.* London: Routledge.

Pawson, R. and Tilley, N. (1997). *Realistic Evaluation.* London: Sage.

Payne, M. (1998). Social Work Theories and Reflective Practice. In Adams, R., Dominelli, L. and Payne, M. (Eds.). *Social Work: Themes, Issues and Critical Debates.* London: Macmillan.

Pearson, G. (1983). *Hooligan: A History of Respectable Fears.* London: Macmillan.

Pecora, P. (1998). *Issues in Evaluating Family Support Services: An American Perspective.*

Paper presented to the Family Support Evaluation Network of Northern Ireland.

Pennie, P. and Best, F. (1990). *How the Black Family is Pathologised by the Social Services Systems.* London: ABSWAP.

Piachaud, D. and Sutherland, H. (2000). Cash in the piggy bank. *The Guardian,* 17.3.2000.

Pinchbeck, I. and Hewitt, M. (1969). *Children in English Society.* London: RKP.

Pollock, J. (1985). *Shaftesbury: The Poor Man's Earl.* Oxford: Lion.

Prochaska and DiClemente (1982). Comprehensive Model of Change. Transtheoretical Therapy: Toward a More Integrative Model of Change. *Psychotherapy: Theory, Research and Practice,* 19: p3.

Pugh, R. (2000). *Rural Social Work.* Lyme Regis: Russell House Publishing.

Quilgars, D. (2001). Child Mortality. In Bradshaw, J. (Ed.) (2001). *Poverty: The Outcomes for Children.* London: FPSC.

Qureshi, T., Berridge, D. and Wenman, H. (2000). *Where to Turn? Family Support for South Asian Communities.* London: National Children's Bureau.

Ramey, C. and Ramey, S. (1998). Early Intervention and Early Experience. *American Psychologist,* Jan: pp109-20.

Reder, P., Duncan, S. and Gray, M. (1993). *Beyond Blame: Child Abuse Tragedies Revisited.* London: Routledge.

Richardson, K. (1995). *A Practical Guide to Working with Rural Lone Parents.* York: National Council of One Parent Families/Joseph Rowntree Trust.

Robinson, L. (1995). *Psychology for Social Workers: Black Perspectives.* London: Routledge.

Rosenbaum, M. (1979). Difficulties in Taking Care of Business: Women Addicts as Mothers. American *Journal of Drugs and Alcohol Abuse,* 6: pp431-46.

Rowe, J., Hundleby, M. and Garnett, L. (1989). *Child Care Now.* London: BAAF.

St Christopher's Hospice (1989). *My Book About...* London: St Christopher's Hospice.

Saleeby, D. (1994). Culture Theory and Narrative: The Intersection of Meaning in Practice Social Work. *Social Work*, 39: p4.

Salford Community and Social Services (2000). *Conducting Family Assessments*. Lyme Regis: Russell House Publishing.

Sanders, M., Montgomery, D. and Brechman-Toissaint, M. (2000). The Mass Media and the Prevention of Childhood Behaviour Problems: The Evaluation of a Television Series to Promote Positive Outcomes for Parents and Their Children. *Journal of Child Psychology and Psychiatry*, 41(7): pp939-48.

Scottish Executive (2001). *Getting Our Priorities Right*. Edinburgh: Scottish Executive.

Seitz, V., Rosenbaum, L. and Apfel, N. (1985). Effects of Family Support Intervention: A Ten Year Follow-up. *Child Development*, 56(2): pp376-91.

Sheldon, F. (1998). ABC of Palliative Care: Bereavement. *British Medical Journal*, 316: pp456-8.

Shucksmith, M. (2000). *Exclusive Countryside? Social Inclusion and Regeneration in Rural Britain*. York: JRF.

Silverman, P.R., Nickman, S. and Worden, J.W. Detachment Revisited: The Child's Reconstruction of a Dead Parent. In Doka, K.J. (Ed.) (1995). *Children Mourning, Mourning Children*. Washington: Hospice Foundation of America.

Silverman, P.R. (2000). *Never Too Young to Know: Death in Children's Lives*. New York: Oxford University Press.

Simons, R., Johnson, C., Conger, R. and Lorenz, F. (1997). Linking Community Context to Quality of Parenting: A Study of Rural Families. *Rural Sociology*, 62(2): pp207-30.

Sinclair, R., Hearn, B. and Pugh, G. (1997). *Preventive Work With Families: The Role of Mainstream Services*. London: National Children's Bureau.

Singh, G. (1996). Promoting Anti-Racist and Black Perspectives in Social Work Education and Practice Teaching in Social Work. *Education*, 15(2): pp35-56.

Smaje, C. (1999). *Health, Race and Ethnicity: Making Sense of the Evidence*. London: King's Fund Institute.

Smith, C. (1996). *Developing Parenting Programmes*. London: National Children's Bureau

Smith, D. (1994). *Working with Volunteers: Recruitment and Selection*. Volunteer Centre UK.

Smith, G. (1994). Parent, Partner, Protector: Assessing Non-Abusing Parents' Capacity to Protect. In Morrison, T. et al. (1994). *Sexual Offending Against Children*. London: Routledge.

Smith, T. (1996) *Family Centres and Bringing up Young Children*. London: HMSO.

Social Services Committee (1984). *Report of the Social Services Committee on Children in Care*. London: HMSO.

Social Exclusion Unit (1998). *Bringing Britain Together: A National Strategy for Neighbourhood Renewal*. London: HMSO.

Social Services Inspectorate (1993). *Children Act Report*. London: HMSO.

Social Services Inspectorate (1999). *Care in the Country: Inspection of Community Care in Rural Communities*. London: Department of Health.

Social Services Inspectorate (1999). *Getting Family Support Right*. London: Department of Health.

Solomon, J., George, C. and DeJong, A. (1995). Children Classified as Controlling at Age Six. *Development and Psychopathology*, 7: pp447-64.

South Lakeland Family Support Service (2001). *Ourselves, Yourselves*. Kendal: SLFSS.

Statham, J., and Cameron, C. (1994). Young Children in Rural Areas: Implementing the Children Act. *Children and Society*, 8(1): pp17-30.

Stein, M. (1997). *What Works in Leaving Care*. Barkingside: Barnardo's.

Stevenson, O. (1998a). It Was More Difficult Than We Thought: A Reflection on 50 years of Child Welfare Practice. *Child and Family Social Work*, 3: p3.

Stevenson, O. (1998b). *Neglected Children: Issues and Dilemmas*. Oxford: Blackwell Science.

Stevenson, O. (Ed.) (1999). *Childhood Welfare in the UK*. Oxford: Blackwell.

Stone, M.K. (1990). *Rural Childcare.* London: Rural Development Commission.

Stone, M.K. (1994). *More Than Child's Play.* London: Rural Development Commission.

Sure Start (2000). *Service Delivery Agreement.* London: Sure Start.

Sure Start (2001). *The Impact of Sure Start – 1 Year on.* London: Sure Start.

Sylva, K. (1984). The Impact of Early Learning on Children's Later Development. In Ball, C. (Ed.). *Start Right: The Importance of Early Learning.* London: Royal Society of Arts.

Tonkin, L. (1996). *Growing Around Grief: Another Way of Looking at Grief and Recovery in Bereavement Care.* London: Cruse.

Travers, T. (2000) 'Town and Country'. *The Guardian,* 12.12.2000.

Trinder, L. (1996). Social Work Research: The State of the Art (or Science). *Child and Family Social Work,* 1: p4.

Tunstill, J. and Aldgate, J. (2000). *Services for Children in Need: From Policy to Practice.* London: The Stationery Office.

Utting, D. (Ed.) (1995). *The Hayle Project on Families and Parenting – A Conference Report.* London: Department of Health.

Velleman, R. (1992). Intergenerational Effects – A Review of Environmentally Oriented Studies Concerning the Relationship Between Parental Alcohol Problems and Family Disharmony. *International Journal of the Addictions,* 27(3): pp253-80.

Waldfogel, J. (1999). *Early Childhood Interventions and Outcomes: CASE Paper 21.* London: London School of Economics.

Warner, M. (1989). *Into the Dangerous World: Some Reflection on Childhood and its Costs.* London: Chatto.

Wasserman, D.R. and Leventhal, J.M. (1993). Maltreatment of Children Born to Cocaine Dependent Mothers. *American Journal of Diseases in Children,* 147: pp1324-8.

Wattam, C. (1996). The Social Construction of Child Abuse for Practical Policy Purposes – A Review of Child Protection: Messages from Research. *Child and Family Law Quarterly,* 8: p3.

Welshman, J. (1999). The Social History of Social Work: The Issue of the 'Problem Family' 1940-70. *British Journal of Social Work,* 29.

Westheimer, I. (1977). *The Practice of Supervision in Social Work.* London: Ward Lock.

Weyts, A., Morpeth, A. and Bullock, R. (2000). Department of Health Research Overviews – Past, Present and Future: An Evaluation of the Dissemination of the Blue Book. *Children and Society,* 5: p3.

White, K. (Ed.) (1999). *Children and Social Exclusion.* London: NCVCCO.

Wilens, T.E. et al. (1995). Pilot Study of Behavioural and Emotional Disturbances in the High Risk Children of Parents with Opioid Dependence. *Journal of the American Academy of Child and Adolescent Psychiatry,* 34: pp779-85.

Williams, H.S. and Webb. A.Y. (1992). *Outcome Funding: A New Approach to Public Sector Grantmaking.* NCVO.

Williams, J. (2000). *Meeting the Needs of Country Children. A Guide to Service Planning and Development.* London: National Council Voluntary Child Care Organisations.

Worden, W.J. (2002). *Children and Grief: When a Parent Dies.* New York/London: Guildford.

Index